Russia: A Long-Shot Romance

Russia

A Long-Shot Romance

Jo Durden-Smith

Alfred A. Knopf   New York

1994

This Is a Borzoi Book
Published by Alfred A. Knopf, Inc.

Parts of this book have appeared, in other forms, in *European Travel and Life* (New York), *Argonaut* (San Francisco), *The Guardian* (London), *Domino* and *Destinations* (Toronto), and *Moscow Magazine, Moscow Times, The Third Estate,* and *Literaturnaya Gazeta* (Moscow).

Owing to limitations of space, all other acknowledgements for permission to reprint previously published material may be found on page 319.

Library of Congress Cataloging-in-Publication Data
Durden-Smith, Jo, [date]
    Russia, a long-shot romance / by Jo Durden-Smith.
      p. cm.
    ISBN 0-394-58257-8
    1. Russia (Federation)—Description and travel.
    2. Durden-Smith, Jo, [date]   I. Title.
    DK510.29.D87   1994
    947.086—dc20   93-19834
                                        CIP

Manufactured in the United States of America

First Edition

For
Yelena, Ksiyusha, Katya,
and Tatiana Samoilovna:
the women in my life

Russia is a country in which things that just don't happen happen. —PETER THE GREAT

If ever your sons should be discontented with France, try my receipt; tell them to go to Russia. It is a useful journey for every foreigner: whoever has well examined that country will be content to live anywhere else. —MARQUIS DE CUSTINE

We have a blood tie with the next world:
Who has ever been to Russia has beheld the next world
In this one. —MARINA TSVETAEVA

We are branded with Russia
By a white-hot blizzard,
By the rhetoric of dark funnels
Of pits made of snow.
—IRINA RATUSHINSKAYA

Amen.
I have killed a poem. Killed it unborn.
To hell with it.
We bury,
Bury poems. Come see.
We bury.
—ANDREI VOZNESENSKY

Preface

On my first trip outside Moscow in 1989, on the way to a small town that had once been the home of two of the Soviet Union's greatest poets, we passed through a scarred and gutted landscape, with pylons stitched and riveted into the earth, and came along the road to a place called Bolshevik. It was, I suppose, a factory-farm settlement of some kind, with the usual slabbed apartment blocks and the usual dreary, parade-ground public emptiness. There were, no doubt, the usual war memorial and the usual photographs of awkwardly smiling workers displayed on the usual board of honour. But that's not what I noticed that spring day. At that time I was almost totally ignorant: I didn't know the road signs; I had no idea, for example, how the end of a village or town was announced. And then I saw it beside the road: the word "Bolshevik" in black with a red line slashed through it, cancelling it, removing it from the running ribbon of the road and from memory. It seemed to me then—as the First Congress of People's Deputies was about to open and enthral the whole nation with what seemed to be democracy-in-action—a vision of a small kind on the road to Tarusa, my own little epiphany.

It still seems so today, as I sit on a verandah in a cooperative village outside Moscow, listening to my Russian daughter complain about having to go to sleep in the afternoon, and wondering how to sum up what has happened here to me and to the country over the past three years. And then I remember. Not long ago, with a friend, I drove the short distance to the six-hundred-year-old fortified monastery at Zvenigorod, and on the way there we passed through another nondescript farm community called by a much older name than Bolshevik: a name that seems to echo with the pain and frustration of centuries of frontier soldiers and peasant serfs forced on to poor land in what was a forgotten corner of Europe. It's called Gryaz, or Mud. There's recently been talk, in the new atmosphere abroad in the country, that someone means to build a Holiday Inn in Gryaz. I can only wish him luck.

                                        Nikolina Gora, 1992

Acknowledgements

I should like to thank Regina Nadelson and Leslie Woodhead for their friendship and support—and for badgering me into going; Craig Horowitz and David Breul of *European Travel and Life* for seeing to it that I could; Artyom Troitsky (especially), Svetlana Kunitsina, and Alex Kan for making sure that I was looked after; and my brother Richard Durden and my sister, Clare Lodge, for taking care of business, meanwhile, at what was at the time home. As for the men and women in the Soviet Union (afterwards Russia) who gave me, not only help, but also the great gift of their friendship, I want to thank above all Nikolai and Larisa Petrov, Sacha and Ina Lipnitsky, Savvely Yamshchikov, Vadim Borisov, Yuri Belyavsky, Anatoly Shevchenko, Martin Walker, Fazil Iskander, Fyodor and Yelena Kasatkin, the late Andrei-Alexandrov-Agentov and his family. Anatoly Shelyuk, Irina Artis, Tomas and Yelena Topadze, Guram and Yelena Mzhavadnadze, Jim and Joanne Hutcheson, Boris and Irina Grebenshchikov, Boris Khmelnitsky, and Yuri Shvalbo. Thanks too, in Britain, especially to Jan Murray, who became my Russian family's mainstay, baby-sitter, landlady, and more besides; Christian and Melanie Wangler, who kept the faith; Ken White of British Airways; and Giles and John Tilley. In America, I want to acknowledge gratefully the help and encouragement of Phoebe Larmore; of my agent Irene Skolnick (of Curtis Brown); and of Ashbel Green and Sonny Mehta of Alfred A. Knopf.

Part One

Getting There

Chapter 1

April 1989

I

I feel oddly apprehensive on the plane. Perhaps it's to do with Yelena: the fact that I haven't seen her for two months and don't know what to expect. Or perhaps it's because I'm going alone to Moscow for the first time, with no responsibilities except to myself. It would be easier—or at least more convenient—if the surroundings were odder, more signal somehow. But the British Airways flight could be going anywhere. The stewards are, as they always are, both solicitous and oddly distant, as if playing their parts behind masks. There are no incidents, no stories. There's no particular laughter or nervousness among the passengers, just an air of routine. Two couriers sit in front of me, weighty professional men who won't pass through customs, for whom the flight is simply a chore; then an American businessman doggedly leafing through papers; then an over-made-up blonde woman trying to get the attention of an Indian sitting across from her with a little laugh that ends on an interrogative note, like a question she knows has no answer. The atmosphere is hushed and orderly, except for the woman's narcissistic trill: quite different from that of the first flight I took to the Soviet Union only fifteen months ago. Then there was a hum of energy, of controlled excitement throughout the cabin.

And now there's just me, this little hole of apprehension in a cathedral calm, thinking about customs, about the clothes I've bought for Yelena and Ksiyusha; the blouse for Svetlana; the pills for Tomas; the sweater for Tolya; the books for Andrei; the guitar strings and capo for Sacha. It's as if for everyone else on the plane Moscow has become in little more than a year just another destination, while for me it's still an amazing departure, an astonishing unknown, like setting out in a jollyboat for an unexplored continent, armed with nothing but trade goods you're not even sure the natives will like.

And yet how quickly in just seven visits I seem to have been assimilated into all these separated lives, to have become a Western extension of them, already a sort of trading partner. They exchange their intensity and warmth and friendship and sense of danger for my . . . well, what? Goods? No, not goods, though I'm aware that a lot of what I bring disappears into the little networks of influence and acquaintance each of them has woven over the years, so that they can get a doctor for their children or a ticket to the theatre or the first news of a new batch of high-quality material at a clothing store in the Arbat. No, what I bring, I think, are things more valuable than these: my curiosity, my strangeness. I take things for granted that they are just beginning to reach towards and hope for. And at the same time I am for them a kind of stage on which they can act themselves out, project themselves, understand themselves better. Joseph Brodsky once wrote that St. Petersburg became the birthplace of Russian literature for a very good reason. For it was only after the establishment of this artificial, European New Town on the edge of Russia that the country could turn around, look back on itself, and begin to see itself whole. The stranger—especially if he's as curious as I am—can maybe play for individuals the same kind of integrative role (particularly in the Soviet Union, where everything, all meaning, all personalities, are today in question). He is the person you can tell things to without them becoming currency. He is the safe repository of secrets, because he is there and not there, because he is going away. If he is a spy, as I am in a sense—as all writers are—then he is an unthreatening spy, a spy only of the heart.

(God, how I love this place I'm going to: its dreams and passions, its struggles with history, its monumental search for a memory! God, how I love its intensity of feeling! We have become dry sticks. The sap of life has been tapped in the West, has gone.)

2

Outside the plane at Sheremetyevo Airport, the corridor is empty, except for a bored soldier avoiding eyes, his identity submerged in his uniform, as if he were merely an announcement, a placard. I struggle down the stairs towards immigration, bottles clanking, books sagging: a one-man merchant navy loaded to the gunwales with plastic bags. Then I stand in front of the immigration booth, rocking from side to side with the weight, trying as usual to arrange my features into some pattern that will roughly conform with the photograph on my visa. "I am me," runs my end of the unspoken conversation on these quintessentially Soviet occasions. "No, you're not," says the guard, as he looks up at me with penetrating, suspi-cious grey eyes. "You are possible." Look down at the visa. "You are plausible." Look up again. "But you are only pretending to be you."

Instead: *"Zdrastvuitye,"* he says this time, smiling, young, the down barely off his cheeks. "Good flight?"

"Da, spasibo." Yes, thank you.

"Film?" he asks, looking down at my visa.

"Nyet, televidinya."

He smiles again, and stamps the pages of the visa with a flourish. And then I'm through into the dark arrivals hall, the first

sighting that visitors have of the glum public landscape of waiting
and queuing in which the Soviet people live. Except that this time
it's no longer locked in its usual grey twilight. For landed in the
middle, like a space ship, is a gleaming new duty-free shop, radiat-
ing light and possibility into the gloom. Smiling Russian sales-
women move to and fro against a backdrop of radios and shavers
and cassette players, all shining with newness. I grin and gawp at
this vision, which seems to me like the Taj Mahal improbably
landed in the back garden of some grimy industrial suburb, and
drop my bags in surprise to the floor. Every time I arrive, I think,
there seems to be some new, impossibly vivid sign that the private
gaiety of Russians is finally beginning to invade the public dreariness
of the nanny state. But then I realize that the duty-free shop is
valyuta—for hard currency only. And the feeling passes.

"*Zdrastvuitye, Jo. Privet.*" Suddenly there is Yelena, pushing
through the crowd behind me, her long dark hair bracketing her
face, her wide green eyes tilted at the corner, as if her vaultingly high
cheekbones were climbing upwards towards her temples and putting pressure on them. She is shy and nervous, dressed carefully and
smartly, as if she were meeting a delegation (as she is: me), or were
herself leaving. She looks at me for a moment, then kisses me
gravely, impersonally. And then she looks down at the pile of bags
at my feet.

"Oh, Jo," she says, erupting into a cascade of laughter. "You
are Geepsy!"

It is going to be all right.

3

Tomas is waiting for us, looking drawn and ill. Tomas is a Georgian who has worked all his life in the film business, and he usually
has about him an air of watchful irony, of a kind of wry mischief

waiting to burst out, that Georgians often have. But today he is subdued; his ulcer—for which I've brought medicine—is playing up. It's partly to do with the new joint venture with the Greeks that he's been setting up, he tells me as we begin the long drive in from the airport. The agreement has not been signed, everything is still up in the air, and he now has to take a job with one of the press agencies under pain of losing his employment status and pension rights. Yelena later tells me in the hotel that there's another reason. "Tomas's wife is very nice, of very good family," she says, tossing her hair. "Her father was chairman of one of the Institutes, and he was not too crazy about this Georgian boy she came home with— always on the streets, always chasing the girls. But she was good for Tomas: she married him; she made him finish school, made him have a career. Only thing is that, *tsk,* I don't know, Tomas just can't stop himself. When he was in Norway with Sovexportfilm, he had an affair with one of the diplomats' wives, someone they were close to. And his wife found out, and something died between them. Now there is Lyena"—a tall, round-faced model with one of the clothing cooperatives who once when we had dinner with her, at the Backstage Café at the Taganka Theatre, said not a word all night. "I said to him when it started, 'Tomas, what are you doing? This is crazy!' And he said, 'Don't worry. It's meaningless; it's nothing.' But now when he's tired of her and wants to leave, she threatens him. She calls his wife. And the other night she tried to commit suicide. Tomas had to go round to where she lives with her mother. There were ambulances, doctors, the *militsia,* everything. She'd taken fifteen sleeping tablets. It was terrible!"

Outside the car window, as we drive, the streets of the city are lined with red flags, like battle standards for May Day. There is an air of holiday, of spring having suddenly arrived. Families are out walking; baby carriages are everywhere. As Tomas talks about the difficulty of doing business with the West when it's so hard to go there himself and close the deal, Yelena and I hold hands on the backseat and smile into the evening sun like conspirators or cats.

4

Later, in the hotel, we make love, surrounded by the things I've bought for her. I've been absurdly quick to press the packages on her, as if it's all I have to offer. And she, usually so happy with presents ("Is it good? Is it a good one, Jo?"), has sat dolefully over coffee and the bottle of brandy I've brought with me. She is like no one I've ever met in the West, I think as I watch her: very coquettish, very instinctive, very close, all the time, to either laughter or tears. You can read her emotions as they pass over her face like the weather. I sometimes think that she's like some prefeminist Western woman of the fifties. But that conjures up something passive and fluffy. And Yelena, though she seems to live as close to her emotions as a child, is at the same time often hard and deliberate, very aware of her value. There's something in her, reflected, of the Russian male's attitude to women that goes back to Dostoyevsky and beyond. Women are both virgins and whores, saints and devils. They are close to the source of instinct and meaning. They are different, dangerous.

After we make love, though, the mood changes. We are going to Yalta for two days, and Yelena finally bubbles with laughter and excitement. She bounds up from the bed, cupping her breasts, arching her body, smiling. I can almost feel her pleasure and relief: "That's done. That's over. We can get on now." And so we can. I repack her presents: gloves and wooden jewellery and pantyhose from a friend at *The Guardian;* sandals and paste brooches from another at *Elle;* a blouse, skirt, and boots from me. And as we walk down the great sweeping staircase of the hotel—where the lift doesn't work—she says to me: "I won't do anything for anyone else now, Jo. Just for you." Some sort of decision, I suppose, has been made.

Chapter 2

January 1988

I

On my first visit to the Soviet Union, the first thing I did was laugh. The KGB man at passport control stared at me for what seemed like an eternity with the bilious gloom of a suspicious meat inspector. The cavernous airport baggage hall looked as if it were lit by a single fifteen-watt light bulb. Even the lobby of the National Hotel—which had been touted to me in London as the best in Moscow—provoked nothing so much as a renewed gale of mirth. It looked like a caricature of itself: too unnaturally like what all my prejudices had led me to expect. There was a grim porter there, a Brezhnev made of tallow lording it over the small world of the entrance; and a dipping, ducking receptionist with transparent-skin whose only English, whispered, seemed to consist in "So sorry." There were giant plaster caryatids; clanking, grumbling elevators; and a constant parade of dun-coated men and women shaking the snow off their boots and the laughter off their faces, as if they were arriving somewhere momentous and dangerous, like a police station or a morgue. The atmosphere, I thought, was that of a midwestern railroad hotel in the 1950s, forty years after the railroad had been discontinued. The famous National Hotel bar, one floor up a once-grand staircase and one of the legendary meeting places of the city, looked to me as if several crimes had recently been committed there—but no one had seen anything or had anything to say.

I had come to Moscow with two friends who worked in British television: one of them anxious to make a film about the shamans of the Far East, and the other in pursuit, for a script she was writing, of the life and times of Dean Reed, an American actor and singer who had been hugely popular in the Soviet Union and had recently been found drowned in a lake in East Berlin. I was merely along for the ride. True, I'd been commissioned to write an article about Leningrad for an American magazine. And true, I'd been doing intermittent research for a number of months for a series of possible films about Russian culture. But I was really there in the end only because my friends had encouraged me, and because it seemed suddenly an interesting place to be. It remained for virtually everyone in the West at the time as impenetrable and incomprehensible as it had always been, a black hole on the edge of Europe. But recently shreds of information had been emitted from it like radiation squeezed out against the odds of the local gravity. Something was happening in Mikhail Sergeyevich Gorbachev's Soviet Union: the beginnings of a civil society were starting to appear. Ecology groups had been set up to fight the polluting of Lake Baikal. Something called Klub Perestroika had emerged from discussions at the Central Economic-Mathematics Institute in Moscow. Young filmmakers, many of whose works had earlier been banned, had taken over the running of the Union of Film Workers with the encouragement of people in government. And in Leningrad there'd been a massive popular attempt to prevent the city soviet from tearing down the old Hotel Angleterre. What was happening at the top, in the Kremlin, remained, for the most part, as Byzantine and unreadable as it had always been. But even here there were indications, if you wanted to look for them, that things were on the move. In June of the year before, for example, a plenum of the Central Committee had announced that a radical reform of the entire economy was needed. And in November, on the seventieth anniversary of the October Revolution, Gorbachev had said in a speech that though collectivi' zation had been a good idea, and though Stalin's victims had numbered only a few thousands, his acts had nevertheless been criminal. We didn't realize then—nobody did—how much even this small statement had cost him. Nor did we realize that, a few days before we arrived, he'd made another breakthrough: he'd started using the word "democracy" in his speeches for the very first time.

2

The three of us met up that first night, after a preliminary exploration of each other's rooms, in a small hard'currency dining room, which shone, unlike the rest of the hotel, with crystal and polished porce' lain. It also looked out over Red Square and St. Basil's Cathedral, that improbable Russian fantasy that Western television newsmen were always using as a backdrop for their evening reports. The snow was gently falling on the cathedral as we gazed through the win' dows, and all the light bulbs that were being scrimped on in the rest of the city seemed to be trained on it.

"It looks like a spaceship," said the Writer, sipping Russian champagne. "A Walt Disney spaceship that's landed in the wrong place."

"Or a giant's coconut'shy," I said, tucking into the caviar, "with oranges, pomegranates, and pineapples instead of coconuts. Lenin comes out of his mausoleum at dead of night and throws snowballs at it."

"No," said the Director, cutting into his sturgeon. "It's not a building. It's more an uncomfortable experience. It's said that Ivan the Terrible cut out the eyes of the architects who built it, so that they'd never be able to build anything like it again." The Director was the only one of us who had ever been in the Soviet Union before, and he'd found it depressing. He also spoke a good deal of Russian, learned when he'd been in the Royal Air Force. And though this mostly took the form of phrases like "My altimeter is on the blink" or "My undercarriage is slipping," we'd decided that it was one of the things we shouldn't let on to in public, since not only had he made controversial drama-documentaries about the Russian invasion of Czechoslovakia and the dissident Soviet general Grigo-renko, he'd also signed the British Official Secrets Act.

We couldn't mention television, then, in front of the hidden microphones which we imagined all round us. Nor could we discuss the Writer's project. For Dean Reed, who'd been known locally as the Red Elvis, was popularly reckoned at the time to have been killed by the KGB because he wanted to go back home to America. So instead we regaled each other, over the pike and chicken *pa-Kievsky,* with all the dredged-up bits and pieces of in-formation we knew about the Soviet Union.

"In Moscow," said the Director, munching, "you're allowed a maximum amount of living space: I think it's nine square metres a person, and another twelve for a family. If someone dies, then you have to fork up more money or move out. The only two ways you're allowed to keep the space you've got and not pay extra is if one of you's declared certifiably insane, or if you buy a show dog that's registered with the Moscow Kennel Club. Then you can claim an extra twenty square metres."

"Twenty square *metres!*" said the Writer. "Then you guys'd better get me a show dog right now. I'm in some lousy broom closet at the back of the hotel; and I want to be in room 101, where Lenin used to give speeches to the crowds from the balcony. If Richard Branson"—the head of Virgin Records and Virgin Airlines— "can stay there, so can I. Otherwise, boys, it's going to be one of *your* rooms. You can play Russian roulette for the privilege of swapping."

"But we're heads of *delegations*," said the Director and I simulta' neously.

"And besides," I said, "you're not going to be in it for long. It's going to be culture, culture every day."

"And shopping," said the Director.

"You've got to go to the Kremlin," I said, "to see the world's largest cannon, which has never been fired, and the world's largest bell, which has never been rung. You've got to see the Cathedral of the Dormition, which was originally built by Russians and fell down after two years, at which point they had to hand the job over to a bunch of Italians."

"As they still do," said the Director, "only now it's Finns and Swedes."

"And then," I went on, "there's the Museum of the Revolution to see, and the Tolstoy House and the Pushkin House and the Pushkin Museum. You simply can't miss the postimpressionists in the Pushkin Museum; they *alone* could take you a whole day. The sugar merchants bought them before the Revolution. They were confiscated and afterwards shown as examples of Western deca' dence. Gauguin was labelled 'taste of the rentier'; van Gogh, 'taste of the small bourgeoisie'; and Matisse, 'age of distorted imperialism.' "

There was a silence. Then: "You cheated, Jo," said the Writer. "You *boned* up." She paused. "But don't think that's going to get you out of giving up your room."

After we paid the bill, we walked out of the hotel, running the gauntlet of taxi drivers and moneychangers, in the direction of Red Square. It was very cold. When we got there, we stood silently and almost alone in the middle of the huge cobbled space, looking at Lenin's tomb and at the soldiers of the guard changing, moving like ghost puppets through the snow. A big Zil car crept like a moth out of the mouth of the Spasskaya Tower.

"It's beautiful," said the Director.

"And creepy," the Writer said.

I said: "It was originally the marketplace. Then it was called Fire Square after the fire of 1493. It wasn't known as Red—or Beautiful—Square until the end of the seventeenth century. Up there by St. Basil's is where state decrees used to be read and where Peter the Great executed the leaders of the Streltsy rebellion. In the same place, Ivan the Terrible told the people how sorry he was for how terrible he'd been, and somewhere else here he started the Russian state tax on vodka. Up there, at the top of the Spasskaya Tower—"

"Oh, shut up, Jo," they said.

3

Only on the surface, of course, was Moscow even remotely familiar. Like everybody else who comes here, I had nothing in my head but a few half-assimilated facts and a few familiar images, mostly of Red Square; a few fragments, perhaps, of Tolstoy, Dostoyevsky, and Pasternak; and a few more or less contemporary anecdotes, mostly about people talking too much and being thrown out of the country. I knew, for example, that the art director of the film *Gorky Park* had spoken up one night in the National Hotel about what he was doing in the city, only to be told the next day that he was persona non grata. I knew that a British television crew, secretly filming the dissident Anatoly Shcharansky, had been arrested after an insecure phone call from London and had had almost all of their film confiscated. I took it for granted from the beginning, then, that the Writer, the Director, and I were being watched. A British correspondent had once told me, with bizarre satisfaction, that the KGB had between seven and ten operatives for every foreigner in the city. And it would have been positively demeaning to believe that we were somehow excluded from its list. This made for a certain self-consciousness, even self-importance—as the Writer and I discovered on our first outing into the city.

This outing was of not the slightest importance: it was merely a walk. But since every other foreigner we could see in the hotel, when we came downstairs in the morning, was standing in line for a guided tour on a tour bus, even the walk quickly took on the character of a singular adventure.

We walked out of the hotel, turned right past the Intourist Building, and were immediately caught up in a fantasy that every foreigner who ever came to Moscow at the time will recognize. We were under surveillance; so we were actors in a film—we were, in fact, stars. And as stars, we were required to give a performance. We slipped and slid through the snow, then, waving our arms to keep balance and laughing too loudly, just as if we were on a film set and the inevitable centre of all the Russian extras' attention. This was actually not too hard to imagine, because in a sense we were. Everyone we passed, dressed in drab bundles of fur and padding, seemed to have eyes for no one but us. We were colourful; we smiled, we laughed; we were curious and larger than life; we were from another planet. "More, more!" the audience seemed to be asking of our performance as it stared at us. "Be more eccentric. Be more Western." We tried to oblige.

It was fun for a while, but it was also, of course, completely isolating. For nobody smiled or approached us. They simply looked. We were locked up in their attention, but locked out from who they were. We were condemned to play foreigners and to be judged on our ability by all those eyes. The people, in fact, were literally *all* eyes. For eyes were all we could see of them, through the swaths and scarves and ear-flapped fur hats: eyes turning and swivelling;

dark, muddy eyes, louring eyes, accusing eyes, coquettish eyes. And the only thing we could satisfactorily do for them all, with their different agendas of blame and envy, was to ham it up.

"Ah," said the Writer, as if sensing what was being required of her, "look at those *clothes*. I'm glad I'm not an extra in *this* movie."

The clothes, though, were just part of it—even though I'd never been so conscious in my life of the way we in the West use clothes as costume and declaration. (All around us were people in various shades of black and brown, while we were as gaudy as peacocks.) There was something else, too, in the charged theatricality of our passage down the street. It was as if the people we saw about us were not only more hidden and more monochrome than we were, but also squatter and flatter and smaller, as if they had only just begun to emerge from some more horizontally biased dimension. The same impression was given by the streets themselves, by the huge expanse of Manege Square and, beyond it, the walls of the Kremlin. Everywhere we looked, the buildings seemed to grow sideways rather than upwards, as if they were designed as barriers, to block out the horizon. However old they were, they seemed looming and ungraceful. It was no wonder, I thought, that no one had ever seen a great postcard of Moscow's ceremonial public spaces. There was a kind of flat, brooding sullenness about it that defied all beautifying.

"All right," I said on the corner of Kalinin Prospekt, getting out my guidebook. "Enough of this. Over there in front of us is the Lenin Library, and just behind us somewhere—in the reception rooms of the Supreme Soviet—is where the Moscow Art Theatre began. In front of us, up here to the right, is the house that's the model for Prince Bolkonsky's in *War and Peace,* and the House of Friendship, which was built for the art patron Morozov and based on the sixteenth-century Casa de las Conchas in Salamanca."

"So where do we get coffee?" said the Writer.

I'd like to say that all kinds of adventures happened to us as we plodded up Kalinin Prospekt on the way to that cup of coffee in the Arbat. But they didn't—and it didn't matter a bit. For slowly we realized, as we got farther from the hotel, that we were in a real city, Gorbachev's city, and everything we saw carried within it some potential burden of meaning: every face, every shop front, every uniform, every bus—even the statues and plaques that we passed, where heroes whose names I tried to decipher from my vanishingly small knowledge of the Cyrillic alphabet were frozen forever in attitudes of intellectual or military superiority. We found ourselves looking at everything as if it had to be a certain sign of change, as if each item and person could be deciphered and their roles read if we only could find out what language they were in. We scoured what we could see of faces. We peered at every bus, every policeman, every shopper. Who was that? Was that a dissident? Was that a hood, a housewife, a member of the Party? What was that? A queue, a meeting, an exchange mart, or just a bunch of people waiting around? We didn't know; we never found out—the guidebook couldn't tell us. But I don't think I've ever felt so concentrated, so greedy for information about people, in any city in my life.

4

That evening Martin Walker burst into the hotel. Martin was the *Guardian*'s Moscow correspondent, and he was wearing the greatest fur hat I'd ever seen.

"Where can I get one of those?" I said immediately.

"You can't," he said. "Unless you go wolf-hunting in Siberia, drink as much vodka as the hunters do, and get given it."

Martin Walker was a short, energetic man in his late thirties, with dancing eyes and a faintly crumpled look, as if he'd been in a bad fight in his youth and his nose and his cheekbones hadn't been set quite properly. (It was the best thing that had ever happened to his face; he looked vaguely like the young Marlon Brando.) He also probably knew as much about the Soviet Union as any Westerner alive. He knew about rock concerts and painters and restaurants and writers—all of which he wrote about in a personal column every week—as well as about the arcana and pecking orders of the Party and the Kremlin.

He and the Director embraced—they were friends. And, one by one, we handed over to him bags packed with lime marmalade and steak sauce and Indian spices which we'd bought in London for him and his wife, Julia. Then we settled ourselves into the unforgiv-ing chairs of the National bar.

"What can I do for you?" he said.

"Explain it," I said.

"The Upper Volta with rockets," he said.

"More," said the Writer.

"O.K. Two Muscovites are in a gallery, and they come across a painting of Adam and Eve. One of them says to the other, 'Look at that. Adam and Eve. They've got to be Russian.' 'Why?' asks the other. 'They've got nothing to wear; there's nothing to eat but an apple between them. And they think they're in Paradise.' "

"So the food situation is bad?" asked the Director.

"It's always bad," said Martin. "You can go up Gorky Street to Gastronom Number One, for example—people still call it Yeliseyev's, after its pre-Revolutionary name. And there's hardly anything there. When Walter Benjamin was in Moscow in the mid-twenties, he said he saw dishes there that beggared the imagina-tion—it was the kind of Harrods Food Hall or Dean & DeLuca of Moscow. Now there's nothing."

"So what do people do?"

"They barter, they bribe, they make deals. They trade at the back door of shops or under the counter. Or else they go to the so-called free markets and pay over the odds."

"And they buy everything they can whenever they can," said the Writer. "We saw all these guys in suits walking through the streets carrying rolls and rolls of toilet paper around their necks."

"Yes," Martin said. "If it's on offer, they buy as much of it as they're allowed. That's why everyone carries carrier bags all the time: *avoski,* 'perhaps bags.' The point is . . . Well, look, one of the first things you have to do is to start seeing the city, not as buildings, but as a kind of gigantic bush telegraph which holds together a network of obligations and counterobligations. So if a Muscovite sees any/ thing worth having, first he queues for it; then he jumps out of line to telephone his friends about it; and then he buys as much of it as he can. And then he uses the information or what he's now bought to oil the next deal, the next trade. And that goes for everything that's on sale here: Hungarian chocolates, Crimean wine, Bolshoi tickets. Everything. The real business in the city is underground trade."

"And no one does any work," said the Director.

"You know the old Russian saying. 'They pretend to pay us; we pretend to work.' "

"So what does Julia think of all this? With two young kids to take care of?" asked the Writer.

He laughed. "She writes a weekly column for a paper in London. And the Soviets think she's the most anti/Soviet corre/ spondent there is."

"And you?" asked the Director.

"I think it's the most interesting place on earth."

"Jo," said the Writer, turning towards me suddenly, "it's half past seven. Isn't Art supposed to be here?"

"If he is," said Martin, "then you'll have to go down and get him past the porter. They don't let in Russians, unless they're hookers or hoods and come in bearing gifts. I don't think Artyom fits either of those categories."

Art was Artemy Troitsky (or Arthur Trinity, as I later came

to translate him), and he was the first fully paid-up Russian I'd ever met. A critic and pop-cultural historian who'd had a rough time during the Andropov/Chernenko years, he'd organized under Gor-bachev a famous benefit concert for the victims of Chernobyl (thus earning himself the title of "the Soviet Bob Geldof"), and he'd written a book on the history of Russian rock music that had been published by a small press in London. When I'd heard that there was to be a launch party for the book and that he was going to be there, on his first visit to England, I'd arranged to meet him. The Director, the Writer, and I had all trooped off to a place called the Moscow Club in London's Soho district to shake his hand and get his book. And the next day the Writer and I had taken him to lunch in a Thai restaurant in South Kensington. ("Where do you want to eat?" we'd asked. "Ethnic," he'd said in immaculate En-glish.) We'd stayed in the restaurant for four and a half hours.

I'd wanted to talk about rock music and intellectuals and the role of the guitar poet in Russian culture. The Writer had wanted to talk about Dean Reed and shopping. In the process of doing both, we'd become friends. Art was sometimes cynical and self-conscious, but he answered our questions with all the good nature of a tour guide for children. The Director later described him as being exactly like one of the street hustlers who hung around outside Moscow's tourist hotels, "only what he's peddling is the truth."

"Hi, big Jo," Art said, stamping his feet. "Welcome to the Evil Empire."

We went back inside past the doorman, who seemed to pay us absolutely no attention, probably because Art was dressed, I could see now—after London and royalty cheques—like a hip London media entrepreneur, all the way down to the designer stubble. We climbed the stairs and went into the bar.

"*Kak ty?* How are you, friend?" said Martin, standing, as we came in. Art had been Martin's guide to the music and art worlds of Moscow when he'd first arrived as a correspondent. And Martin had been Art's best man when he'd married a fashion journalist at what was said to have been Moscow's best underground party of 1987.

We stood around for a while embracing Russian-style. The Director, the Writer, and I handed over more bags of tribute—this time videotapes and records of obscure English thrash garage bands with names like Mercury Poisoning. Then Artyom, which was what Martin called him, said abruptly—with the rising inflection he always used when issuing orders—"O.K., people. It's time to go."

"Where are you going to?" asked Martin.

"Gorky Park," said Artyom.

5

At the entrance to Gorky Park there were huge gates, a Ferris wheel, and a large ice rink, where loudspeakers were incongruously blaring out "Volare." *"Nel blu, dipinto di blu,"* sang the Writer happily, along with the canned music. She couldn't hit a single note; but she was a skater: she knew about things like double axels and camel spins, and she wanted to look at Moscow's skating form. I, meanwhile, thought about the film *Gorky Park* and shivered. This was the rink—recreated by the director, Michael Apted, in Helsinki—where three friends had gone on a skating picnic on a winter's night like this one, only to end up in a snowdrift, with their faces cut off.

The memory of the film persisted as we plunged away from the lights of the rink, pursuing Artyom into the darkness. We were all three (I learned later) for some reason immensely scared. So far Moscow had seemed unthreatening: we'd been insulated from the real thing by each other's company. But now we were on our way, through a murderous film set, to see Oleg Smirnov, Dean Reed's longtime interpreter, who, we'd been told, had "good KGB connections." (I was later to hear the same thing about half the people I knew in Moscow.) We wondered if we'd been followed from the Metro station and across the Krimsky Bridge; we wondered what we were getting into. We felt unreal, as if we'd once more found ourselves in a movie—only this time one with no happy ending. The tinny music from the loudspeakers, as it ebbed away and we were lit now by no more than moon and snow, served only to intensify the mood: it was as eerie as a soundtrack in the buildup to some impossible horror. Low, distant voices came out of the shad-owy trees in front of us; there was menacing laughter behind us. We walked on, increasingly nervous, with the Writer calling out: "How far are we going?" And then suddenly—whoosh—a dark, goggled figure rose up out of the darkness on our left and hurtled past us, materializing out of the night into close-up like an apparition or an evil genie.

"Jesus! What was that?" said the Director, watching as it disappeared again into the night.

"Oh, a speed skater," said Artyom from twenty yards in front of us. "I forgot to tell you. They ice down the paths and use them as runways."

"Gee, thanks for telling us, Artyom," said the Writer.

Artyom walked on ahead obliviously, while we three followed, silently clustered together as if for protection. It was bitterly cold. There seemed to be no one at all in this part of the park, except for the speed skaters with their sharp blades and sudden, ghostly arriv-als. I reminded myself that the Soviet Union was a police state and promised myself that I would never again take it less than seriously.

Finally, after what seemed like an hour of increasing paranoia, we arrived at our destination: Stas Namin's Hard Rock Café. We stumbled out of the darkness towards an anonymous front door with a dim light in front of it, and had our coats taken by a wizened, toothless old man who cackled greetings at us and laughed. He pointed out the lavatories, still laughing, and then ushered us down a narrow corridor lined with travel posters, into the restaurant.

I don't know what I'd expected, but it was certainly totally unlike any Hard Rock Café I could have imagined. It was a faintly sinister room, as if it had just been put together by a rather desperate design department out of available props. There was a high bar along one wall; pictures that looked as if they'd been recently painted; and an arrangement of tables of various shapes and sizes covered with a job lot of pink patterned tablecloths. At one of the tables sat four young men who seemed to be disguised as rock musicians. And at another, set with appetizers and jugs of fruit juice, sat the interpreter Oleg Smirnov and Artyom's wife, Svetlana. Oleg Smirnov was disguised, the Writer later said, as a 1950s American college boy—with large, round glasses and a jacket pocket lined with pen tops—while Svetlana was got up as herself, which was tall and graceful. I remembered what Artyom had said about her: that she hadn't been allowed to leave the country with him, in case they both defected. And I remembered that the things she'd wanted him to buy in London for her were leather riding boots and a man's dinner jacket. So I sat down next to her and said hello—it seemed enough information to go on.

This left the Writer and the Director with Oleg Smirnov. And I could see immediately that it wasn't going to be an easy evening for any of them. All three were intensely nervous of their upcoming conversation—as was I. I realized that in the long burn-down of my marriage I'd almost never met socially a woman I didn't already know.

It turned out, indeed, to be an uncomfortable evening. Svetlana didn't have much English, and I had less Russian. Artyom went off early to talk to the rock musicians (who turned out to be real) and wasn't available for any translation. So I spent most of the evening pretending not to be there, while I listened to snatches of the conversation the Writer and Director were having with possibly-KGB Oleg.

It didn't start too promisingly. They were pretending to be innocents abroad, with only a passing interest in doing something about Dean Reed. And Oleg somehow knew they were lying. "How can I tell you are who you say you are?" he said. "How can I tell you aren't out to destroy the memory of Reed and aren't telling me the truth?"

He was also (was it?) pretending to be in the know and to be keeping his options open on some valuable information he possessed. At a later stage in the cat-and-mouse game, when the Director asked whether he thought Dean Reed had been killed, "Yes," Oleg said knowingly, "I think it very possible."

"Who by?" said the Director.

"The CIA," said Oleg. It wasn't clear whether it was a statement or a question. "Or maybe the KGB," he added teasingly. "Because he knew too much."

"What did he know?" asked the Writer.

"Ah," said Oleg. Apparently that would be telling.

At this point Stas Namin arrived in a smiling flurry of Armenian goodwill. He was a short, tubby man, black-bearded, with a chaos of long, curly black hair that looked like a fur hat that had been left untrimmed. And he was the owner, with his sister—to whom he soon introduced us—of the Hard Rock restaurant. He was also the grandson of Politburo and Praesidium member Anastas Mikoyan. And it was this that was generally reckoned to have been responsible for his long career as a more or less officially countenanced rock musician. In the seventies he'd started a band called the Flowers (soon changed to the Stas Namin Group), which had made records for the state-monopoly recording organization, Melodiya, and had been allowed to travel abroad. Now he was not only one of the first private restaurateurs in Gorbachev's Soviet Union; he was, he said, the first independent rock entrepreneur.

He was every bit as charming and foxy as his grandfather was supposed to have been. But I soon realized that our meeting was a setup: I was in Gorky Park as one of the trades Martin had talked about. I, after all, had made films long ago with the Rolling Stones and the Doors; I was thinking of making a film now with the man called "the Russian Bob Dylan," Boris Grebenshchikov. And this was apparently enough for me to be presented by Artyom to Stas as a gift, a potentially valuable Western contact. Stas played his part in this fiction to the full; I was given the business. Hauled up from the table where the Writer, the Director, and Oleg were still hud-dled together, I was rushed across to the musicians' table and introduced. Then I was taken outside to the outdoor theatre Namin wanted to lease on a permanent basis, and to a series of dingy rooms inside, which were soon to be transformed, he said, into rehearsal rooms and recording studios. Finally, back in the restaurant, he pushed a tape into a beat box and played the music of a band he said he was grooming for American stardom. He played it very loud and snapped his fingers to the beat. What did I think of them? he asked.

"They sound American—a bit like Bon Jovi," I said.

"Great. That's the idea," he said. "What shall I call them?"

"Gorky Park," I said. "Definitely Gorky Park."

6

Later, back at the hotel, while the Writer and the Director went for a walk in the snow, to confer about Oleg Smirnov away from the hidden microphones, I went upstairs to the bar. Martin Walker had said it got interesting late at night; and indeed it had. As I came in, two blowsy women in one of the corners were standing up, hitting one another with what looked like Western handbags, and no one seemed to be paying any attention. The place was thick with cigarette smoke and noisy with drink. It looked like a convention of double-glazing salesmen out for a toot with their out-of-town molls.

I stood at the bar with a man in a suit, who turned out to be Danish. "I've been coming here for twelve years," he said sadly, sipping a Scotch. "Do you see that girl over there, the one in the white dress? She used to be in here once in a while just to have a glass of Coca-Cola. And now she's turning tricks just like everyone else."

Later—much later—I got into a conversation with an English-man, who said he was involved in building a condom factory near Tallinn. "Do you know," he said, giving a glum once-over to all the sexual transactions going on in front of him, "how many condoms they make here a year for every active male in the population?"

"No," I said.

"Three," he said morosely. "Just three. The main method of contraception is abortion."

7

The next morning, I went off alone to the Pushkin Museum and the Tolstoy House; and then I left for Leningrad. On the plane, I sat next to a Texan woman with a card announcing her as a member of the President's Commission on Drugs, with an office in the White House, and watched her as she walked down the aisle, cheerily handing out candy and sticks of gum to any Russian who would take them. She was immaculately groomed and as unstoppa-bly enthusiastic as a wartime GI liberating an Italian township with Hershey Bars. The passengers accepted her offerings with good-natured puzzlement, as if she were mad. I found the whole thing achingly depressing.

I was driven in from Pulkovo Airport, in a chauffeured car I'd hired in London, to the Yevropeiskaya Hotel, just off Nevsky Prospekt. It was hemmed in by a corral of tour buses, and was full of Finns and Germans: big, florid men and women in multicoloured parkas who were clearly there to do nothing but drink. They carried bottles in the tiny elevators, stuffed into them like dumplings, and laughed a lot.

In my room, I telephoned everyone in the city for whom I had a number: members of Boris Grebenshchikov's band, Aquarium; a teacher of English; a TV director; an actress. There was no reply except from the actress, who said she would come to the hotel after that night's performance. To kill time, then, I went downstairs, and walked through the slush and the street hustlers to the restaurant next door. The band, on a dais at one end, was playing "I'll Be Loving You" as I came in: two guitars, drums, and an electric organ making a little sizzling noise, like someone frying. Old women were peeking out from doorways at the few, clumsy dancers, and giggling, as if nothing like it had ever been seen in the city before. The bread in the restaurant was stale; the service, gloomy. Of the hundred or so items listed on the menu, only about fifteen were available. When I left an hour and a half later, the band had graduated to "Rock Around the Clock" and then, joined by an accordionist, to a polka, which the customers seemed to prefer. They jounced around on the floor noisily, kicking up their heels. I found it odd that the band should play nothing but American and German music, the music of the Soviet Union's two greatest enemies.

At about ten o'clock, the actress arrived. I met her at the door of the hotel, where her internal passport was carefully scrutinized. She seemed to be about nineteen or twenty, though she must have been older. She was a friend of a Russian emigrée I'd met in London. She was very nervous.

I took her into the almost empty bar and settled her in a corner. In the light and stripped of her coat, she seemed as delicate as a nineteenth-century consumptive. Her green eyes were large and feverish; her skin was pale and almost transparent, as if a dim light were shining through it. Her English was good, but tentative, as if it came from long ago. There was an air of bewildered desperation about her.

She'd graduated not long before from drama school, she told me, and now she worked in a comedy theatre as a juvenile. It was far away from the centre; it was terrible. "But perhaps you will come to see me there," she said, gripping my arm.

I said that I would try. Then: "It is safe to speak here, do you think?" she asked.

I looked around the bar, which was empty, except for a group of noisy Germans at a large round table. "I suppose so," I said, shrugging.

"I must leave here," she said in an excited whisper. "I must go to the West. Perhaps you will help me. Perhaps we will do things together. Perhaps you will give me things, help me. Perhaps you will take me with you when you leave."

"Well," I said slowly, "I don't think I believe in getting married on the first date."

She seemed not to hear me. "I cannot live here anymore," she said. "You cannot know how we live. We live like animals."

"Even now?" I asked. "Under Gorbachev?"

"He is just for the window," she said. "For the West. There is no future here, only more of what has been. I will do anything to leave. Anything."

We sat in silence for a while. And then I walked her to the Metro station at the end of Brodsky Street. Before she left, she kissed me briefly on the cheek and said sadly: "I think you are a good man. You will telephone me?"

"Yes," I said. "Of course." I never saw her again.

Back in the hotel, an Irishman was standing over the floor lady, who was settling in for the night on a couch in front of a small black-and-white television set. "Well, my little treasure . . ." he was saying as he drank from a bottle, which he offered me as I passed.

He turned out to be an actor from the Abbey Theatre in Dublin, in Leningrad to perform a play which I'd seen at the Edinburgh Festival the year before. And when the floor lady finally proved resistant to his charm, we went to his room, where I tele-phoned the teacher of English, who said, yes, he would take me to see Boris Grebenshchikov on the following day. The Irishman, sitting down on the bed, asked me what I thought of Russian girls.

"Beautiful," I said. I couldn't think what else to say.

"Yes, beautiful," he echoed, and proposed a toast. "Here's to Leningrad, comrade," he said. "It's a fine city. A beautiful city. But . . . sad."

8

The next morning, I walked up Nevsky Prospekt to the Intourist Building near St. Isaac's Cathedral and waited in a room where a French businessman was complaining about his mail being inter-fered with. "I'm so sorry, I'm sorry," said the man who was dealing with him, his eyes watery with indifference. He could not say it had nothing to do with him.

"Leningrad," said the woman who finally came to pick me up and offer me coffee, "is on the same latitude as the city of Vancouver. It is situated in the mouth of a river as wide as the river Hudson in New York. It is made up of twenty-five canals and a hundred and one islands. It has sixty-eight museums, eighty cinemas, fourteen permanent theatres, and twenty free markets. There are more than two hundred places in the city associated with Vladimir Ilyich Lenin." "And there's not a single guidebook to the Hermitage," I said. On my way I had stopped at the hard-currency shop on

Herzen Street, next door to the building which had once housed Fabergé. The salesgirl, when I'd asked, had told me no guide to the Hermitage was available.

"We *ask* them for them; we *inform* them," the woman said, hunching her shoulders and throwing out her hands, in that invoca-tion of fate and the authorities that makes every Russian functionary, however dour, look like a refugee from a Jewish comedy theatre. "But the books are sold out as soon as they are produced. There are never enough. I'm so sorry. But maybe I can help you with other things."

"The docks," I said. "I'd like to see the docks."

"Oh no, that is not possible," she said. "The docks are closed to foreigners."

"Or a meeting of the city council."

"So sorry."

"Well, what else do you recommend?" I asked.

"You will see the museums," she said. "You will have dinner in the restaurants. And you . . ." She was lost for a moment. "You will write about the city." She segued back to her set text. "The city, you will say, is twinned to the city of Manchester in England, and there are talks about twinning with both Boston and San Francisco in the United States. Oh, and the five millionth inhabitant of Leningrad is about to be born. There are many discussions on television about what the child should be named."

No name suggested itself, and I couldn't bring myself to tell the woman that her precise statistics weren't exactly what I was after. So I gave her a back copy of the magazine I was writing for (which I later learned was worth a week's salary on the black market) and fled out onto the slushy street. I slithered and sloshed my way down to St. Isaac's Cathedral, and there was suitably impressed by its "columns of jasper and lazurite," its "congregation of thirteen thou-sand," and the fact that it was built on "twenty-four thousand piles sunk into the marsh." Then I walked across Decembrists' Square, with the slim spire of the Admiralty on my right, to the famous statue of Peter the Great: the Bronze Horseman.

The Bronze Horseman, I knew, was a sort of lodestone: a magnetic point through which flowed the two great electric charges of Russian history and Russian literature. It had been commissioned and paid for by Catherine the Great, the German-born woman who became empress in 1762, after her husband, Peter III, had had his brains beaten out (with a stool) by her lover. Though Catherine was every bit as autocratic as any of her predecessors, she was much admired by the leading democrats of the French Enlightenment— she'd taken the sound precaution of paying them a pension. And it was they who had in return suggested, as sculptor for this act of homage of hers, a Frenchman, Etienne Falconet. Falconet, after his arrival in St. Petersburg, was said to have enlisted the aid of a Russian general, who was required each morning to gallop up a specially prepared ramp of sand before bringing his mount to a halt and rearing it up in a display of paddling hooves and a mouth snarling into the bit. The result was the enormous statue I was now looking at: a horse and rider on a granite rock twenty-five feet high and weighing sixteen hundred tons, the rider's arm stretched out towards the river Neva and the university buildings on its other side. Alexander Pushkin, Russia's Shakespeare, turned it, in one of his greatest poems, into a symbol of the city and of the power of the Russian autocracy: a figure out of nightmare. The Communists made Peter retrospectively a sort of honorary Bolshevik, and the statue a place of pilgrimage. It was one of the two or three most famous sites in Russia. At the foot of its base lay neat rows of red carnations, and while I was there, two wedding parties from a Wedding Palace down the embankment arrived, to lay down more flowers and wave bottles of champagne up at the garlanded figure.

I'd been told by Artyom before I'd left Moscow that this statue should be my first port of call in Leningrad. "Why?" I'd asked him.

"If you want to know about Russia," he'd said in his brusque way, "then you must know about Peter."

But in fact I already knew about Peter. When I was about six, I'd read about him in a child's *Book of Knowledge:* this huge, almost seven-foot-tall Russian alien who'd come to the West (according to the pictures) to study shipbuilding in Holland and to pretend to be a gardener in the grounds of Hampton Court. And ever since then I'd been fascinated by him. He didn't live long: he died in 1725, at the age of fifty-two. He was barely literate: his handwriting was indecipherable, his spelling wretched. He was plagued by epilepsy and nervous tics. But he was one of the most energetic and contradic-tory men who ever lived. In some ways deeply religious, he neverthe-less held blasphemous orgies and made the church subservient to the state. He celebrated the weddings of his court dwarfs in debauches that could go on for weeks; collected freaks and human organs; and organized masked balls for twenty thousand people where noblemen and peasants were forced to rub elbows together. He seems never, ever to have been at rest. While conducting the longest war there has been in the last three hundred years—against the Swedes—he worked as a craftsman, mastering the arts of engineering and fortifi-cation, papermaking and stonemasonry. He made his own boots and books and furniture—not to mention the first ship in the Russian navy. Meanwhile, he completely transformed Russian soci-ety. He created the country's first standing army. He founded the Russian Academy of Sciences—as well as a particularly virulent secret police force under Prince Romodanovsky. And in the process of all this, by sheer force of personality, he frog-marched Russia into the modern age. When he began his reign, the country was back-ward and enslaved. But by the time he died, it had become a European power—what that canny old toady Voltaire called a brand-new model state—based here, on the cold lip of Western Europe, in the brand-new city of St. Petersburg.

I paid my respects to the Bronze Horseman as another wedding party came up; walked down the embankment behind the Admiralty, and crossed over a bridge to the tip of what I found out later was Vasilyevsky Island. I jostled my way through the tourists coming out of their buses, and looked out over the river. To the right, according to the guidebook, was the Winter Palace, a long complex of ornate baroque buildings hunched in the snow like old ladies crouched under a blanket; to the left, on the other side of the Neva, was the spire of the Cathedral of the Peter and Paul Fortress, shining out over the squat ramparts like an obstinate affirmation, a suggestion of grace. I walked down a ramp to the edge of the ice to take a closer look. And I tried to imagine what Peter had seen here; I tried to think myself into the phenomenal act of will that had created this eighteenth-century Brasilia from scratch. Somewhere behind the fortress, according to my guide, there was a little wooden hut that Peter had had built for himself in 1703 when nothing had existed here but swamp and sky. (It had been given a stone coat eighty years later by Catherine the Great, and Nicholas I had turned its little study into a shrine.) And yet, using this (at first) as his headquarters, in the twenty years that followed, he'd conjured up out of nothing a port, a naval base against the Swedes, and a new capital city. I'd read somewhere that in pre-Christian and mediaeval Russia men and women were buried alive in the foundations of cities, as a sacrifice to guarantee their future growth and prosperity. And by the lights of this old custom, St. Petersburg from the beginning should have been a prosperous city indeed. For, though no one knows how many conscripts and prisoners of war died fulfilling Peter's dream, the population of the country was said by a Russian historian to have dropped by about a quarter during the period of his reign. St. Petersburg was not just a city (or a port or a base); it was the first Russian Gulag.

"Hello. Can I help you?" said a voice behind me in English. I turned. It was a young man in spectacles, a flapped fur hat, and a Western-style anorak. "No," I said, and added, without thinking: "I was thinking about Peter the Great."

"You wanna change money?"

"No," I said. "Thank you."

"You want military watch? You want caviar?"

"No."

"You a tourist? Where you from?"

"Yes," I said. "I'm from England."

"You need a guide? I can show you. He's buried over there, you know."

"Who?"

"Peter. In the cathedral. He was a crazy man. Only he could have built this crazy city."

"What do you mean?"

"He wanted to make us Europeans. And in the end he just made us slaves."

I couldn't think what to say. Had he followed me? Was he just a hustler? I looked around. Another wedding party, I could see, was getting out of cars at the top of the quay. I began to walk slowly up towards it, away from the river. He followed me, still talking.

"All the things we have today, Peter made: internal passport, first efficient secret police, state monopoly of industry, huge bureaucracy."

The bride and groom (both impossibly young) were moving down towards us, hand in hand—she with a fur coat wrapped round her white dress, he in a shiny suit and a thin gestural moustache. Then, suddenly, the people around them broke into a strange taunting chant.

"What're they saying?" I asked.

"The people shout: 'It's bitter. Make it sweet,' " he said. "Then the man and woman have to kiss." I'd read about it in *Doctor Zhivago,* in the passage where Lara marries the student Antipov.

"Your English," I said. "Where did you learn it? Why's it so good?"

"I'm a student," he said.

"Where?"

He shrugged his shoulders.

"But if you're a student, then why do you need to sell things on the street?"

"Nobody can live on forty roubles a month."

"What's your name?"

There was a pause. Then: "Andrei," he said quietly. I suddenly realized that, unless he was a provocateur of some kind, he probably felt as exposed as I did. Any contact between Westerners and Soviet citizens was, I supposed, if not illegal anymore, then at least suspicious.

We walked on, past the tour buses. He was indeed nervous, I decided. He kept glancing around—as I did—to see if anyone was watching us. But he still showed no signs of wanting to go away. Instead, playing the tour guide, he pointed out two huge columns, symbolizing the port; and across Pushkin Square, a Doric-columned building which was once the Stock Exchange. "Now it's the Naval Museum," he said. "You can see in it the first boat in the Russian navy, which Peter built with his own hands. Round here was the original port area. Peter dressed up in a pilot's uniform to meet the first ship."

"Look," I said, stopping him in full flow, "I don't mean to be rude, Andrei. But I don't want to buy anything. I don't want to change money. And I don't need a guide."

"But you are with a group?" he said.

"No."

"What do you do in Leningrad? What profession are you?"

"I'm a writer. But—"

"Then you must know about the city." He stopped at the

approach to the bridge back to the mainland, and looked down at the buckled ice below. "It is artificial place, completely. Look." He pointed towards the spire of the Admiralty and then to the long reach of the Winter Palace. "There was nothing here at all but swamps and fever. There wasn't even any stone. So Peter made every person, every ship, every wagon bring stone here. He forced his aristocrats to build houses. And then he cut off their beards and their kaftans and made them wear European clothes and wigs, and do European dances, just like performing monkeys. In fifty years, most of them forgot how to speak proper Russian. They spoke in German and French. They were like foreigners in their own country, an occupying power. They had nothing in common with the people anymore." He turned back to me suddenly. "Maybe you got clothes you want to sell? Jeans? Tapes? Something like that?"

"No," I said.

"It was revolution from the top," he said, almost without pausing. "Just like now. Peter said Russians were too stupid to do it for themselves. So he forced them. Poor dumb Russians. They became fake Europeans and got a police state in return. Same under Stalin; same under Gorbachev. The only difference is name of tsar."

"Look," I said pompously. "I'm a friend of this country's and an admirer of Mikhail Gorbachev. When I hear you talk like that, I think you can't be trusted."

"But if you only want to hear good things about the Soviet Union, Mr. Writer, then how will you find out truth?"

It was unanswerable. So I walked with him a little further, while he talked his faint sedition, and finally bought him a drink at a Pepsi-Cola stand incongruously set beside the Winter Palace. I asked him where he came from. Vologda, he said: a town some-where to the north of Moscow. He hated Leningrad, he said; Vologda was real; Leningrad was superior and self-conscious. Leningraders were always telling you that they spoke the best Russian and had the most beautiful city in the Soviet Union. "And look at it," he said, pointing up at the Winter Palace. "It's all official beauty, all for the glory of the Russian state."

"It's like a film set," I said.

"Yes, but for big propaganda film. It's facade."

"And behind it?"

He shrugged. "Poverty, bad housing, the people who do the work. I can show you, if you like. I can show you the real Lenin-grad," he said, suddenly enthusiastic. "I can introduce you to my friends. I can introduce you to girls."

"Well . . ."

"Here," he said, fumbling in his pocket. "I will give you my telephone number."

"No," I said. "Wait." I didn't want to be seen taking anything from him in public. So instead I wrote his name and telephone number down on a page in my notebook, and five minutes after we said goodbye, I threw it away into the snow. I was probably being paranoid, but it seemed a good idea at the time. Besides, paranoia is flattering: it makes you feel important. It was hard for me, a Westerner, not to feel important then.

Chapter 3

April–May 1989

Outside the hotel. Savva the filmmaker is waiting by his car, drumming his fingers on the bonnet. We are late. Varya, his wife, shrugs her shoulders, says it doesn't matter, she understands. Then we race across the city, with Savva literally driving his impatience away, a radar detector he got in America peeping out a warning from the dashboard every time it senses *militsia* on the prowl. Savva is intensely proud of it, balancing it carefully on a glove. "See, see," he says, pointing to a parked car or a *militsia* man standing beside the highway holding out a long white radar gun, as he slams on the brakes once more. "They are everywhere. It's a holiday weekend and there are lots of people coming into the city. There. There." Then he's away again, accelerating through law-abiding traffic, laughing, lost in the game. I find myself thinking of him—as I have before—as Italian: this intense, funny man whom Yelena calls one of her Three Musketeers. But it's France he really loves the most. He tells me a long story in the car, between the beeps of the detector, about the imagined rivalry between Tarkovsky and Bresson at one of the Cannes Film Festivals he's been to: how they finally embraced on stage at the end of the festival and put paid to the overheated theorizings of the French critics. Then he describes his latest film, which was shown at the Leningrad Film Festival and will be shown in France later in the year. It's had a mixed, rather confused reaction so far from the newspapers and journals. But a young girl stood up for it when it was shown at the Moscow House of Film not long ago. She said (and was quoted in *Komsomolskaya Pravda*) that it was the right and duty of every serious artist to experiment, to push at the barriers. He laughs. The girl was Yelena's sixteen⁄year⁄old daughter, Ksiyusha: proud, passionate, political Ksiyusha.

We stop at Yelena's parents' flat on Vorotnikovsky Alley, just up the street from Pushkin Square, where the great demonstrations for Boris Yeltsin began. Ksiyusha is out, for her English lessons with a private tutor. But Mama, as I call her, is waiting for us with painted Easter eggs, a traditional domed Easter bread, and a giant *kulibiak,* made with cabbage and meat. She's a funny and imposing woman who works as a grader in a film processing laboratory. But in this cramped little apartment she is always dressed in an apron and carpet slippers, bustling from kitchen to dining room to bed⁄room, calling out to Ksiyusha or Yelena that their food is ready, or that someone's on the phone, or that it's time to go out. Where she gets her energy from, I have no idea. She cooks and shops and queues for the family. She works daily eight⁄hour shifts. And yet she never seems to go to bed before one o'clock in the morning. I can't help thinking of her, whenever I see her, as a hen: busy, beaky, clucking, broad⁄beamed, down⁄bottomed, holding her hands clasped in front of her and using her elbows for gestures, as if they were wings. But there's much more than that in her: some tempered iron that I can only guess at. Ksiyusha once told me that she was, when she was young, a very talented mathematician. And for her last birthday, she gave Yelena a thousand roubles—roughly five months' salary.

Gennady, Yelena's father, is also there, though I might have missed him in the packing of the food and the stowing of presents. He's a strange figure, Gennady, existing, somehow, on the fringes of this noisy female family: jowly, droop-eyed, lost in a strange sadness, like a man who has forfeited some once-great authority and doesn't know why. He has the air of a petitioner, of a man permanently looking over the shoulders of others, trying to get attention. Perhaps it's just his family he's trying to attract, I think as we talk together in the courtly, slightly stilted French he likes to practice with me. Or perhaps it's something to do with the times, the turbulence of the new freedoms he must see around him and sense in his daughter and granddaughter. I remember as we talk that he once worked as a journalist in Belgium, and that the last time I saw him he was in a clinic in the north of Moscow, suffering from some obscure bronchial complaint. He told me then, with some pride, as we walked in the corridor, that this was the clinic where they treated Leonid Brezhnev. And he seemed happier there, amid the privileges of the old guard of the Party, than he ever seemed at home.

2

Night is beginning to fall outside in the courtyard and the children are called in from play. We drive to Varya's family's dacha in Peredelkino, through streets and past buildings crowned and lined with flags. We stop only once, to pick up a woman with a deep cigarette-laugh who's been staying with Savva and Varya: a Frenchwoman, I think I hear Savva say. In fact she turns out to be a Russian. And only much later do I realize that she's the novelist and playwright Nella Biyelski, who moved to Paris in the sixties and has recently written (about her first visit to Moscow in four years): "I had one immediate impression which affected everything. The fences have been dismantled. For me, the symbol of Moscow has always been the contrast between the immensity of the city, its streets of huge modern buildings, and the intimacy of the interior courtyards, with their grass and trees and the small kitchen windows looking onto them. Before, the little courtyards were fenced off, as if they refused the change of regime. Today, these barriers are down and it is as if old Moscow lives once more, and has opened itself to the outside world."

I hadn't really looked at the courtyards before.

3

We drive up to the gate of the old wooden dacha at Peredelkino and Varya disappears through a postern. Then the gate swings open into a garden full of jasmine and raspberry bushes, pear and apple trees. We're only twenty minutes from the city, but we're immediately in another world: a private, Chekhovian world of echoing voices and trailed-away sentences; the world of the countryside, which broods over Russian art and literature like a requiem. As we unpack the car, other houses along the lane seem distant and remote; our laughter threads away on the evening breeze, to be scattered over half-lit porches and balconies. When Varya opens the front door with a large, iron key, the house is full of an old, remembered peace, as if it's rousing itself slowly and comfortably from winter: smiling.

"Isn't it beautiful, Jo?" says Yelena, carrying an armful of lilies, and her toothbrush like a talisman. And it is: like a ship becalmed in a sea of trees. She leads me through the rooms: a hallway with a long, battered oak table and trestle benches; a sitting room with worn throw rugs over sofas; and a dining room, the heart of the house, where you almost expect to see holes dented in the table by generations of people leaning forward in the night: arguing, making a point, toasting. Varya is shaking a peasant-patterned tablecloth over it, and it is soon laden with cakes and bread and *kulibiak,* and a *pashcha,* a beheaded cone of pressed cottage cheese, stuffed with raisins and pistachios, which is traditional at Easter. We sit down and look at the spread—Savva and Varya have been fasting through Lent and will not eat till midnight. And then we toast each other solemnly with little glasses of Armenian brandy, looking forward: "Happy Easter."

A few minutes later, the poet Andrei Voznesensky and his wife, Zoya, arrive from their dacha nearby, bearing in triumph yet another domed Easter sugar loaf. Andrei is, as usual, wrapped in a double smile: one smile for the outside world, and one smile for the joke he seems always to be listening to inside. "Andrei's such a sweetie," Artyom Troitsky says of him. But he's also a survivor—he's re-mained from Khrushchev's time onward one of the two or three best-known poets in the Soviet Union. The elfin gentleness he radiates has something tougher within.

We shake hands while the others embrace—we like each other, I think—and I give him a book of Derek Walcott's poems that I have brought. He is pleased. ("Joseph Brodsky admires him very much, I know.") And then I ask him why I haven't seen him in England, where he was supposed to come to deliver a new book. He laughs. "Oh, I can't seem to come to grips with it," he says. "You know? There's too much going on here." He is chairman of the committee for the centenary of the birth of Boris Pasternak, whose apprentice and protégé he was; and he's on the editorial board of *Yunost* (Youth), which is competing with all the other so-called "thick journals" to publish the lost backlog of Russian literature and history. The last time I saw him was onstage at a poetry reading at a palace of culture, where he was introducing to a packed audience some of the unpublished poets of the Brezhnev era, as well as scabrous young punk poets from the city's universities and high schools. He looked tired. He didn't read his own poetry; he just sat there smiling. But he was bombarded with a steady stream of fan notes and written questions passed hand to hand, from spectator to spectator, down through the long ranked seats of the hall.

Zoya, his wife, I haven't met before, though I've talked to her on the phone. She's the writer Zoya Boguslavskaya, and she's just finished a book on American women. (The manuscript is leaving in a few days' time for New York, she tells me, with Hedrick Smith, the author of *The Russians.*) We toast the book, the new child going out into the world. And then, sitting next to her, I watch her as she talks about the women she's interviewed in the United States (among them Nancy Reagan), to see if I can see why she's not universally liked (as I have heard). Perhaps it's only because she doesn't *look* like a writer—or at least like a Russian writer: the often considerably down-at-heels tribune of the people. She's urbane and carefully groomed, her hair pulled back in a chignon. She carries herself beautifully. But her clothes and manner seem better suited to the world of the Kennedys and the Rostropoviches, the world she and Andrei inhabit in the West, than they do to the ramshackle informality of this writers' colony at the beginning of summer.

In a lull in the conversation, I talk to Andrei about a story of his, "O," which he thinks might be filmed. And then I ask him if he's given any readings of his own poetry recently; and if so, whether he had any trouble from Pamyat, as he did in Odessa at a reading of his two or three months ago. (Pamyat, an organization originally founded to fight the destruction of Moscow's historical and cultural monuments, has become over the past two years or so Russia's equivalent of the fascist National Front. Pamyat people broke up the election meetings of liberal candidates like Vitaly Korotich, the editor of *Ogonyok.* And the movement's chief spokes- man, Dmitri Vasiliev, is now much given to announcing that war is the only way to save Russia's soul.)

"Yeeess," Andrei says, raising his eyebrows, gathering atten- tion. "I gave a reading recently, and Pamyat created a big distur- bance. There were only about two hundred of them in an audience of two thousand, but it was impossible to continue. They are crazy people, I think." He splays his hands and shrugs. "But . . ."

There is a sudden irruption of talk. Liberal intellectuals are made very nervous by Pamyat, by the idea that something dark and very Russian is being dragged up by the new freedoms: an echo of the old Panslavism, the old Black Hundreds; a nostalgia for the mission of the Holy Mother Country and the virulent, chauvinistic Stalinism of the postwar years. I am too tired to follow what they are saying: Nella, the wry and pungent Parisian; Savva, urgent and declamatory; Yelena, always asking soft questions; Andrei, as softly answering. And instead I simply listen to the ebb and flow of their language as the night deepens and we become more and more isolated in a tiny circle of light. This, I think as I sit, is where Russia has always lived, round a table in a pool of light, surrounded by night and distance and the grip of bad weather. And at the table, there has always been the plash and music of this most beautiful of languages, creating landscapes of mood and whole armies of ideas to launch against the challenge of the future. This is the *kruzhok,* the circle, and out of it has come both the millennial clash of the Revolution and the shining obstinacy of the poets and writers who lost their lives in its aftermath.

4

Near midnight, we drive to Peredelkino's little onion-domed church. In the darkness of the lane up to it, hundreds of people seem to be milling about us, and at the top, the *militsia* have put up a rope to keep back the curious. In the churchyard, there is no one, just an amazing stillness: the sound of the wind and distant chanting. The church, dimly lit, looks like a cluster of improbable rockets rising from the launching pad of the asphalt around it.

We find a side door and squeeze in at the back, among a huge crowd of old and young, most of them carrying between their hands thin oxblood-coloured candles. All we can see from where we stand is a sea of backs, topped by another sea, of faces, in the porch across from us. Then the great music of the Russian liturgy washes around us: the arching monotone of the priest answered turn by turn, first by the nasal, reedy, almost keening voices of old women, and then by a mixed choir, in which a deep bass voice rumbles and turns like an acrobat. There is a constant movement in the congregation, a ripple of heads bowing, the sudden swing of hands from head to navel to shoulders in the great rhythmical sweep of the Orthodox cross. And though from where we are I can't see the embroidered, peasant splendour of the priests or much of the painted, vaulted roof of the church, I know that there is something here, something old and atavistic, that still—despite all the years of persecution and murder and neglect—touches the heart of Russians, whether they know the words of the liturgy or not, or whether they think of themselves as believers or not. I remember, two months ago, Yelena saying to a young priest, Father Vladimir Rusak—who had just been released from a twelve-year prison sentence for having written a three-volume twentieth-century history of the church—that she felt a longing to be baptized. I thought at the time that she was just making a gesture of sympathy, of solidarity, and I didn't take it seriously. But now, as I watch her face shining in the half-light, I think that, like many Russians, she would really like to be reattached in some way to this charged, emotional, Byzantine old world, where the difficulties of day-to-day living can be given up in the interests of an afterlife, and where *sobornost*—a kind of self-forgetful together-ness, for which most Russians seem to have a limitless yearning—is still available.

Just before midnight, the church falls silent. There is a rustle of movement, as people lean together, passing a flame from candle to candle across the congregation. A young boy, wrapped in a great-coat, turns and offers candles to Yelena, Nella, and me from a nest in his hands. I smile and make a small namaste as thank-you, and he lights them for us from his flame. Then I look up to see the church dancing with tiny, flickering points of light. "Christ is risen. Christ is risen." The priests, carrying icons, move down below the great central dome of the church. The congregation pours in behind them and the doors are thrown open. A long procession, singing, makes its way out into the night, to proclaim to those behind the *militsia*'s barrier that Christ has made his way to heaven and hum- drum mortality has once again been conquered.

We follow the procession out from the church through the watching graves, cupping our candles against the wind. And then we stand aside, and make our way down to Savva's car, keeping them alight until the last moment.

5

We raise champagne glasses. "Christ is risen." And after dinner— of chicken and a huge ox liver, which I've cut into pieces, grimac- ing, and fried—we walk in the lanes and listen to people singing in distant houses. Then we sit upstairs in the darkness, sipping brandy, looking deep into a fire which Savva has lit from gathered branches. Nobody speaks. Then Nella says in English quietly: "Nowhere in the world do they have such wonderful homes. I don't mean houses. I mean homes."

As we go finally to bed, Savva slips an arm round my shoulders and says: "You know, Jo, you and me, we're on the same team. We're the last generation of seekers. When the computers are turned off or break down, that's when they're going to need people like us."

I feel ridiculously moved. Later, in the little upstairs bedroom, where Yelena's necklaces are hung across a mirror like a valence, we fall asleep making love without speaking.

Chapter 4

February 1988

"Excuse, please," said a middle-aged man in a fur hat and torn sheepskin coat, as I was fighting my way through the crowd at one of Leningrad's so-called free markets. Downstairs I'd seen out-of-season tomatoes at astronomical prices, and now on the second floor I was in a bruising conga line, trying to shuffle my way past racks of clothing that was new but looked old, like fifties' museum pieces.

"You are American?" he said.

"No," I bellowed over the hubbub. "English."

"One minute." He beckoned me, then pulled me by the elbow into a corner. "You must help me," he said in an urgent whisper, his mouth close to my ear. I could smell the garlic and toothpaste on his breath. "Here," he said, pointing at my camera. "You have film?"

"Yes."

"You have other film with you?"

"No. Why?"

"I am dissident," he said. "I need thirty-five-millimetre film. For important thing. Then maybe you take out of country."

"No," I said, fighting free of him. "No," I said, rejoining the conga line quickly and looking around to see who'd been watching us. He could have been the real thing, of course. But I immediately assumed that he was a KGB plant.

The KGB was still very much on my mind—as it was on every foreigner's mind at the time. It contaminated every contact I might have made in Leningrad. I didn't know until later (until Yelena, in fact, told me) that every tour guide and interpreter who dealt with foreigners had to write special reports on their charges for "the friends," so I was probably less of a blip on their radar than most travellers. But I remembered Martin Walker saying that I shouldn't have anything to do with the street moneychangers, the *fartsovchiki,* or with the hookers, the *prostitutki,* since some of them, inevitably, were informers for the *militsia* or the KGB. (He'd even talked about his Russian assistant: "A terrific, intelligent woman—such a pity she has to report to the KGB too.") So I exchanged no more than a few words with the men who were constantly sidling up to me on the streets, offering me roubles for my pounds or jeans or cigarettes or records. I smiled vacantly at everyone who called out "Mister!" or stopped me to ask why I wasn't part of a group. I wanted to demonstrate to my watchers that I was a harmless travel writer, an innocent abroad, and I played the role during the day as convincingly as I could. I appeared, notebook in hand, at all the mandatory stations of the tourist's cross: I paid my respects to Dostoyevsky and Tchaikovsky, Borodin, and Rimsky-Korsakov in the Tikhvin Cemetery; I plunged, like a conspicuous swimmer, into every church and cathedral I could find.

For my work for the American magazine had become what I thought of as my cover for what I now did at night: which was to make my way (by a roundabout route) to Boris Grebenshchikov's eyrie of an apartment on Sofia Perovskaya Street.

2

"Boris," I said to the English Teacher when he came to the hotel. "Tell me about Boris." He took off his coat and closely examined the small beer in front of him. He was a slight man in his thirties, with a patriarchal ginger beard which seemed too old for the young face that peeped out behind it. He earned eighty roubles a month in an art school, he later told me, and he was an expert on Soviet jazz. His voice was soft and high-pitched. He was very cerebral.

"Well, I don't know what you want to know exactly," he said slowly. "But Boris is, well, a very important figure—I'd say the most important on the whole Soviet rock scene. His band, Aquarium, was among the first to perform in Russian. They were the first to put out underground cassettes. Boris was a major force, too, in setting up the Rock Club that we have here in Leningrad. And he produced the first rock magazine."

"And his music?"

"Well, he's made every sort of music," said the English Teacher. "Maybe like Bob Dylan. He's had a punk phase, a reggae phase, folk rock, acid rock, everything you can think." Then, as I looked bemused: "You see, Jo, it's different from the West. Rock music here isn't about dancing or sex. It's still very pure. What matters is the melody, and especially the lyrics. I remember when I first heard Boris. I wasn't into rock music at all then—it was the seventies, and there were all these Beatles imitators. It was very boring, even in the West. But then somebody persuaded me to go to this concert by Aquarium, and I remember thinking: 'This is amazing! We've finally produced something that can stand on its own. Rock, but real *Russian* rock.' Boris is a poet like Dylan—a guitar poet, as we say."

"And a hero?" I asked.

"I suppose, yes: an antiestablishment hero. Harassment, ban-nings, the usual thing. Then, in 1980, he took Aquarium to a festival in Tbilisi, and they did some, I don't know, antics on stage which the organizers thought were homosexual. When the authori-ties here heard about it, he was sacked from his job as a computer operator. He lost his rehearsal facilities, everything." He laughed. "It was probably the best thing that ever happened to him. Now he is . . . well, tolerated."

We left the hotel and walked through the snow past the audi-ences coming out of the Philharmonic Hall and the Maly Theatre. "And Melodiya's finally produced a record of his," I said.

"Yes," said the English Teacher. "But all they did was to take the material from two of his old underground cassettes. The only thing Boris had to do with it was to get Andrei Voznesensky to write the liner notes."

We crossed a footbridge over one of the canals and then turned towards the entrance of a building. I caught a glimpse of a dark, ruined courtyard, and then the English Teacher beckoned me to-wards a hidden door off to the right. He opened it. There was a strong smell of urine. We were at the bottom of a high stairwell. Five or six teenagers were at the foot of the stairs, smoking, talking quietly, looking upwards.

"Fans," said the English Teacher softly.

"How far up is it?" I said as I moved past them, nodding.

"All the way to the top."

We clambered slowly upwards. It was extremely cold. On the fourth landing, I called a halt, panting and muttering something about the need to establish a base camp before attempting the summit. Then I looked around. Every available surface was covered with graffiti. "What do they say?" I asked.

"Boris is known as Bob," he said, and then pointed. "Here. 'Bob Equals *Bog*': Bob is God. Here, 'Long Live Tsoya Bob

Culture.' It's a pun. Soya Bean Culture, or Boris and Viktor Tsoy, the lead singer of a band called Kino. The rest," he said, "well . . ."

At the top, when we finally made it, another group of fans was waiting outside a door facing out over the stairs. The English Teacher stopped to speak to one of them and then translated what he said for me. "He says he comes from Siberia," he said. "He first heard Boris on one of his underground cassettes, probably an eigh-teenth-generation copy by the time it got to Siberia. He's come to pay his respects." He paused to talk to another. "This one," he said, "comes from Vladivostok." Then he rang the bell. There was a pause, and then Grebenshchikov appeared at the door, wearing a kaftan. He shook hands with the English Teacher and embraced him. Then: "Hello," he said. "You must be the Englishman."

Boris Grebenshchikov was in his mid-thirties, with long pale-brown hair, soft, penetrating eyes, and a mouth wry with irony. He talked softly, and had a habit of pausing before he said something and then pausing again afterwards, with his head cocked sideways, as if to measure its effect. He spoke astonishingly good English, and he had all the qualities that were necessary to make him hugely attractive to Westerners like me: he was light in touch; he made jokes; he paid flattering, but never slavish, attention. He had, I thought as he chatted with his fans and then ushered the boy from Vladivostok inside for something to eat, all the charm and confi-dence of a scholarship winner or someone who has an important secret known only to himself and God. He also had the most variable face I'd ever seen in a man. In repose or when his attention strayed, he could look, with his bad Soviet teeth, as coarse-featured as a docker. But then he would draw on some hidden well of energy, smile, and transform himself immediately into what looked unset-tlingly like a comic-book Nordic god. When I later recognized how private and chameleonic and Russian he in fact was, I began to call him, because of these instant transformations of his, Perun the Mighty Wonder, a sort of mediaeval Russian Clark Kent.

We followed him down a dark, narrow corridor, and then sat round a table in a little room littered with tapes and posters, paint-ings and ikons, drinking Irish whisky that I'd brought from En-gland. "Look. Liquid heaven," he said, raising his glass. Then: *"Slon giobagh."* He drained it in one toss. He had been to the West only once in his life, when he'd flown to New York to discuss making a record with CBS. But he spoke about the Chieftains and the Clancy Brothers and the Dubliners as if they were close friends. "We Russians," he said a little later, "are really just Irish-men who got lost somewhere along the way. Look: same love of drink and poetry; same madness; same endless argument with God. *Na zdaroviya!"*

I asked him why on earth he'd become a rock musician. "Oh, that's easy," he said. "Because of the Beatles, of course!" Then he sang a snatch of "She Loves You" constantly interrupted by the machine-gun hiss of static. "Voice of America. The BBC. You could only just hear them through the jamming. But they'd found the promised land—you could hear it in what they were playing." He shrugged his shoulders. "After that, there wasn't anything to do but follow them. Ask any Soviet musician of my generation. He'd say exactly the same thing."

"There was total Beatles madness here," said the English Teacher, leaning forward. "You can't imagine. Sailors, dancers, athletes—anyone who could get abroad—brought back Beatles LPs and sold them on the black market for enormous prices. If you couldn't afford to buy one, you could maybe hire it overnight."

"You could even hire a *photograph* overnight," said Boris, laugh-ing. "And if you couldn't afford that, then you did the next best thing: you went to a Beatles concert. There were probably four thousand bands in the Soviet Union who played nothing but Beatles music, like human jukeboxes."

"All in English, of course," said the English Teacher. "I remember one of the first bands in Leningrad ever to sing in Russian, like Aquarium did. They were booed off the stage by the audience."

"So what kind of living did you make when you started?" I asked.

"*Living?*" They both burst out laughing. "I'm an *amateur,* Jo," said Boris. "To be professional, you have to be O.K.'d by the state. You have to audition in front of artistic councils and have your lyrics approved by the KGB. Aquarium would never go through any of that shit. So from the state's point of view we simply didn't exist. We still don't exist: which means no touring, no decent instruments, and no records until a few months ago. Until a couple of years back, we couldn't even charge money for admission. It was illegal. So we gave concerts in people's apartments or in a lecture room in one of the Institutes, with everybody chipping in what he could afford. Later someone might be brave and hire a hall and sell handmade tickets—"

"Absolutely underground, without any publicity," said the English Teacher.

"—and maybe we'd have enough in the end for a couple of bottles of vodka."

At this point, all formal talk disintegrated in the room under the eaves, as the bell rang and people began to pour in, waving offerings of chocolates or vodka or vegetables or bread, to be accommodated on rickety chairs around the small table, or else perched on the arms of armchairs in the corners, peering into the candlelit centre like birds with their wings crimped. Boris's wife, Lyuda, bustled through the room among them, big-breasted and cheerfully loud-mouthed, emptying ashtrays and plonking bottles and glasses down on the table. But apart from her the company was all male— extravagantly male, in fact: bearded and stubble-jawed, long-haired, noisy and argumentative. I fed them my Western cigarettes as they arrived, while those who could speak English fed me questions and opinions about writers and musicians, philosophers and painters in the West. They were, it seemed to me, astonishingly knowledgeable. They knew of Western bands that not even other Western bands had ever heard of. They could quote Marcuse and Salinger and the lyrics of Marc Bolan, which they argued over with the intensity of seminarians. They were opinionated, too; they treated me with a mixture of truculence and ironic deference, as if I knew both nothing at all and (just perhaps) a whole lot more than they—which was close to the truth. They were, though, I noticed, universally deferen‐ tial and placatory to Boris. For it was he who through the long night refereed their spats and shushed them when they became too raucous; it was he, never shifting from his chair, who passed round the food and drink. This was my first *kruzhok*—made up, in part, of some of the aristocracy of Leningrad rock, I learned later—of which Boris, I soon realized, was definitely the still centre.

Not much else remains in my mind of that first evening except a few patchy impressions: of the English Teacher sitting carved at his place at the table, stirring only when the talk shifted (with Boris translating) to the politics of the Leningrad Rock Club or of the Cultural Democratic Movement; of a large drunk—once genial, now glowering—being led sombrely from the room; of Boris quietly singing; and of my opening doors down a corridor on the way to a lavatory, and finding behind them craned necks and wide eyes, people coming awake. Somewhere in the middle, though, of the long hours of floating, eddying, squalling talk—none of it small— Boris and I agreed to try to make a film together. And I remember thinking, as I listened to him talking and reminiscing about the way he'd been banned and forbidden to tour and declared a public enemy, of a lyric of his quoted in Artyom's book: "We drank that pure water / And we'll never grow older." It was a pure sixties line. And the atmosphere in the little room was unmistakeably like that of my own sixties in the West—except perhaps for the drug of choice. It was intense, lofty-minded, innocent, conspiratorial, and, above all, I thought, brave. I could have been in London, Paris, or Berkeley in 1968.

Before I left, and after most of the circle had gone, Boris told me a story: slack-eyed, facing the dawn. I wrote it down, rather blearily, when I got back to my hotel. "In the seventies," he said, "when I was still a student, there was a man who encouraged me more than anyone else to write my own songs. He was a physicist. He lived in a communal apartment. And he spent his time doing nothing but drinking and listening to Miles Davis and Jimi Hendrix. It was a sort of weird communal apartment, full of mysterious people— Syrians a lot of them. But then I suppose it had to be. My friend'd sit there in his room, smoking his pipe, and be surrounded by people: poets, other physicists, young punks, everybody. He'd play Jimi Hendrix full blast at five o'clock in the morning.

"Anyway," he went on dreamily, "one day I went to see him. He had two young hoods there, who were on the run from the police. They wanted shelter and he gave it to them. And the next day they showed up with two cases of cognac which they'd stolen from some liquor factory, to thank him. Well, the cognac was terrific, and there was an enormous drunken party. And the *militsia* came and broke it up. But the odd thing was that they didn't arrest anybody but him. And from that point on, he was arrested again and again and constantly harassed, and he finally had to move out of the communal apartment. He found another place to live, but not long after he moved in, he was found murdered on the stairs— his stomach had been carved up, really mutilated. They arrested a friend of his: a kind of a violent guy, but not a guy who would ever have attacked someone he cared about. He was killed, I think, by the KGB."

3

Two days after my first meeting with Boris, my friend Marjie arrived in the city. Marjie was an American, a child psychologist whom I'd known since the time she'd had a house in Miami Beach in which a plot was hatched to steal Jack Kennedy's portrait from the 1972 Democratic Convention. She now lived in London, but she remained what she had always been: a by-the-book Jewish-American princess, intelligent, wry, and very observant. Her first night in the city, I took her to see Boris. The next morning, we went to look at the Peter-Paul Fortress.

"This is a strange place, boy," she said, looking out over the river Neva. "Look at them. They cut holes in the ice to go swimming. They queue up in the slush for ice cream on Nevsky Prospekt. And their kids use buckets and spades to play with the snow in the parks. What do they think this is?"

"The summer of *glasnost?*" I said.

"That's the trouble with you, Jo," she said, turning. "You're already in love with this place. You want everything to stand for something, to mean something good." Later, when I painfully deciphered a word on an architectural plan on the wall of the fortress's cathedral, and it turned out to be *perestroika,* or reconstruction, she said: "Um, I might have known."

She was right, of course. I did think—at first, at any rate—that Leningrad was one of the most romantic places on earth. Everything in it seemed charged with emotion, full of historical sorrow and hope, like the memory of an old love affair at the beginning of a new one. The services at the Alexander Nevsky Monastery that we went to were almost impossibly moving. The meals we ate at the first of the city's private restaurants were a triumph, I thought, of individual willpower over the levelling indifference of the Soviet state.

Everything I saw, in fact, as we walked along the frozen spools of the canals, seemed saturated in significance. Everything represented something I'd read about: the bleak monochrome of the Piskaryov´skoye Cemetery (where the dead from the siege of Leningrad were buried), the limitless, epic suffering of the Russian people; the shrinelike museum in Pushkin's last apartment, where he died after a duel, their worship of poetry and their veneration for the dead. As we endlessly crisscrossed the city, everything was grist to this inner interpretational mill of mine. I wrote down every smile I saw and every scrawny chicken and orange being sold on the street, and thought of them as the beginnings of private enterprise and of freedom after repression.

This was all right with Marjie, as far as it went. But she had come to Leningrad for the art and the architecture, about which she knew a good deal. She was also a great reader of guidebooks: a gutter, a disemboweller, of facts and figures. So our daily tours through the city were soon accompanied by a host of names and ghosts. It began almost as a game. "Look," she'd say, "the Summer Gardens . . ."

"Where Peter built his palace . . ."

"And Lisa was pointed out to Herman in Pushkin's *Queen of Spades.*"

Or: "This is where Father Gapon led his march of supplicants towards massacre in 1905 . . ."

"Looked down on from a balcony by Pasternak's Dr. Zhi´vago . . ."

"And turned into music in Shostakovich's Eleventh Sym´phony."

The names and references slowly piled up around us as we paced through the museums and huge architectural landscapes of Leningrad: Peter and Lenin, Pushkin and Tchaikovsky, Dos´toyevsky and Gogol and Catherine the Great. History and music and literature and opera began to supervene on each other in our minds, bleeding into each other like the layers of a Viennese torte. Here was where General Yepanchin in Dostoyevsky's *The Idiot* lived, a near-neighbour of the exiled poet Joseph Brodsky, not far from where the emperor Alexander II was assassinated. There was where Vladimir Nabokov looked out in his youth over the domes of the churches seen through Tatiana's window in Tchaikovsky's *Eugene Onegin.* "The problem," I finally said to Marjie one day, after we'd spent hours tracking down the house where Raskolnikov murdered the money lender in Dostoyevsky's *Crime and Punishment,* "is that Leningrad's a fictional city turned into brick and stone, rather than a real one turned into novels and verse and music, like London. Historically speaking, it's a puzzle or a bad joke. There's no real reason for its existence."

"The problem," said Marjie wearily, rubbing her feet, "is that there's simply too much Here here."

It was a remark that stayed in my head for days. A fictional city with too much Here here. That was exactly right. The city was not only unnecessary—as a fortified port, it had become an anachronism even in Peter the Great's time—but also, psychically and architec-turally, somehow out of kilter. There were just too many colonnades in the city; too many porticoes and pilasters and triumphal arches. Nowhere else on earth had the classical and the baroque been given such scope, such space in which to deploy themselves as in this made-to-order place. Nowhere else had the royal and noble clients been so free with their money, so anxious to show themselves off as civilized and European. And the result was an excess born of insecurity: the gigantomania of a people who were making them-selves up from scratch. It had produced a literature that was often surreal and haunted, and an architecture from which (on foot, at any rate) you simply couldn't escape. The combination had the effect of seeming to eliminate time and reality, making the history (and fiction and myths) of the place omnipresent and simultaneous.

One night in Boris's apartment, I asked him whether he thought this was true. "Yes," he said. "There is too much history here. Too many ghosts, living among the living. Leningrad must be the saddest and most self-conscious place on earth."

4

We went, of course, to the Winter Palace. You couldn't avoid it. It was the hub of the city, the place where the sustaining myths of the tsars and the Revolution met. It was also huge—so huge, wrote Catherine the Great to her poodle Voltaire, that "only the mice and I can enjoy it all." Peter the Great had lived relatively modestly by the royal standards of his time, amid the cupboards and stoves of the wooden Summer Palace the other side of the Hermitage. (He ate porridge, it was said, and cabbage soup and disliked being waited on at table.) But not so his successors in this enormous palace, built for the empress Elisabeth and then reconstructed after a fire in 1837. It was, I thought as Marjie and I climbed the great sweep of the Jordan Staircase day after day, an orgy of ostentation, of marble and porphyry, alabaster, gold, and amaranth. Scrolls and mouldings, lion masks and caryatids seemed to decorate every surface. There were forests of columns of every size and shape; and whole zoos and pantheons of gods and animals writhing and trumpeting their presence overhead. Each of the state rooms was an elaborate stage set: the huge Nicholas Hall, where balls for five thousand were given in the winter season, and where the last tsar made a speech early in his reign about "the senseless dreams" of those who wanted to limit his power; the Pavilion Hall, where his doomed daughters used to skate across the birchwood floor, amid fluted pillars and fountains, to see birds spin and crow and spread their wings in a fantasticated eighteenth-century clock given to Catherine by one of her lovers; and the Malachite Hall, with its bright green columns and pilasters, where the Kerensky government held its cabinet meetings until arrested by the Bolsheviks in the White Dining Room next door. These rooms were backdrops for a cast of giants—or gods. And the presence, in galleries around and above them, of some of the world's most beautiful paintings did nothing to soften the impression it gave: of a manmade Valhalla, built by a religion which worshipped nothing so much as the splendour and audacity of its own high priest. It made dwarfs of the modern tourists who clustered here. It must have made progressively smaller dwarves in the past of all those who had stood further and further away from the holy of holies of the tsar, whose glory and power it represented. When the imperial family, I read in one of the guidebooks, made its passage to the cathedral every January 1, it passed through an enfilade here in which exactly this pecking order of progressive shrinkage seemed to be symbolized. Next to the great central accumulator of the family's apartments stood the court in the Concert Hall, followed by military officers in the Nicholas Hall and the Fore Hall (where champagne buffets were usually given). After that came the mayors and mer-chants in the Field Marshals' Hall, followed, in the Armorial Hall, by lesser officials and their wives in national costume. In this case, as in life, it was distance from the tsar that defined social status (and vice versa). Only contact with his mystical electricity could confer any authority at all. "The mad Tsar Paul got it right," I said to Marjie, "when he said to the Swedish ambassador: 'In Russia, only he is great with whom I speak, and only while I am speaking to him.' " It could have been Stalin talking.

5

"He's my favourite tsar, Paul," said Boris, looking out of the window over Sofia Perovskaya Street. "You know, he created a special regiment of guards who all had to have snub noses exactly like he had?" He laughed and sat down at the table. "He used to have visits, too, from the archangel Michael, who told him to build a castle where he'd be safe from his enemies. So he built it, the Engineers' Castle. He was murdered there six weeks after he moved in. You can never tell, with archangels." He laughed again.

Almost every night, after the Winter Palace or the Smolny Convent, after a concert or the ballet, Marjie and I would climb the steep stairs, past the fans and the graffiti, to Boris's nest under the eaves. The rest of the building seemed eerily empty. (We later found out that it had been abandoned, vacated.) There was just Boris's little nighttime kingdom at what seemed the top of the world, a kingdom he shared (we also found out) with the janitors and odd-job men from the school in the courtyard below. We would sit around the little rickety table as a stream of people ebbed and flowed around us, and hold in a fug of cigarette smoke long, earnest debates about everything under the sun: about Tolkien and the Tao and the Egyptian *Book of the Dead;* about the Doors and the Beatles and drugs and who should play on the record he was going to make for CBS. Religion and mysticism were never far away from Boris's mind. (He was clearly his circle's spiritual guru.) But he almost never talked about politics, except dismissively. Only once do I remember him putting aside his easy charm, when Marjie asked him one night about the Brezhnev years, the so-called era of stagna-tion. "What was life like then?" she said.

"It was a time," he said slowly, "when everybody died. Inside or outside, it didn't matter. A lot of people died of drink. Some of my friends became prostitutes or black-market dealers. Others emi-grated or were forced out of the country. Others just took what was offered, and became cynical bureaucrats. It was a time of great . . . sin," he said finally.

"What about now? Under Gorbachev?" I asked him quietly.

"I don't know," he said. "You see, Jo, I think we've done you in the West a great favour. For seventy years, we've been a laboratory in which this experiment called socialism was run. The people at the top tried everything to make it work. They did genetic experiments—they killed off all the best people. They cut out the brain of the society; they cut out its heart—they destroyed the culture. Well, it still didn't work—so now you don't ever have to try the experiment for yourselves."

"But what about Gorbachev?" said Marjie, insisting.

"He took part in the experiment too," he said. "But, well, what the hell, he seems to be a good man. And look," he said, reaching for a shelf, "I have a record put out by the state. I'm here. You're here from the West. We can visit each other. We have something to eat, we have something to drink. For the moment we're safe." He raised his glass in toast.

6

"It still doesn't feel particularly safe," I said to Marjie. "Or rather, it probably *is* safe, but only because it's under such close surveillance. Which makes it *un*safe, if you know what I mean." We were getting ready to go to the American Vice-Consul's apartment, to meet some "unofficial" painters.

"Yes," she said. "Inside your apartment is probably the only safe place there is. Outside is a no-man's-land. I don't think Boris ever goes out there."

"It belongs to an occupying power."

"Right."

"It's been fictionalized by propaganda."

She turned towards me a sceptical look. This was the woman who had conned our way into the vaults of the Russian Museum on nothing but sheer chutzpah. "Maybe," she said, then patted my hand. "Maybe," she said, and laughed.

We went outside and turned up Nevsky Prospekt. The street

was almost deserted. There were footsteps behind us: metal heels on the cleared pavement. I stopped to light a cigarette. The footsteps stopped. We walked on, and then I stopped again, listening. Same thing. The hairs stood up on the back of my neck. "Look, Marjie," I said quietly, "I think we're being followed."

I pulled her down a side street. The footsteps echoed behind us. We crossed the street at a curve and I stopped again to look back. There was no one there, but when we walked on, the sound of the footsteps started up once more. It was impossible to tell whether I was being paranoid or not. And I thought: "That's the point. You can *never* tell: never tell whether you're being followed or not, watched or not. So you have to behave all the time as if you are."

After a while, of course, as we quickly zigzagged through deserted side streets, the footsteps disappeared. But by that time we were both—as I had been in Gorky Park in Moscow—very fright- ened. We telephoned the Vice-Consul to ask him to come down- stairs and let us in to his building, and ducked past the guard who was posted outside. Perhaps meeting "unofficial" painters, I thought as we went in, was regarded as some sort of enemy action. Perhaps lists of visitors were made.

The Vice-Consul—to whom the English Teacher had intro- duced us—was a bluff, cheerful man, with the sort of open, outdoorsy face which firmly discouraged paranoia. And the "unof- ficial" painters could hardly have been described, except in my imagination, as a very subversive group. They were in fact faintly hangdog: they watched a slide show by a visiting American weaver with a rueful envy at all the techniques and technology she had at her command. And after it was over, they shyly approached me and Marjie and showed us photographs of their work, fishing for our interest. They told us vague stories of persecution. Foreigners, I realized, were probably the only buyers they had.

I overdid my interest in their work, which wasn't great. And then I gathered together plates and glasses and took them into the kitchen, leaving Marjie behind. As I came in, the Vice-Consul looked up from the sink and said: "You know, before I was posted to Leningrad, I was in Poland, where there's hope, there's a future: you can see it in their faces. Here it's all over: they're beaten and resigned and glum."

I said: "I think they're forced to play needy and persecuted because it's the only way they can get our attention and our money. They pretend to be downtrodden; we pretend to be sympathetic millionaires. It's a locked-in two-step, some kind of awful post-*glasnost* dance."

He laughed. "No," he said, "I don't mean the painters outside, Jo. I mean the people on the streets."

"Maybe it's the same thing," I said. "They don't own anything out there; they have no stake in it at all. So they play a game for all the watchers and the hidden cameras. They hurry through the streets with their heads down, and act doomed and beaten so the state has no reason to infringe on them at home. Perhaps, in the end, it shows, not how resigned they are, but how defiant. What you see is just a performance."

As I look back now, I think it was the first completely Russian thought I'd ever had. Such-and-such was true and unarguable; but the opposite was also true. Three years later, Ksiyusha was to put the matter neatly, when she described a praiseful end-of-year speech by one of her teachers as "absolutely sincere . . . well, Soviet sincere."

"You mean, also *in*sincere," I said.

"Yes," she said. "Exactly."

7

Our last night in Leningrad, we went behind the imperial facade of the city, to a palace of youth in a back street where Boris's band, Aquarium, were to perform. As we arrived with the English

Teacher to meet the Vice-Consul and his wife, Joanne, there was a crush in front of the doors, much waving of tickets, and *druzhinniki* (volunteer police helpers) in red armbands busily keeping order. Inside the hall there were more *druzhinniki;* and since they were at least twice the age of most of the people in the audience, the whole affair had the enforced sedateness of a chaperoned high-school prom. The audience was quiet; No Smoking signs were everywhere; and the impression of being in a time-and-space warp was enhanced by the stage lighting, which was harsh, universal, and flat. It called to mind those American gyms and community halls in the early sixties, where celluloid teenagers were forever putting on bright, well-behaved concerts against the torpor of the suburbs and the hostility of their parents (who always came round in the end and joined in in the last reel). Whether the *druzhinniki* would join in on this occasion seemed from the beginning doubtful. Dour and offi-cious, they moved through the muffled chatter of the audience as if they belonged to another species.

When the band finally walked onstage to polite applause, and the concert began, it became extremely hard to focus on the here and now: to shift the idea that this was indeed somewhere else and another time. It wasn't that Aquarium's performance was well behaved—though it was. It was that, by Western standards, it was, well . . . before: before the days of the choreographed performance, when the costumes became elaborate disguises and the amplifier mountains began to soar. Boris was wearing jeans and a leather jacket; and the band—drums, flute, percussion, lead guitar, two violins, and a cello—were wearing no more than slightly gussied-up versions of their ordinary street clothes. They looked exactly, that's to say, like their audience, just as bands had in the sixties, when the music, and the music alone, was what was important. They played what I thought of as I sat there, looking for analogies, as Andean-Celtic music: sometimes plaintive, sometimes pulsating; sometimes dark, sometimes jiglike. But the audience, however driving the beat,

didn't respond by shouting or screaming or dancing in the aisles—
all the different methods audiences had in the West of calling
attention to their own importance. They simply sat there, gently
rocking to the rhythm and mouthing the lyrics, or furiously writing
down the lyrics of whatever songs were new. The concert was, above
all, an act of communication. And I found myself recording, with
the help of the Vice-Consul, some of the messages: "So many
babushkas and each one wears a tie. .'"; "Our fathers don't lie /
Like wolves don't eat meat / And birds don't fly. . . ." Among the
songs was one which Artyom had called one of Russia's most
resounding underground anthems: "Rock and Roll Is Dead (But
I'm Not Yet)." Another, "The Generation of Night Watchmen
and Street Cleaners," spoke, I thought, for everybody who was
there, condemned to whatever meaningless or marginal jobs they
were assigned to by the state, living their true lives at home, in
kitchens and bedrooms, well away from its prying eyes. The whole
concert seemed, in the face of the octopus of central authority, which
had lost none of its power since the building of Petersburg's first
palaces, both immensely serious and ridiculously brave.

As Marjie and I took a plane the next morning to Moscow—
and then on to England—I knew that I had to come back. Whatever it was that I had been looking for since I left America in
1985—perhaps since the sixties—I thought I had found: heroes and
an enemy with its roots deep in history, and the smell and taste of
freedom. For the first time in years, I found myself remembering a
line that was much quoted in the West in the 1960s: "When the
mode of the music changes, the walls of the city shake."

When I got back to London, I met a Russian-emigré friend of
mine who worked for the BBC's World Service Radio. He took
one look at me and said: "Oh-oh, I've seen that look before. They've
done it to you. You're hooked, aren't you?"

"Yes," I said. "I'm afraid I am. Yes."

Chapter 5

April–May 1989

Yelena has lost her internal passport. We're in the car on the way back from Peredelkino, and suddenly she's hollow-eyed with anxiety. She fumbles in her bag. Could she have left it at the dacha? "No," I say, "I checked the room. There was nothing." Everyone in the car focusses his attention on her. "Where could it be?" "When did you last see it?" "Quick, Yelena. At the hotel?" "At your parents' apartment?" "Don't worry. You'll find it," says Savva the filmmaker uneasily.

Back at the apartment, she rummages through the chaos of her little bedroom: ashtrays and makeup, newspapers, clothes, and thick journals strewn everywhere. She kneels to peer under the pullout sofa-bed, as her mother clucks comfort behind her. "It'll be all right, Mama," says Ksiyusha, round-eyed, dressed like a London punk. But Yelena is crying. I lift her up. "Look, it's all right; it's all right. Nobody died. We'll get a taxi and—"

She interrupts me, exasperated. "You don't understand, Jo. We can't go to Yalta."

Then I understand. She can't go anywhere without her internal passport: it's her identity as a Soviet citizen. It gives her the right to live where she lives; it shows that she is who she says she is. It is she, as a public rather than a private person: as an extension and expression of the state. I find myself wondering what the passport says. Nationality: Jew? (Her mother is Jewish.) Or, Nationality: Russian—like her father? It's never occurred to me to ask. Nor has it occurred to me that to get another passport, she'll have in effect to reconstruct her identity, out of something other than just an idly taken photograph, as I would.

I tell her that we'll take a taxi and retrace our steps of yesterday; we'll even go out again to Peredelkino to check—we can stop and look at Pasternak's dacha. But then the phone rings. It's Tomas the Georgian: he says he's just found her passport beside the backseat of his car. She whoops out in delight and relief, half-laughing, half-crying into the phone. It's over. But it's been a sobering, ugly little episode, one that I don't find easy to forget. It occurs to me that, if Yelena is so quickly devastated by the loss of her documents, then she probably doesn't work directly—as she might—for the KGB.

2

We find Artyom's wife, Svetlana, at the National Hotel, curled like a snake in a round chair in reception. As she and Yelena kiss, I wonder how on earth she's managed to get past the doorman. But then she uncoils herself and stands. She's wearing an immaculately cut trouser-suit of black worsted, a cream linen shirt, and a little multicoloured bow tie of shot silk. Pity the poor doorman, then, trawling for Russians in these increasingly confusing times of *glasnost* and foreign travel. She could only, of course—dressed in these clothes—be foreign.

We hug and laugh. Svetlana has learned more English in the last year; she's writing a book on the history of Soviet style for a Finnish publisher; and she's finally been allowed to go to the West at the same time as Artyom. In my visits to Moscow over the past

year, I've sometimes stayed (illegally) in their flat near the Vagan-
kovskoye Cemetery, where the actor-poet Vladimir Vysotsky is
buried; and at a dacha they've been renting to the north of Moscow,
where Vysotsky and his wife, Marina Vlady, once had a country
house. I've seen Artyom twice in London (the last time two days
ago), and them both, eight months since, in the United States.
Though Artyom was slightly dazed by, and therefore withering
about, the embattled glitter of New York, Svetlana sailed through
it all—the reception for her at *Ms.* magazine, the dizzying material-
ism of the music and fashion businesses—as if it were merely some
lost extension of her birthright.

We go upstairs to the bar, which over the past year has begun
blazoning itself with decals and dispensers from Western salesmen.
The hookers aren't in yet, just a few tired businessmen and an
American girl writing postcards, though the television is, as usual,
blaring. The place makes Yelena nervous, I realize as the two
women sit and I order drinks. She deals a lot with Western film
producers and film crews; and she once, she's told me, had a long,
secret affair with a Western businessman, for which she could have
been sent to the camps. Like any woman, then, in this xenophobic
country who sits with Westerners and talks their language—
especially any beautiful woman—she's constantly being appraised,
approached, and insulted as if she must be a hard-currency hooker.
It's why she has a constant longing for Western clothes too good for
the black market the prostitutes have access to: so that she can look
like a Western woman herself. She recently worked, over a long
period, for an American woman producer based in London. She
was paid virtually entirely in English and American clothes.

And Svetlana? I suppose I think of Svetlana as being fearless,
untouchable somehow, ever since the day I saw her take on a KGB
man in the Ukraina Hotel. The agent had been assigned to a
Swedish woman film director who was trying to make a film about

the thousand-year anniversary of the Russian Orthodox church. And Svetlana, whose friend she was, could no longer stand this man's obstructions, rudeness, and cunning delays. She shouted at him about his "closed-mindedness," his "rotten nostalgia for the old way of doing things," his "paranoia," and his "total failure to understand what is happening in this country." The man stormed out of the restaurant, and a few minutes later Svetlana was warned by a waitress that "they" were waiting for her outside. Sure enough, just like in the movies, "they" were in the lobby when we emerged, a bunch of thick-set men wearing identical leather jackets. Svetlana and Artyom (who had arrived by now) were waylaid and then dragooned upstairs to a locked, unnumbered room next to a hair-dresser's, pursued by me and the ululating director. For ten minutes she and I waited outside in the corridor, speculating about what we'd do if they were arrested. And then finally the door opened, with Artyom smiling an accommodating smile and Svetlana, be-hind him, silent and morose. "It's all over now," said Artyom. "We're all friends." But Svetlana shot a baleful look at the men behind her, and then spewed out a stream of fractured, furious Russian at Artyom on the way downstairs. He must have said that she was an emotional, overexcitable woman, who needed to be protected from herself by her husband. (I've never asked them to this day what really happened.)

There is, though, I think, a buried anger in Svetlana, just as there is a prickliness, a defensiveness in Yelena. In Yelena's case, it's to do with working in, and being attracted to, a world that can only compromise her in the eyes of her countrymen (except for those who inhabit it themselves). But in Svetlana it goes deeper. I think she would actually like to move to the West, not just because of the constant, throttling presence here of the apparat and its spies, but because her life as an intelligent, ambitious woman is so frustrating and difficult in the Soviet Union. Like almost all Russian men,

Artyom does nothing in the house; he doesn't seem to care where he lives, so long as there's a place for him to work; and he barely notices when food Svetlana has travelled and queued miles and hours for is put on the table. I remember once visiting with Svetlana (after a lunch that I had bought and cooked) at a dacha a few doors away, where a funny, mercurial man from the Committee of Youth Organizations was holding court to a group of friends: composers and academics, mostly. After dinner, which the women (once more) had bought and served, I brought up—at first tentatively, and then more vehemently—the subject of the Russian Woman: working, taking care of children, shopping, cooking, controlling a network of *blat* (influence) and exchange to get what she can for her family; then ageing, before her time, into a lined, round, still hardworking babushka; all the while being idolized and excoriated (in Russian literature) as a savior-virgin and a fleshly canker that can corrupt men's souls. The man from the Committee of Youth Organizations egged me on, laughing. But the reaction of the other men was one of horror. How dare a Western man lecture them about the plight of Russian women? What could he possibly *know* about the nature of their arrangements and transactions? Perhaps they were right. But as we walked back through the snow, Svetlana said fiercely: "They'll *never* understand!" Artyom is always first at their computer.

When I return, carrying drinks, to the table in the corner where Yelena always sits, as if hiding out, Svetlana looks up and asks me about my mother. There is little to say. My mother is slowly dying of cancer in a small house in England, where I and my brother, an actor, live with her by turns. Because he was away working, I lost touch, after shooting, with the film on Boris Grebenshchikov, which was cut in New York.

"And the film, Jo," she says. "How is it?" It's about to be shown on British television.

"It's fine," I say, "but it's, I don't know, Western. It simply can't deal with what Boris means *here.*"

3

Outside the National, we hire one of the moonlighting official drivers to take us to the Taganka Theatre, the other side of the Yauza River. The Taganka is a kind of shrine to the work of actor-turned-director Yuri Lyubimov, whose Romeo Andrei Voznesensky once saw with Pasternak, and whose productions during the Brezhnev years were among the most daring in the Soviet Union. (It's said that Yuri Andropov, then head of the KGB, turned a blind eye to what was going on at the Taganka because Lyubimov had once dissuaded his son—without knowing who he was—from becoming an actor.) Lyubimov is in exile now, driven out, among other things, by the banning of his production in memory of Vysotsky, who was a member of his company. But in an upstairs office, whose walls are filled with the signatures of visiting stars (Laurence Olivier and Robert Redford among them), his coat is still draped over a chair; his books and papers are laid out on a desk, waiting for his return. In January, when he paid a brief visit to Moscow to celebrate what would have been Vysotsky's fifty-first birthday, and to see his own finally permitted production, a thousand people were outside the theatre to greet him, while two hundred more were clambering over the roof trying to find a way in. At the end of an evening filled with Vysotsky's songs, he mounted the stage to a standing ovation, and conjured up again for those who were there the man he once described as "our bard, the keeper of the nation's spirit, of our pain and all our joys." As he talked, people came up from the audience to lay red carnations on a lone guitar leaning against the back wall of the stage. Many of those who watched and listened were weeping. He later told me that he'd always wanted to mount a production of

Vysotsky in English, in the West. But it would require, he said, shrugging, the combined talents of, say, Joseph Brodsky, Charles Bukowski, Tom Waits, Randy Newman, and Robert De Niro.

The theatre is emptying as we drive up. And we go next door through the crush to the Backstage Café, where the company held a banquet for Lyubimov the night of his return. Yelena is usually expert at wheedling a table here—people always seem to remember her; they smile at her with pleasure. But tonight there is a party upstairs, and none of the musicians who are our friends are in town. Tamara, the elfin violinist in pixie boots who can play anything from Magyar folk songs to concertos, is in Finland, on tour. And Sacha, the big bear who sings the romances Yelena loves—as well as settings of the poetry of Pasternak and Tsvetaeva—has gone to Canada; no one seems to know why. I think sadly of something Savva said at the dacha: "People have to leave, you know? We've spent so long pushing against the barriers, living within strict limits, that half of us don't have any idea what to do now that they've been lifted. Take Lyubimov, for example, with his elaborate stage machinery and his heavy, symbolic effects. Or Grebenshchikov, with his rebellious stance and his sideways lyricism. It was time for them to go abroad. They needed to. Here they were just repeating themselves, repeating their own pasts. They'd run out of ideas."

They finally lay a table for us downstairs in the Vysotsky Bar. But the evening is not a success. The musicians play Russian folk songs that even I know. They grin too much. The place is becoming a parody of itself. And I miss Sacha: his beautiful, still tenor voice and his long, earnest toasts to Yelena's eyes. The first time I met Sacha, he said to me lugubriously: "Jo, I think my wife no longer loves me. What shall I do?" The next time I saw him, he was divorced and as mischievous as a kitten: he was about to open his own opera theatre. Later—one night during my last trip—I said to him that I had never heard any good balalaika music. And twenty minutes afterwards, he announced that "the greatest balalaika player in the Soviet Union, Oleg Davidov," was on his way. Davidov turned out to be a small, cadaverous man, with large, round eyes and an astounding skill. But he mostly played Bach and Beethoven on his balalaika, which was (as Dr. Johnson said) rather like a dog dancing or a woman giving a sermon: not in itself particularly revealing or appetizing; just astonishing—on a three-stringed instrument—that it could be done at all.

Svetlana, too, is not happy. Artyom has not called from London in the ten days that he's been there, and she can't understand why. Yelena tries to cheer her up, finding excuses—though later she says to me: "But, Jo, it is not correct." (It is one of her favourite phrases.) The food, too, is slow in coming. And Svetlana picks out from the bag of presents I've brought for her a box of chocolates that the Writer has sent. "Let's have a chocolate while we wait," she says.

"No, no," says Yelena quickly. "No, Svet, you'll need them. For a doctor. Or something. Jo, you know . . . ?"

But I'm looking at Svetlana. She shrugs her shoulders, smiles, and puts the chocolates away. Three days later, I hear that Artyom's mother has just gone into hospital to have a hysterectomy—Svetlana hasn't wanted to tell me and spoil our trip to Yalta. Instead, Yelena tells me on the plane on the way back. And the next day, we go together to the hard-currency store at the Mezhdunorodnaya Hotel to buy other presents—newly published books—for the doctors who are treating her mother-in-law: Pasternak's *Doctor Zhivago,* Vassily Grossman's epic *Life and Fate,* the Avkhazian stories of Fazil Iskander, and books of poetry. I'm not sure which I find more distressing in the end: the fact that we have to buy these gifts to make sure the Soviet doctors do their job, or the fact that the books we get cannot be found anywhere in regular book shops—just here, supplied for hard currency for foreigners like me who cannot read them.

4

The next day Yelena picks me up at the hotel with another member of her seemingly endless network of friends and acquaintances: Oleg, a Sovinfilm driver who needs hard currency to buy for his wife a swimsuit he's seen in a hard/currency shop. We drive through the early/morning streets, with the May Day flags snapping and quarrel/ling in the wind around us. Though it's only seven o'clock, cars are already pouring into the city for the holiday.

Yelena is curiously silent, though I know she's been looking forward to this trip for weeks. She bet me, as I went through the laborious process of trying to book rooms from London, that we'd never find places at the Oreanda Hotel in Yalta. And then, when I succeeded, she whooped with joy over the telephone. She's obvi/ously had to use a good deal of influence herself to get us on the first flight out. She clutches the Aeroflot tickets in her hand like a petition.

At Sheremetyevo—named for a nineteenth/century aristocrat whose serfs created the first Russian textile industry—Oleg hustles our bags into Intourist reception, and then leaves, two/fifths of the way nearer his wife's swimsuit. Our passports are inspected and we're herded into the waiting area, where a guard takes a grim delight in seeing my pockets progressively emptied, my jacket and watch taken off, as I endlessly set off the metal/detector alarm. Finally I decide that a tooth filling or my metal belt/buckle must be the culprit. But he's not satisfied until we've exhausted all the possibilities of humiliation that his little bailiwick allows. We never do find out what is responsible. In the end, the guard, who must be about eighteen years old, just gets bored and waves us exasperatedly on into the bleak little room where infectious foreigners are still kept away from Soviet travellers. We're finally taken to the already full plane—along with a young Czech mother and child and a black student from Ghana who's going to play in a band concert in Simferopol—in a bus that could carry at least seventy people.

As the Ilyushin lumbers and creaks down the runway (I sud-denly imagine it's made of wood, like an old ship), Yelena holds my hand hard, till her knuckles show white. Then she falls asleep on my shoulder, while I try to hold steady in front of me the BBC journal which is the only reading matter, I realize, that I've brought with me—except for a book I want to give Sakharov's friend Lem Karpinsky. The journal has a review of *The Third Truth* by Leonid Borodin, which it glowingly compares to Solzhenitsyn and Che-khov. The people around me will never have heard of Borodin, I know—any more than they'll have heard of Karpinsky, a subtle old man who's spent most of his life trying to understand the nature of socialism. Borodin was recently released from a long jail sentence for anti-Soviet agitation and propaganda—he'd published a volume of short stories in the West—and has never, as far as I know, been published in the Soviet Union. And Karpinsky, who twenty-five years ago was number two in Komsomol (the Young Communists' League), has only just begun to find a voice again—after arrest and long silencing—in journals like *Twentieth Century and the World*. I remember him walking slowly and stiffly down a corridor in the National, saying: "It's the system, the system. I tell everyone. It's no use making cosmetic changes, fussing about with the periphery. It's the *structure* that's got to be changed." There is about him the shining clarity that I've sometimes noticed in so-called dissidents, as if they've been burned clean by persecution.

5

At Simferopol Airport, the television is on in Intourist's echoing reception hall, showing the May Day parade in Moscow. There is dancing in the streets, then an interview (in Russian) with two correspondents from *Time* magazine. There are no soldiers or tanks in evidence. It's more like a people's festival: a welcoming of spring. The faces are smiling; the children dressed, as always, in their Sunday best: better than their parents. I remember something Sacha Tirov, Boris Grebenshchikov's bass player, said during the making of the film: "Our children, perhaps, will be the first generation to be free. We are not free—we were raised in oppression. But for them it is possible." It is as if the children are being groomed for freedom: made the repository of all the hopes that have been lost along the way.

I remember too something that Vitaly Korotich, the editor of *Ogonyok,* said to me the last time I was in Moscow: "My grand, mother died believing that *I* would be happy; my parents, that my *children* would be. I woke up one morning thinking, 'Why not *me? Why not now?'* " Korotich runs the most iconoclastic current, affairs magazine in the Soviet Union, a lot more antiestablishment than *Time.* I later hear a story about him, which I believe to be absolutely true: In 1988, at almost exactly the time I first went to Leningrad, he gave a speech there attacking Yegor Ligachev, the leader, it was supposed then, of the Communist opposition to *glasnost* and *pere, stroika.* And when he got back to Moscow, he was immediately summoned to the Kremlin, where, for an hour, Gorbachev bawled him out like a docker for what he had said. In the middle of his tirade, though, he suddenly stopped and made an odd gesture, as if what he was saying shouldn't be taken entirely seriously. In a corridor afterwards, Alexander Yakovlev told Korotich why: the whole thing had been a charade, he said, for the benefit of the KGB's hidden microphones.

We go upstairs in the terminal to drink thick, sweet coffee, and then come down to reclaim our bags. Yelena asks me, do I have a voucher for a car to Yalta? "No," I say. "I didn't think it was

necessary." "Well, Jo," she says, staring at me coolly, almost chal-
lengingly, "you'd better arrange a taxi then." I go outside, leaving
her chatting to the Intourist superintendent. And as I walk to the
other end of the airport—the one with people in it—I realize what
her look means. It means that she is no longer going to be the
interpreter and organizer; I, the poor foreigner who has to be taken
care of. Our roles will have to change. I'm going to have to take
charge, if we're to be together. I also understand why she was so
silent on the way to the airport, and has seemed withdrawn since
then. This is the first time we will ever have been alone together,
apart from snatched moments in hotel rooms or in her tiny, crammed
bedroom. She's nervous, wondering if she's doing the right thing,
wondering what her friends will think, what people in Yalta will
think. She tells me later that though it's no longer illegal to associate
with foreigners, it's still illegal to stay in their hotel rooms after eleven
o'clock at night. I had no idea.

In the bright sunshine outside the regular terminal, I negotiate
in Russian with a weatherbeaten old taxi driver. Finally: *"Da, da,"*
he says. *"Spasibo." "Nezashto."* I clamber in and we drive back to
Intourist, where Yelena is standing in the doorway, still talking with
the superintendent. "How much was it, Jo?" she asks, looking up
as I get out. "Fifteen roubles," I say. She laughs. "But, Jo, it's a
hundred and forty kilometres. He must have said *fifty!"* Then she
reaches out and ruffles my hair, still laughing. "Poor Jo. You didn't
know." Another of her idiosyncratic Rubicons seems to have been
crossed. For as we drive away, she says dreamily, holding my hand:
" 'They hailed a cab and drove to Oreanda.' " It is a line from
Chekhov's "Lady with a Little Dog," which comes just after
Gurov has made love to his lady for the very first time. It was written
in the place we are going to almost exactly ninety years ago.

6

Yelena is silent for most of the journey. She has this capacity—I've noticed it before—to disappear into her own thoughts for hours on end, as motionless as a lizard. So I look out of the window as we drive south: at cows and goats tethered by the roadside, at secret little dachas, small runs of orchards, and then apartment buildings rising suddenly and improbably out of screed hillsides. This was the home of the Crimean Tartars, the descendants of the Golden Horde who once ruled Muscovy. But in 1944 they were deported to Central Asia on the questionable grounds that they had collaborated as a people with the Germans during the Great Patriotic War. Those who survived the journey had Stalin's charges against them with-drawn in 1967. But they've been blocked from returning in any large numbers ever since. I look in vain among the bus queues in the villages and the gaggles of bicyclists along the road for the high cheekbones, the olive skin, and the strange, almost feral look of my New York friend Rennat. All I seem to see are the same stolid, flat, open faces that I see on the streets of Moscow.

Further south, vineyards begin to appear beside the road. But the vines are all new, I notice, as if they've just been planted. I ask the driver where the old vines are. He turns and grins. "They aren't. When the law against alcohol was passed four years ago, most of them were cut down. The tasting hall in Yalta was shut, and the deputy director of the Wine Institute committed suicide. Now they're having to start again from scratch." He laughs uproari-ously—as well he might. The Crimea has always been one of the great wine-producing areas of the Soviet Union. But now that there's no wine—and precious little vodka—available, people all across the country have turned to sugar, for making moonshine, *samogon*. Last year, in just four months, the country ran out of its

entire year's supply of sugar. And the Soviet Union—the largest
producer of sugar in the world—had to import the rest from abroad.

7

"The sea! Look, Jo, the sea!" Yelena awakes from her reverie. And
we begin to descend through a ring of hills to Yalta, which stretches
down the coast for eighty kilometres on either side of us. The road
opens out into a wide boulevard. There are horse chestnuts in
blossom; cherry trees and lilacs everywhere, cloaking nineteenth-
century villas and pillared sanatoria—Stalinist people's palaces—
where favoured union and Party members come for treatment and
relaxation. There's a Mediterranean feel to the city: a lushness and
laziness in the air. Young girls are walking hand in hand along the
pavements, and there are glimpses of winding, ramshackle lanes
curling up and away from the leafy main streets. Near the sea, along
a narrow road lined with cypresses, we have to inch our way
through crowds of strollers and sightseers and a cluster of people in
shirtsleeves and summer dresses looking at secondhand books laid
out on a white wall over a canal.

8

The Oreanda is a nineteenth-century building faced with white and
cream stucco, with blue canopies hanging like eyelids over the
top-storey windows. In front of it is a shingled beach where gener-
ously fleshed men and women are laid out on wooden slabs for the
inspection of the sun. Across the street is the squat, modern shoe-
box of a people's exhibition hall. The hotel itself, though, is curved
and graceful; and beside it and in front of it are two seafront
walkways alive with flags and swarming with families out for the
holiday. "Isn't it *wonderful,* Jo?" says Yelena, getting out of the cab

and stretching in the sunshine. Though she's been to Yalta several times, she has never stayed at the Oreanda (which like most good things in the Soviet Union is largely reserved for hard-currency travellers); only at the Yalta Hotel, a monumental chunk of white on a distant hillside that boasts three swimming pools, seven bars, and rooms for twenty-three hundred people.

The taxi driver and I carry the bags into the entrance hall. I pay him his (expected) fifty roubles, and then present myself at the reception desk, where I'm confronted with a large, blonde woman wearing a dress made up of huge black and white squares, like a chessboard made of cloth. I hand her my London-bought vouchers for our two rooms. She studies them carefully, then looks in a book and says slowly: *"Nyet."* A pause. Then she waves the vouchers in the air dismissively, as if they could be used only for an improvised fan. "We don't know anything about you, Mr. Smith," she says, looking up. "London has not communicated with us. There are no rooms in the hotel."

Yelena sags into a little heap. "I *knew* it! I *knew* it!" she says.

"Then you have a problem," I say measuredly to the woman. "I've already paid for them."

"I *knew* this would happen. I told you, Jo." Yelena is suddenly like a child who's had an ice cream snatched from her just as she's about to take the first lick. I almost expect to see her face begin to crumple behind her Ray-Ban glasses: on the long, silent route to tears, like a child's. It's time, I think, to do the business my new role demands.

"All right," I say as I take her by the arm and lead her away. "I'll take care of this." I sit her down in an unforgiving little armchair and buy her a mineral water from the bar in the foyer. And then I return to the chessboard. I'm not sure on this occasion whether to play the Understanding Friend of the Soviet Union—an unthreatening little pawn move that sometimes works—or the

Noisy, Demented Foreigner—a frontal attack with a big gun. I decide on a combination.

I tell the woman patiently in English that I am a travel writer and that I've sent some pieces (to prove it) to Intourist in London. I tell her that I am here to write about Yalta for the greater glory of the city and the greater cramming of its hard-currency coffers. I invent some huge number of British and American readers who will be put off forever if I breathe so much as a word of this extremely poor—but surely correctible—first impression. Then, when I see her face settle slowly into the frowning, focusless look that sooner or later Russian bureaucrats adopt when faced with something not of their own making or choosing (it means: "It's not my fault; it's not my job; and besides, what you see in front of you is not me—I'm not even here"), I noisily demand to see the administrator, the head of tourism, the Party chief, the mayor. I bellow for a telephone so that I can call Moscow, London, and the British embassy. After a few minutes of this rant, the woman's face begins to unglaze a little and then to form itself with agonizing slowness into a tentative, forced half-smile. "Why don't you and your translator," she says finally, wearily, "go and have lunch and I'll see what I can do."

I haul Yelena up and we go to the dining room, which is dominated by a six-foot nude, vaguely reminiscent of the Venus de Milo, but made, it appears, of reinforced concrete. Suddenly the situation seems to me utterly hilarious. As we sit, I begin to invent possible future scenarios, of us camping out in a bathing hut or building cairns of shingle on the beach. I make up life histories for the stolid Finns and Germans who paddle around us, just up from the swimming pool. And soon Yelena is laughing too, eagerly joining in. Even the young waiter, who brings us caviar and mush-room soup, is smothering laughter whenever he comes near us, though he hasn't the slightest idea what we're saying.

After lunch, I once again deposit Yelena in the cordon sanitaire of her armchair and make for the reception desk But this time there's a slim, dark-haired woman lying in wait for me. "Are you Jo Durden-Smith?" she asks in perfect English. "Yes," I say. "How do you do?" she says. "I've just arrived. I'm from Intourist in London, and I was told before I left that you were going to be here. The trouble is there seems to have been a mixup. There aren't any rooms."

"So I've heard."

"There's really only one solution. We could put you up in the President's Suite on the fourth floor."

"Yes?" I say calmly.

"The problem is that it will cost another forty roubles a day."

"No, it won't."

"No, I suppose under the circumstances it won't." She looks up. "And of course it's only got one bed."

"Ah."

"Though we could put another bed in the small room," offers the chessboard behind us.

"Well," I say slowly, "I shall have to consult Miss Zagrevskaya and see whether she has any objections."

"Yes," says the dark-haired woman. "Of course."

I walk across to where Yelena is sitting anxiously, biting her fingernails. "All right," I say. "I want you to look serious. They don't have any rooms. All that's available is the President's Suite, and it's only got one bed." I look into her skittish green eyes. "Though they could make up another one in a small room."

"I don't know, Jo." A pause. "Will it be all right?"

"Yes."

"But, Jo, I want to see it first."

I trail back to reception. "Miss Zagrevskaya would like to see the room." The chessboard hands me an enormous bunch of keys— there must be five or six of them—and gives me directions.

We go upstairs, Yelena silent, peering at the floor numbers over the lift's door as they light up one by one: counting down. We get out and I open an unmarked door with one of the keys. "Jo, Jo—quick," I hear her calling as she goes down a corridor. I follow her. To the left, a sauna, a shower, and a small pool. Then, a big bedroom with a bathroom beyond; a small L-shaped room, where a maid is already making up a pullout bed; a kitchen area with a bar; and a huge formal dining room with a television in the corner, glaring out into veiled sunlight. I finally find her on a wide balcony, planted with hydrangeas and roses, overlooking the intersection of the sea-front walkways.

"Jo, it's wonderful," she says, looking out over the sea. "Wonderful. Will we always stay here?" She turns and throws her arms round my neck. The suite is a lot larger than her family's Moscow apartment.

I go downstairs to pick up our bags and tell the chessboard that we will somehow make do. And when I get back, Yelena is beneath the sheets in the big bedroom, naked and languorous: smiling. As I put down the bags I think for some reason of something I've read: that the Russians, as well as having had no Renaissance, Reformation, or Enlightenment, have no tradition of romantic love. I wonder whether it matters as I take off my jacket. It's created nothing but trouble in the West.

9

In the late afternoon we walk along the beachfront promenade through the May Day crowds, past kiosks selling souvenirs and wooden jewellery, and street photographers posing whole flotillas of families against cutouts of cartoon pirate captains. Old men with walking sticks and breasts full of medals sit contemplatively on benches amid boxes of white flowers, while teenagers in Western

T-shirts and jeans skip and scurry round them. There are people queuing for pizza on board a wooden ship moored in concrete on the esplanade beside the hotel; and, further down, a brass band playing military music in front of a giant statue of Lenin. There's a kind of innocence about the crowd, I think as we walk. They're not really here to buy things or to chase some sensation not available at home. True, there are oranges and nuts and ice cream for sale in little booths. And at the far end of the bay, there are Dodgems and roundabouts. But the roundabouts are sedate, ceremonial affairs, and the Dodgem drivers are less than ferocious. Going out has not been commodified here as it has in the West: nothing seems to cost more than ten or fifteen kopecks. And the music, booming out of loud-speakers along the sea front, competing with the brass band and with announcements for excursion trips—and at one moment careering, I swear, into a number from the Dizzy Gillespie Big Band—is free.

We leave the coast and the crowds and walk inland. The air here is resinous—slightly sticky from the pines in the mountains—and full of the sound of birds. The lanes climb upwards and then twist sideways along the rims of the hills. The road surface is chalked every twenty yards or so with the markings for hopscotch. And amid the wisteria and lilac trees, behind rickety fences, there are secret courtyards filled with garden furniture and potted flowers. Cats clamber lazily over corrugated iron roofs jumbled together. Wooden verandahs lean out at distorted angles into the roads. There is not a soul in sight. We could be anywhere in the northern Mediterra-nean—in Provence, say, or Corsica—except for the stark modern buildings that we see below us along the coast where the vista opens out at street corners.

We walk for an hour trying to find an Orthodox church we've seen perched somewhere above us. But we somehow lose it in the maze of little lanes. And in the end we run down a steep flight of steps towards the Yalta Hotel. The hotel is set in a park just above the *dom tvorchestva* (creative house) of the Actors' Union, amid pines and plane trees, and beds planted with violets. But it's a brutal intrusion on the lush slopes of the hills behind it, heavy and frown-ing, with windows like gun sights. Hundreds of people seem to be waiting for taxis in the concrete forecourt, and the reception area is like an airport terminal. We wander along corridors as wide as a highway, and find a bar that is mysteriously, magically empty. "Why?" I ask as I get drinks. The waitress shrugs. "The tape player broke and nobody seemed to like the silence."

Outside in the forecourt as we leave, the cab driver Yelena has jumped the line for jerks to a halt and lets in a young, unshaven man who has weaved his way across to us, waving. He turns and leers towards me as we drive breakneck down the hill. *"Amerikanets?"* *"Nyet, Anglichanin."* "You want change money?" "No." His eyes flick towards Yelena. "You want caviar, good time?" "No." We almost crash into the back of a lorry, and he roars with demented laughter. When he finally gets out of the car, the driver says fiercely as he gets into gear: "Scum. Drug-addict filth. They should put them in a pen up there in the mountains, along with the whores." I wonder why he picked him up in the first place.

10

That night, we go to a cooperative restaurant, the Gourmand, up an arched stone stairway by the sea. By law, any three or more people now have a right to start a cooperative in the Soviet Union. And there are said to be between seventy and eighty thousand of them, ranging from scrap-metal dealers to hairdressers to the twenty-three luxury public lavatories near the Communist Party headquarters in Moscow. But cooperative restaurants like the Gourmand are among the hardest businesses to start. First, a licence and premises have to be wheedled out of the local district soviet—which requires bribery, or huge *blat*. Then the place has to be decorated and furnished and provided with cutlery, crockery, napery, and kitchenware. And even then, the cooperative's troubles aren't over. For much of the food—especially the vegetables—has to be bought at the free markets, like the one in Leningrad I visited, where tomatoes were on sale for the equivalent of ten dollars a pound. They're extremely expensive to set up and maintain, then. But they're also highly profitable. So those that aren't set up by the local Mafia or black marketeers in the first place sooner or later attract their "protection." (Vitaly Korotich said: "All the coop restaurants in Moscow have to pay protection money now. It's like Chicago in the thirties; there's shooting in the streets.") They often provide the best cooking to be found in the Soviet Union, it's true. But they can be as eerily empty as a front for white slaving, or as raffish as speakeasies.

The Gourmand (Russian, inexplicably, for "gourmet") doesn't promise well. There's what looks to be a near-riot on the cobbled street outside it, with men in jeans jackets and sunglasses and their brassy women jostling for attention. We dive in at the front and ask for our reserved table and then dither around nervously, looking at each other, waiting. Then a gate in a picket fence is opened quietly behind us and we are ushered in through a back door.

The restaurant is a succession of small rooms, decked out with flocked wallpaper (like a London curry house) and a huge colour television set (as if to show that the proprietors can afford it). We sit, under the watchful eyes of the other diners—not to mention the Cyclops eye of the flickering TV behind us—and order salad and mushrooms and lamb stew. And then Yelena begins to talk about Tbilisi.

Like most Westerners, I suppose, I've assumed that what happened in Tbilisi three weeks ago, when twenty-one people were killed at a Georgian nationalist demonstration, was a case of ill-disciplined soldiers panicking in the face of threats from the crowd

and then running amok, rather than of organized murder. I know
that Yelena stayed up half the night with Ksiyusha when the news
came in, comforting her, and that she was herself desperately worried, weeping down the phone to me. But I've taken it for granted
that they were just anxious about Yelena's friend Maya and her son,
Sandro, a tall, placid boy who is Ksiyusha's first boyfriend. The
family lives in Tbilisi and couldn't be reached by telephone for five
days. Ksiyusha once described Sandro approvingly to me as "a
nationalist fanatic."

"No, no, Jo," says Yelena. "You don't understand. I was
crying because it was *deliberate!* They were Ministry of Defence
soldiers, and women were beaten to death with shovels as an example to us all." I think—and say as much—that there are some cities
in which when you hear a car backfiring, you assume it's a bullet;
and some where when you hear a bullet, you assume it's a car
backfiring. It simply depends on the past history of the place,
whatever the present truth is.

"Jo, you're such a romantic," she says. "You think the bad old
days are over. All can you see is people demonstrating and publishing books and putting on plays. You think it's the sixties in the
West all over again. But we know what it is. After Tbilisi, people
were up all day and night, talking, telephoning each other. We
thought it was the *end,* don't you see? That's why I was crying. We
expected tanks. We didn't know what to expect. I met with the
Three Musketeers. They said the women should go to the West if
they could—Savva said Varya should go. But they said that *they*
had to stay, to fight, to do something. It was the same talk all over
Moscow. It was the same with Artyom and Svetlana. It's the same
today."

I mutter something about chains of command, misunderstood
orders, accidents. "Jo," she says, interrupting, "two years ago, I had
a lover. He was a deputy minister, very important, a Gorbachev

man, strong for *perestroika*. He used to come round to the apartment
from the ministry, from the Kremlin, and talk to my father. He
wanted me to be his official mistress, but I said no. And he said to
me: 'Yelena, all right. But you should make arrangements to go to
the West while you can. Because, if what I think will happen
happens, I'm going to be shot. And I won't be able to protect you.'
Now do you understand?"

I digest that for a while along with the mushrooms. I know that
a number of men have wanted to set Yelena up. I remember a story
someone told me about an official who would hold parties in her
honour and then dismiss all the guests so that he could be with her
alone. I remember a story she once told me herself about being
pursued by a famous, much-collected painter of what have always
seemed to me overblown illustrations. (I saw him in a Leningrad
hotel four months ago while we were filming, sitting next to one of
the most beautiful women I have ever seen, as Boris Grebenshchikov
and a session singer from Los Angeles wailed into a microphone
and I watched Russians dancing and applauding like Westerners
for the very first time.) But I've never had to confront the fact before,
or face how skin-deep and precarious Gorbachev's revolution really
seems to those who've staked everything on it. I know that Mikhail
Sergeyevich (as everyone calls him) is more popular in the West
than he is at home. I've seen the queues; walked through the
Mother Hubbard stores; heard the grumbling. But I've been caught
up in something else: the sheer intellectual excitement of people like
Natan Eidelman, a history professor at Moscow University, and
Yuri Afanasyev, the co-chairman of Memorial, who've paced the
floor in front of me, building shining pictures of the future out of
words. They're people like me, and they have power, a voice, for the
first time. It's never occurred to me that the whole edifice they are
trying to build could be torn down overnight, or that their ultimate
protector, Gorbachev, could be sidestepped, ignored, and even sum-

marily executed—along with however many Gorbachevite deputy ministers. I've bought the image of the adroit, crusading survivor which the West has tended to promote.

"How shaky do you think he really is?" I ask.

"Completely."

"But what about the elections two months ago [for the new Chamber of People's Deputies]? Dozens of the old Party bosses were defeated, thrown out on their ears. Half the people we met in January are now deputies, for heaven's sake. What about Afana-syev? What about Korotich? What about Yeltsin?"

"The bosses will never forgive Gorbachev, never. Elections in March, massacre in April. They'll never allow him to take away their power."

"But what can they do?"

"You don't understand, Jo," she says, almost weeping. "They can do anything—*anything.*"

We talk of other things for a while. And then I say quietly, almost out of the blue: "Your father. You have to forgive your father, you know." I think I mean: "For his Stalinism, for going along, for helping create what you're now trying to shuck off." But I also mean for whatever it is that seems to haunt him and stand between him and the rest of his family.

Yelena looks at me. "How did you know?" she says.

"I don't know. I'm a writer. I'm supposed to notice these things."

"It's hard, Jo," she says. "He left us." Then, with her head in her hands: "When I was a little kid, Jo, and we were in Belgium, he loved me. He bought me everything. Everything for me and Mama. I was his little princess. When we came back to Moscow, I remember wearing white gloves to school every day and the other girls staring at me as if I was from another planet. But then when I was ten, he went off with another woman. We had nothing. We had to live in a dacha—we couldn't afford to live in Moscow. Well, he came back, but then he left for someone else. We were poor, Jo, very poor. There was just Mama and me. Mama used to knit all the time, to sell things. I remember once when my father came for a visit, there was a tinker, a Gipsy, who came to the door. And I sold him my father's coat, just so I could buy cakes and ice cream."

Little by little, it comes out: how her grandfather worked for "Iron Felix" Dzerzhinsky's Cheka; how her father, though he was ostensibly employed after the war by Sovexportfilm and as a journal-ist, worked, one way and another, for the KGB. "He was recalled from Belgium and sacked around the time of Stalin's death," she says. "But I think, once you work for them, you can never really stop. Once, when I was a student, I was involved in a demonstra-tion against the invasion of Czechoslovakia, and they wanted to make me an informer. I asked him to help me, and he made them stop. He said I should never, ever have anything to do with them." She laughs ruefully and looks up at me. "He says he thinks you're probably a CIA agent, Jo. But he says: 'It doesn't matter. I respect them. They're professionals.' " She grasps my hand. "You're not an agent, are you, Jo?"

"No," I say. "If only . . ."

I remember something Marjie wrote on a postcard she was sending from Leningrad: "Russia is a perfect holiday. No eating, no shopping, no psychoanalysis." There doesn't seem anything more useful I can say.

11

We spend another day and a half in Yalta. And Yelena is suddenly as perky as quicksilver: smiling and laughing and cocking her head like a bird to watch me out of the corner of her eyes wherever we go. She is as happy, I think, as I've ever seen her. Something has been exorcised. She swims in the hotel pool with her head held steady and high over the surface of the water as if she were dancing, watching me as I sit in a chair making notes. And when we dance that night between the clunky Finns and Germans in the hotel dining room, she floats among them, her head never leaving the line of her body, as if she were swimming. She has become very graceful. What she feels betrays itself in the way she sits and the way she holds herself, as well as in her face. Her head and her heart seem one system: transparent. In the afternoon, when it rains, she forces me to buy her a red plastic macintosh in a hard-currency store along the esplanade. Then she bursts with an odd rapturous delight, as if it were the first present she's ever had.

12

On our last morning in Yalta, we walk hand in hand, through the constant chatter of the birds, to the house Chekhov built here, next to a Tartar cemetery, at the end of the last century. "Nothing will be needed apart from the house," Chekhov wrote to his brother, Mikhail, "no outbuildings of any sort; it will all be under one roof. . . . The hens lay the whole year round, and no special house is needed for them." And so it proves: the White Dacha, as it is known, is simply there when we arrive, exactly as it was when its builder was alive. And I find it, for some reason, inexpressibly moving. In the garden are the wisteria and the lilac that he planted, working alongside his Turkish gardener and being followed about by the crane and the stray dogs which had adopted him. In the sitting room is the piano which Rachmaninov played and beside which Chaliapin sang romances. And everywhere, in a large room kept for displays, there are photographs of this supremely gifted and good man, who saw Russia more clearly than almost any other writer, but thought nothing of putting his writing aside to help people in need. In Yalta he helped set up a pension for consump/ tives; he was on the board of a girls' high school; he acted as a clearinghouse for doctors looking for somewhere for their patients to live in the town. But he still found time here to write *The Three Sisters* and some of the greatest of his great short stories—and to entertain the Moscow Art Theatre actors when they came visiting with Stanislavsky.

There's been an attempt in the house to Sovietize Chekhov: there are posters of productions of his plays made after the Revolu/ tion, and of later films and ballets based upon his work. And since Lenin once said that it was reading Chekhov's story "Ward 6" that made him a revolutionary, "he," I write sniffily in my notebook, "gets in on the act." But none of these efforts can pollute the simplicity and goodness that radiate from the place, or the im/ mediacy of the photographs—capped, hatted, formal, laughing with Gorky—which make him seem contemporary, and the house as if he has just left it. In a glass case, there are his gardening gloves and pruning scissors; in another, his stethoscope and medical bag. It is as if everything were waiting for his return. And the fact that he is not here seems unaccountably like the loss of someone very dear.

We go outside and sit on a bench in silence, facing the dacha. Then I read from my notebook a remark of Chekhov's that's just been published in the Soviet Union for the very first time: "Just you wait. . . . Under the flag of science, arts, and suppressed free thought such toads and crocodiles will come to power in Russia, the like of which were not even seen in Spain during the Inquisition." Yelena sits quietly for a moment, and then leans across and writes beside it: "This happened in Yalta, Jo. We met each other, not to lose."

Part Two

Misunderstandings

Chapter 6

April 1988–February 1989

I

I first met Yelena on my second trip to Moscow, when I came back with the Hollywood Director. I was laden down with trading goods: Chinese ingredients for the brave Chinese restaurant in Moscow which didn't have any; lettuce and lemons and yoghourt for Martin Walker; videotapes and records and magazines for Artyom and Svetlana; and malt whisky for Boris. The Hollywood Director was laden down with a pilot's bag—and no more. I was impressed.

"Damn! They wouldn't let the videotapes through," I said to Artyom when he met us outside customs. "They said they had to have an official letter."

He said: "All right, people. There's no time to check in at the hotel. There's a première tonight and Boris Grebenshchikov is playing."

The Hollywood Director (H.D.) was my ticket to Moscow: my way of making sure that I'd come back, and that the film with Boris Grebenshchikov would be made. He had a reputation as a documentary maker. He also had slightly mournful good looks, a stubborn chin, a roving eye, and a way of looking at you straight, but from sideways on, as if you were peripheral to whatever tack he was taking. It was one of a number of distancing devices (irony was another: a sort of extreme mock gravamen) which he must have adopted, I thought, when his basic English shyness met the demented hoopla of the California dream machine. With a greying head slightly too big for his body, he seemed taller than he was; he jogged, he kept fit; he exuded a wry self-confidence. He was like a man who was successfully imitating the sort of man he'd decided he ought to be.

"All right," he said to Artyom, whom he'd met at a dinner party I'd given in London, "let's go then, let's go."

The House of Culture, where the première was, belonged to the Moscow Electric Lightbulb Factory; and it was surrounded, when we arrived, by people and a cordon of *militsia*. Everybody seemed to be on the move: waving, dealing, peering, prowling, denying passage. It seemed astonishing that so many should be allowed onto the street at the same time; there was the air of something very important happening. H.D. looked around as we got out of the car. "I guess this is tonight's hot ticket," he said.

We clustered in front of one of the *militsia* men as Artyom barked incomprehensibly at him, pointing towards the entrance. The *militsia* man listened dourly, then shook his head: there was, apparently, a problem. Only after a lengthy consultation with a steward was Artyom finally allowed up the steps and into the building, and then only so long as H.D. and I were left hostage down below. Feeling ridiculously exposed, as large as Gullivers, we waited as the last lingerers paired up with late arrivals from the Metro, and tickets changed hands furtively at what I later learned was up to fifteen times their face price. "It's amazing," said H.D.

"It's like 1965," I said.

At that moment, the waters of the crowd going in parted and a woman in her thirties came down the steps towards us. She was wearing a black-and-white check jacket and a short black leather skirt. She had high, dimpled cheeks, slanted eyes, and a long black waterfall of hair on either side of her face. She was very smart and very good-looking. "Good evening, gentlemen," she said coolly, with a little inflection on the "men." She held her hand out. "Here are your tickets."

"This is Yelena—Yelena Zagrevskaya," said Artyom, coming up behind her, waving.

I suppose I should say that I was immediately captivated, but it was H.D. who first responded. As we walked into the House of Culture in her wake, he looked across at me and raised his eyebrows. His skewed, askance self-mockery, which tended to distance men, acted with women, I realized, as a sort of continuous flirtation: the amatory equivalent of a Moscow shopper's "perhaps bag."

The première, we knew by now, as we followed her inside, was for a film called *Assa,* for which Boris had provided the incidental music and a number of songs. But what we might not know, said Yelena as we climbed ornate stairs, was that it was the first, "abso-lutely the first," première of its kind "in these times." Bringing together a whole community of musicians and filmmakers and painters, it was essentially, she said, "the underground coming up from below." We saw some of the painters' work when we stopped on a landing. It looked a lot like the work of the New York graffiti artists, and it seemed to be painted on large pieces of plastic. Artyom later told me that to him, it was the perfect conjoining of medium and message: the medium was acrylics on cheap vinyl tablecloths; the message was easy to fold or roll or stuff into a suitcase when it came time for a Western gallery owner to smuggle it abroad.

In a green room at the top of the stairs, a crowd of people was waiting, among them Artyom's wife, Svetlana. Yelena briskly intro-duced us to them: our hostess. There was Sergei Soloviev, the director of *Assa,* a beaming, fubsy, bearded man: all roundness and bonhomie, not a straight line in him. There was a droop-faced man called Dmitri Zakharov, "one of the presenters of our best new television programme, 'Vzglyad.' " And there was someone I recognized from a picture in Artyom's book: Alexander Lipnitsky, the founder and bass player of the band Zvuki Mu (the Sound of Moo-sic), a (once) collector of icons with a long black beard which exploded out from beneath his chin like a hairy bib. There were others, too: a man from State Television and Radio, who said he would write Artyom a letter so that he could retrieve the videotapes stranded at the airport; the nervous director of the House of Culture, to whom we were invited by Yelena to be particularly cordial (i.e., Western and impressive); and then, finally, Boris, coming through the door oddly quiet and on edge. I introduced him to H.D., of whom much shy fuss was being made, and he said: "Well, it's good to see you—very good that you came." Then, to me: "But look, Jo, it's chaos here; it's impossible to talk. Why don't we wait till you come to Leningrad." Boris was on edge, I realized later, because it really was an important concert, the first of a week-long series of *Assa* showings which were to bring onstage and up into the air for the first time the best "unofficial" bands in the Soviet Union. At the time, though, it was almost impossible for Westerners like me and H.D. to read.

Boris's performance, when we were finally ushered downstairs by Yelena, was fine. His music was full of echoes of music we knew; his melodies soared; and the audience responded, as if to dictation or to a message from the mountaintop, with all the passionate attention I had seen in Leningrad. (He sang a song written in exile by a man named Vertinsky, and when the audience applauded a line about Russia being a land with no gifts, he stopped to rebuke them, saying: "Don't applaud! How can you *do* that? The country is *us,* the country is *you,* and it has plenty of gifts. The question is: Are you prepared to *use* them properly?") He was magisterial, shamanic, I thought: a Norse god, a star.

But what was one to make of Bravo, the other group on the bill? They were a rockabilly band (one of the musicians wore a red gingham shirt as if to prove it), and they had a punchy woman singer called Zhanna Aguzarova, who looked a bit like Barbra Streisand. They had, by our standards, almost no performance skills at all; and they looked to our eyes—as we peered at them through a mass of heads in a crammed balcony—either entirely derivative or else involved in some elaborate East/West parody the point of which we could not get.

And what were we to make of *Assa,* when it finally started? There were no seats to be had in the cinema (for love or fame), so we were forced to stand in one of the entranceways, with Yelena standing between H.D. and me. And though she translated every/ thing that was said on the screen, we still couldn't make head or tail of it, however hard she tried to explain. It was set in Yalta, and on the face of it it was nothing but the kitschiest sort of melodrama: The hero, a young innocent, had a job singing in a café, where he was seen by a young girl who was living with a middle/age Mafioso in a hotel. They were drawn to one another; and at her insistence, he was hired by the Mafioso to entertain the passengers on a private cruise. The hero, though, made a fool of the Mafioso by singing a Grebenshchikov song about "the old goat Kozlodoyev who tries to seduce young girls." The Mafioso was offended, found out about the two of them, and tried to buy the young hero off. He refused; the Mafioso had him killed; and when the girl found out about it, she killed the Mafioso and was arrested by the *militsia.* A more aggressive, tougher band took over at the café.

By the time this long farrago ended, I was tottering with fatigue. And I was astonished when the audience applauded wildly, just as they had applauded every time Boris's voice or music had come up on the soundtrack. I muttered to H.D., who was flirting ponder/ ously with Yelena, something about the Soviet Union having dif/

ferent traditions, a different narrative style. And when Artyom arrived, saying, "Yup, not bad—our first successful youth-exploita- tion movie," I couldn't understand what on earth he meant. Only much later, when rock music had lost much of its force and drive, and when I saw the film again, did I understand why it was so important, and why, because of it, the Moscow Electric Lightbulb factory's House of Culture became an almost legendary venue. First of all, it was (as Yelena said) the first collaboration between the straight world and the underground, and the underground had found through it a focus and a presence that it had never had before. The director, Sergei Soloviev, had set up a special stadium concert for Zvuki Mu and the Leningrad band Kino (as well as for twenty thousand spectators) so that he could shoot the sequence of the tough band at the end; and he'd opened up to Boris professional recording facilities at Mosfilm, where Boris had recorded on the side enough new material for two whole albums. He'd made a deal with the state recording monopoly, Melodiya, to have *Assa*'s soundtrack released all over the country; and he'd cast as the innocent hero a young New Wave painter known as Africa, who performed, together with Boris, in a bizarre jazz orchestra called Pop Mechanics. He'd also delivered up in the film, alongside the music and the melodrama, an extremely direct and simple message. Africa (the young hero) was the pure spirit of rock culture, while the Mafioso represented the money, corruption, and cooptative power of the state. The spirit of rock reached out (from its café hideout) to permeate a whole genera- tion—even touching the young girl who lived in luxury in a hotel. And when that generation was destroyed, by murder or by its own desperation, another, tougher and stronger, arrived to take its place: singing triumphantly and defiantly, as Viktor Tsoy of Kino did at the end: "We are waiting for changes, we are waiting for change."

We couldn't decode it that evening, H.D. and I: we were too busy trying to translate it into our own language. But it was what we had come for.

2

Around midnight, Leonard, the man from State Television and Radio, drove us back to Artyom and Svetlana's, dropping Yelena and her daughter, Kseniya—a sixteen-year-old flash of bright eyes and dark hair who had suddenly appeared—off on the way. H.D. got out of the car and shook Yelena's hand with grave punctilio, smiling and waving after her into the darkness. When he got back into the car, he asked Artyom who she was.

"Translator, interpreter," said Artyom gruffly. "She works for Sovinfilm, a branch of Goskino that deals with foreigners. Does the competitions and festivals. Gets all the boring fancy stars: Burt Lancaster, Carol Burnett, Rod McKuen, people like that."

"Ah," said H.D. "I'm not surprised: she's very handsome. But the daughter, her daughter—now that's real jailbait."

I said nothing. I wasn't about to get into a contest with him. I had four and a half days to make him fall in love with the Soviet Union—any way it took.

3

It didn't take much, as it happened. At first, I tried to keep H.D. entertained. I took him off to see the Matisses in the Pushkin Museum, and to a hilarious meal in the Ukraina Hotel, among Orthodox priests and visiting African dignitaries, where the waiter offered us, at the end of the proceedings, everything (such as caviar), which he'd announced hadn't been available on the menu a half-hour before. But in the end none of it was necessary. The city itself was enough to enthral him. Whether it was heaving a collective sigh of relief after the recent attack on *perestroika*—published in the newspaper *Sovietskaya Rossiya* in the form of a long letter from a Leningrad chemistry teacher—had been publicly rebuffed, I didn't know. Perhaps it was just the first coming of spring, when the catkins and lilac were beginning to seep in from the country. But Moscow seemed, even to me, after just two months, to have changed immeasurably—as it was to go on changing, in astonished spurts, over the next two years. To H.D., who had visited it once years before, on a corralled package tour, it was a revelation, if only of his own freedom to move about in it. The streets we walked bustled with life; the people we saw in the Metro even smiled at us shyly. And it was full, suddenly, of firsts: the first exhibition since the 1920s of the great painter Pavel Filonov; the first documentary about contemporary rock bands; the first film about the veterans and wounded of the Afghan War; and the first apparently unattached Soviet woman either of us had ever met. Little by little after that first night, in the short time that was available, Yelena began to take us over.

We were grateful enough for it. For she could do all the things at which Artyom was terrible: like flagging down private cars and taxis and persuading them to give us a ride, or charming the way to the head of a line and through any obstruction. She never queued; she never travelled by Metro or bus; she behaved in every way like a Western tourist who happened to know the local language astonishingly well. Artyom, in many ways, actually *was* Western. He was brusque and cerebral and impatient; he felt more at home with the faster pace of Western cities. But Yelena, though she was Slavic all the way through—from cheekbones to sentimentality—and had never once been to the West, played the part much better, as if she'd learned it extremely carefully. She was almost, in fact, too good to be real. She was as defensively ladylike as any class-climbing Englishwoman. She dressed like an Englishwoman; she even flirted like an Englishwoman, as if it was all part of some extraordinarily good game: of wit and stop-go and daring.

She also did one other thing that Artyom was often too bored or distracted to do: she took pains to translate. So when we arrived, on our second evening, to see some films at a huge, distant cinema, and found her there—looking, once more, impossibly smart against the drab files of the audience, and with Kseniya in tow—we were delighted. I wasn't so glad, however, with the division of responsi⁄ bilities she'd clearly decided on for the evening. For after we'd been introduced to the cinema manager and the director of one of the films, and after Artyom had wandered off to who knew where or to what purpose, Yelena immediately commandeered H.D. and drew him off (him with elaborate what⁄can⁄I⁄do? gestures) into the main body of the hall, leaving me on a jutting upstairs balcony with Kseniya.

I sulked for a while, I suppose, at being excluded, but I shouldn't have bothered. For Kseniya, or Ksiyusha, as her mother called her, was enchanting company (fey, eldritch; big round eyes under a thick pelmet of black hair) and almost as good a translator as her mother. She was funny and sharp; and she was soon as wrapped up in the two films we saw as I was. For this was the first public showing of the cinema documentaries about Leningrad rock bands and returned *Afghantsi* that I'd heard about; and they were riveting. It wasn't that either of them was any great masterpiece. They were (especially the rock film), like most Soviet documentar⁄ ies, achingly slow⁄moving and indulgent of their subjects. But it was astonishing, to my eyes at any rate, that they'd been allowed to be made at all. The Afghan War, after all, was still going on, in murderous stalemate; and the veterans of the war were an embarrass⁄ ment: they were kept away from the public eye or else simply forgotten to death. Rock musicians, too, though the public cam⁄ paign against them had ended, were still marginal people, living on the edge of tolerance. And yet here they both were: first, five rock bands enshrined in separate segments (except for Boris, who seemed to wander among them freely), playing, rehearsing, and talking from their jobs, as stokers and janitors, as if they were literary figures, acting it up, speaking about change and music and the West; and then the *Afghantsi,* crippled and whole, speaking straighter and more angrily—this one anxious to go back and avenge his mates, this one turned religious, that one disgusted at all the hypocrisy and the useless killing, a group of them trying to build an orphanage for the children of dead soldiers at Zagorsk, just outside Moscow. At the end of *The Abyss,* the veterans' film, Kseniya said quietly: "I didn't know. I had no idea. The war is right here."

The most extraordinary part of the evening, though, came at the end. For after the applause had died down and the lights had gone up, no one in the audience stirred. Then Artyom and the director of *The Abyss* stepped onto the stage in the silence to answer questions.

"What do they want, those players we saw?" asked an old kerchiefed babushka angrily.

"A normal life," said Artyom into the microphone.

"Do they want to leave, to go to the West?"

"They want to be free in their own country."

There was anger in the hall, talk about honour and patriotism: a row between a jowled pensioner with slicked-back black hair and a boy in jeans. And then the Afghan veterans began to stand and talk. They spoke into a hush about the convoys, the boredom, the deaths of their friends, the killing and maiming, and the void of silence into which they had stepped when they came back home. "Do you see me now?" said one of them, standing, his voice shaking with emotion. "Do you see me? Then tell me, go on, tell me: what is it all *for?*"

We didn't eat that night. By the time the questions and answers had finished, the city was shut tight as a drum. We seemed hardly to eat at all in the five days we were there, H.D. and I. There was simply too much happening.

·

4

He said yes to the film, of course. How could he not? When we finally left for Leningrad by overnight train, the station was wrapped in mist and steam and darkness, hopelessly like a stage set for the arrival in Moscow of Anna Karenina. In Leningrad, the lemon, ochre, and turquoise of the buildings shone in the morning sunshine as if the old ladies had decided to put on new frocks. From then on, the city shuffled time and history for us like an accomplished old card sharp. There were hippies clustered in front of a baroque building on Nevsky Prospekt; there were guitarists in the parks. And every Orthodox church we went into seemed to have been primed for our arrival: to be reaching upward towards the climax of the ancient liturgy, or else holding a wedding, with the bride and groom bravely challenging the present under traditional ceremonial crowns. Beneath the eaves on Sofia Perovskaya Street, Boris held charmed court for us, weaving fantasies about the people he would work with in the West, and singing new songs with lines like "This land was ours; now it's time to reclaim it," or else "The people who killed our fathers will come for our children." The whole thing was dizzying. We ran to the Vice-Consul's apartment; we met musi-cians and a young man about to emigrate with his American student wife. We were snatched up and taken by bus to an apartment at dead of night where there were sitars and mandalas and homegrown grass. It was as if we had succeeded in boring through the guard walls of the city and its past to find a whole generation emerging like moles, patting themselves down, brushing themselves off, getting ready for the new. When we finally took the plane back to Lon-don—after a last lunch with Yelena and Svetlana, at which I allowed him to give them the presents that I had bought for them myself—H.D. said: "Thank you for that, Jo. I don't think I've ever

met so many courageous people in my life." At London's Heathrow
Airport, when a ground steward said to him idly, "Nice to be
home, sir," H.D. said: "No, not particularly. No," he said again,
walking on.

5

As the film with Boris lurched towards life and the deals began to
be made, it was plain that, however H.D. and I might feel about
the Soviet Union, it would have to be shot almost entirely in the
West. It was *for* the West, after all, so it had to have (said the money
men, and we agreed) Western production values. It had to be big;
to have stars; to be the story of the Bob Dylan from Mars who was
shuttled through a time-and-space warp to confront the glamour,
the high tech, and the dollars of the Western entertainment business.
Its focus was to be the making of Boris's record for CBS, with
attendant guest performances from sympathetic Westerners: a record
which Boris's New York manager—a onetime inventor with the
scattergun brilliance, total egocentricity, and petulance of a child—
insisted, when I met him, would certainly be "as huge as the
Beatles."

I had my doubts about this, especially after I saw with H.D.,
soon after we got back to London, a live TV link-up with Leningrad (which Yelena had helped to organize). It was yet another first:
the first conversation between representatives of the two countries'
rock communities—and they didn't seem able to find common
ground at all. The people in London (Brian Eno, Peter Gabriel,
Chrissie Hynde, and the manager of U2) were embarrassingly
apologetic about the glitz and hype of the business they found
themselves in; about the fact that Western music had lost its cen-
trality, its force. They were overrespectful of the price the Russians
had had to pay to keep the music alive, and wistfully jealous of the

role they now seemed to be playing in Gorbachev's new Soviet Union. Meanwhile the people in Leningrad (Boris, Artyom, Zhanna Aguzarova, and the leaders of Televisor and Pop Mechanics) seemed hardly to know what to say to all this, except to agree. Boris talked quietly about the mystical spirit of rock, the inheritance Soviet musicians had had from the West. But the others appeared to squirm with the seriousness of it all. It was as if they were saying underneath their forced complaisance: "Hey, come on! We did it for fun, for laughs, just as you did when you started. All we want now is a chance to become professionals and have influence and make money—like you." Each side paraded past the other, that's to say, saluting, misunderstanding: unable to find a common language, yet wanting in a sense to *be* each other. It was a comedy, I thought, of mutually reinforced errors: neither side, through the blinkers of propaganda and wishfulfilment, could see the other straight.

I should have thought more about it at the time. For it was exactly this that bedevilled the whole project (both record and film) when it finally got under way. Though the Western stars who in the end produced and lent their voices to Boris's record were incredibly kind to him, even a little in awe of him, they still couldn't recognize him for what he actually was: someone who had in isolation confected out of all the styles of an essentially illegal music a vehicle that was precisely right for his own audience—melodic, poetic, lyrical, sometimes earthy, sometimes filled with almost childlike fantasies. The problem was that, apart from its tunefulness, this did not translate into English well, because English and American rock had no longer any tradition of poetry or the exaltation of the everyday. It had other fish to fry: the mass fish of teen sex, dancing, and identification with the warrior star. It would have been different, perhaps, if the record had been smallscale, throwaway, an independent release. But there was a second problem: the hype promulgated by the Onetime Inventor and the money that he'd succeeded in getting up front as a result. The record had become an expensive event, CBS's investment in Gorbachev and Western Gorbymania; and the rules of the game meant that it had to be an enormous success or else a (more or less) total failure. The pressure was on, then; and what began life in New York as a modest-sounding album, ragged at the edges, was gradually overlaid, in London and Los Angeles, with the sort of artificial perfection and synthesized instrumentation that Western audiences expected. Instead of being given help with the archness and fragility of his English lyrics—which was all that he needed—Boris was abandoned: little by little his whole musical persona was drowned.

Boris himself, it has to be said, connived in all this: he deserted his own band, Aquarium; he became fascinated by all the things a high-tech Western studio could do. But in New York (for the second time), as the record progressed, he began to retreat into himself: he went out very little; he tried to recreate the *kruzhkovy* intimacy of his apartment in Leningrad. He hung out with dippy mystics, the last ripples of the sixties; he took a lot of Ecstasy. And I shall never forget him, in Los Angeles, starting to paint, beside a swimming pool, naive landscapes of forests, lakes, and onion-domed churches as arguments about the record and the film swirled about him. He said he was painting them to make a little extra money. I knew he was trying to get back to where on earth he'd started out from.

The film didn't help, of course: it forced him to perform. *I* didn't help. I was distracted by my mother's illness and increasingly alienated from the film, which had spiralled out of control into a million-dollar enterprise. I hated the feverish, manipulative bluster of the Onetime Inventor, and the careless predatoriness of the music business at his back. I even started to loathe New York, where I started a doomed, nonsensical affair with a woman who deserved much better than me. I missed what I thought of as the simplicity and brave innocence of the Soviet Union. When we finally went to Leningrad to shoot, I did my best to try to inject them into the portrait of Boris that was taking shape. But even here my attempts were a failure. Under the bright lights of the crew, Boris's *kruzhok* on Sofia Perovskaya Street looked like a drunken, self-indulgent rabble. In church he seemed stagey; in a cemetery, talking about the attitudes of Russians to death and magic, out of synch and unconvincing. H.D. carefully filmed and interviewed every member of Aquarium. But when we put them all together at a dacha near Komorovo, where the great poet Anna Akhmatova was buried, what started out as a picnic quickly turned into a horrid psychodrama: Boris's wife got drunk and hysterical, and the musicians turned their collective back on him. Leningrad, the city which I disliked, was the one star which survived the experience: it was picturesque; it hogged the lens like a mocking old pro. By the time we moved on to Moscow, where Boris finally, ceremonially signed his contract with the Russian authorities and CBS, I was thoroughly depressed.

6

All through the making of the film so far, I'd kept in touch with Yelena. From the studio in London, I'd seen her wave goodbye from Leningrad at the end of what had been rather grandly called "the rock-and-roll space bridge." I'd telephoned her from time to time, and I'd asked H.D. to find out the whereabouts of a friend of hers: a Georgian brain surgeon who was studying and giving lectures at the University of Southern California. At the "space bridge" I'd beckoned H.D. to follow me into the lights to say hello to her, even though he no longer seemed interested. And it was his name I signed to the telex giving her the brain surgeon's address. It was as if I were using him as an excuse: involved in a competition with him in which I wanted to give him every possible edge. I was being either a bawd or a perfect gentleman, which sometimes amount in England to exactly the same thing.

In Moscow, then, when we arrived with our huge crew, I called her on behalf of both of us—I had become a sort of skivvy to the film—and invited her to dinner at the Ukraina Hotel. But though H.D. flirted amiably enough with her when she arrived, carefully got up, he wouldn't move from his political, surrounded seat at the head of the enormous table. So the two of us were forced to sit together, below the salt of his attention, near where the Onetime Inventor was holding forth in a more than usually self-congratulatory vein. I was depressed, but H.D.'s behaviour made me angry. I was upset for Yelena (in a strange way for Russia): H.D.'s immobility was careless, I thought, and besides, a rule infringement in whatever game I imagined we were playing. I was even more upset when, at the end of the meal, he airily left it to me to find her a taxi. So when he and the crew left for New York, I took her—after a stunning exhibition of the avant-gardist Kasimir Malevich—to the best restaurant I could think of, hoping to make some kind of crazy amends. Afterwards, though I hadn't considered it on the cards or menu, we went back together to her apartment. It was empty.

"Jo," she said when I kissed her as I thought I was supposed to, "I'm sorry, I have my period."

"That's all right," I said, and kissed her again. I didn't believe her at all for some reason. But the ground rules had been set.

It's hard now to describe what happened that night. She was in her late-thirties; I, in my forties. But we were like two teenagers anxious to hold on to our virginity at all costs. Everything else was permitted but that final act of consummation, of commitment. So we wrestled together through the whole night in a weird, desperate sensuality that came from misunderstanding, mutual suspicion, and the edgy conviction that we were doing something wrong, illegal. It took hours for me to undress her, by which time she had come three or four times, clenching her teeth and shaking her head from side to side: "No! No!" It took hours more for me to explore the unknown land of her body as she lay on the pullout sofa-bed, sometimes attacking me and sometimes stretching out spread-eagled, dazed, in a state of suspension. We said almost nothing to each other. There was nothing to say. We were strangers dismantling each other, taking down barriers. It was as if, in the end, we weren't there at all, just our two bodies, distended by touch, fighting, out of control. It was one of the scariest and rawest and most shaking experiences I've ever had. As I fell towards sleep at dawn I wondered what I would wake up to, whether the door would crash open and I'd be caught, floundering awake like a sacrificial fish, in the flash of the KGB's cameras.

In the morning, exposed, I fled, leaving Yelena half-awake. I said that we should have lunch together; it was the day I was due to fly back to England. When we met later at the Ukraina Hotel, we were distant, too bruised for much talk, and I gave her an expensive bottle of perfume I'd bought in a hard-currency store. She later told me the perfume made her feel banal and bought: like one of the hookers who crowded the bar in the National Hotel.

7

Life is not neat. It doesn't come in orderly packages. Causes and effects sometimes belong to different universes of discourse (especially in Russia). I didn't forget Yelena, but I began to think of my night with her as an exorcism: an ending, not a beginning. And I itched to get back to the Soviet Union, not because of her, but because of the film with Boris, which I sensed was getting deeper and deeper, as we progressed, into a kind of betrayal. I badly wanted to have another chance to get the country right. So I worked on the proposal for the films on Russian culture; I lobbied a television company in England—and got its agreement—to help organize a season of films and documentaries on what was happening in the Soviet Union. And meanwhile I read wolfishly, gulping down every book I could lay my hands on. In the country cottage in which my mother was now more or less bedridden, I listened endlessly to Vysotsky and Zvuki Mu and Mussorgsky and Rimsky-Korsakov. Wherever I was, in England or the United States, I bought three or four newspapers a day and simply threw away everything that wasn't about Gorbachev or the climate he was busy creating. I immersed myself in the preparations for the thousand-year anniversary of the Russian church; I followed, day by day, the proceedings of the special Nineteenth Communist Party Conference as, bullied and coaxed by Gorbachev, it finally approved political reform and the shunting of power from Party to government. I watched television astonished as Soviet artists fetched astronomical prices at a Sotheby's sale at a Moscow hotel; and as experts debated the constitutional amendments that were taken up in October: to turn the Supreme Soviet into a semipermanent legislature and to allow, for the first time, multicandidate elections. It was all, of course, too much for me really to take in. (It was a magnificent symphony playing three rooms away.) But I was convinced that the Soviet Union, as Martin Walker had said, was the most interesting place on earth: a place that offered, though I couldn't have articulated this at the time, a sort of salvation.

8

In November, the logic of the film with Boris finally Spanish-walked us like condemned pirates back to Leningrad. It was time for us to show off the new album, and the Western musicians he'd worked with on it, to Aquarium and to the local fans. It was to be the climax of the film: rock‑and‑roll détente in action, a concert to show that East and West could work together and be friends through music. But to effect this, of course, and to make it work on our (Western) terms, we had to bring with us, into the giganto‑ manic eighteenth‑century city, all the gigantomanic paraphernalia that the Western music business had become heir to: lighting, riggers, gaffers, designers, mixers, stage managers, six camera crews, and a twenty‑four‑track sound unit from Germany or England. (The Russians weren't to be trusted.) As the preparations for this invasion engulfed everyone involved, I wondered what Boris thought of it all. I remembered him saying in California—where he'd had his bad Soviet teeth capped during the recording—that he wanted finally to take Ecstasy with H.D., to make him relax and get in touch with his soul, like a Russian. When I walked into the huge hall of the Leningrad Sports and Culture Complex, though, there was precious little Russianness about. As the imported techni‑ cians swarmed over the huge stage, it struck me that we were using the sledgehammer of all this Western efficiency in an attempt to crack open a small nut. It was, I thought, our final misunderstand‑ ing. We had, in our well‑meaning, ignorant way, outdefined Boris and left him with nowhere to go. We wanted to show him to the West as the star he was in his own country. And that meant (for us) that he had to be surrounded with other stars, have perfect teeth and publicity, heroic, state‑of‑the‑art concerts, and the best record‑ ing and other equipment money could buy. But this was bound to alienate him from his people, his circle, his own amateur band; and in any case it had nothing to do with what had made him a star in the Soviet Union in the first place. Artyom, in his laconic way, later got it absolutely right, when he said after the first concert: "Well, Jo, we gave you a poet, and you sent us back a professional." At about the same time, in the House of Culture of the Moscow Electric

Lightbulb Factory, there was held a Week of Conscience, in which the names of Stalin's victims were memorialized and people who had been prisoners tried to reach one another. It was much nearer to the spirit with which H.D., Boris, and I had started out our journey in the same building.

The only time I had a chance to talk to Boris alone, the night before the first concert, I tried to tell him something of all this—and to address (sidewise) the rumours I'd heard: that he was having an affair with his bass player's beautiful, graceful wife, Irina. But I couldn't really articulate it; and after I left in the small hours of the morning, Boris's wife, Lyuda—I was told later—tried to throw herself out of the seventh-floor window. Boris turned up at the Sports and Culture Complex the next day with his wrists cut by broken glass. The whole process had gone too far to be stopped. When Aquarium went into retreat at the complex and we complained that they were more than an hour late for a sound check, one of the Russians suddenly spat and screamed with fury: "How dare you people criticize them! How dare you impose on them your wretched Western timetable! They're their *own* people, not yours! They are artists!" We filmed little, of course, of Aquarium's Russian set; we concentrated on the second part of the evening, when they were swamped by the Western stars and Boris sang in English.

9

In Leningrad for the concerts were the Writer and the Director with whom I'd first come to Moscow. (H.D. and the Director were old friends.) And after the concerts were over, I went with them to the capital for a few days. On the second day, I called Yelena and invited her to dinner with us at a new cooperative which we'd heard had a cabaret of some kind.

I didn't know what to expect. But from the first minute, she was totally impossible. She was dressed very smartly, but with a kind of fuck-you casualness; and she'd arranged her hair so that it shrouded her face, as if she'd decided to shut out the place she was going to. She wanted to do everything that no one else wanted: to sit in a corner and talk secretly to Svetlana; to dance with me when everyone else was ordering dinner. The only time she seemed cheerful was when a magician started pulling handkerchiefs out of Artyom's ear. Through all this, she more or less ignored the Writer and the Director; she made it plain that she resented them, and they looked back at her at first with bemusement and then with a faintly super-cilious air of superiority. No doubt they were right: her behaviour did seem slightly mad. But when I saw their response, I suddenly felt an overwhelming sympathy for her. The Writer and the Director were among my best friends. But I was sick of Westerners like them (and me) by now: sick of all their tendentious assumptions, their right thinking, and their good manners. Madness seemed at least satisfactorily foreign. The chances were, there was echt Russianness in it.

When dinner was over, and I walked her home, Yelena said aggressively: "How could they sit there looking down their noses at me? Who do they think they are?" I defended them; I said that she had behaved appallingly badly. But my heart wasn't really in it. It was years before the Writer, the Director, and Yelena could see each other straight, and then only when she had learned to hide what she felt beneath a Western veneer. I tried once more to put them together that week: at the Blue Bird Café, the only jazz joint in the city, where the Director and I sat enthralled, listening to musicians who had obviously studied black-market records with the huge intensity of Talmudic scholars. But she was again aloof and haughty: lost, while the music was playing and the attention had strayed away from her, in the sump of some impenetrably dark gloom. Afterwards the Writer said mockingly that manners weren't what they might be

in the Soviet Union—either that or Yelena was absurdly in love
with me.

I doubted that. For though we again made love, creeping after
midnight into her little room on Vorotnikovsky Alley, our love-
making was filled, as before, with the tremendous desperation of two
people who couldn't quite remember each other's name. And when
we were alone together in public, she began to be as impossible with
me as she was with the Writer and the Director. It was as if all the
hounds of her emotions had somehow been unleashed and were
careering around her, demanding, one by one, her immediate attention. Her moods were mercurial and titanic: she was by turns
imperious, childlike, loving, dismissive, airily happy, and continen-
tally sad. It was fascinating, foreign, but it was a trial in both senses,
like something out of one of those mediaeval ballads in which the
knight, to prove his constancy, holds beneath his cloak a woman
who becomes, one after the other, lion and leopard, eagle, antelope,
and snake.

10

She came to London less than a month later, on her first-ever visit
to the West. She was travelling on a *komandirovka,* or business trip
(complete with special business passport), to act as translator for two
of the heavy men from Sovinfilm, the organization for which she
(mostly) worked. It was all supposed to be absolutely routine. But
for some reason they'd made a mess of their British visas, and I'd had
to spend days on the phone to the Foreign Office and to the British
embassy in Moscow to help unsnarl them. By that time, I was
convinced that Russians were children: though their country might
be a great nuclear power, as individuals they couldn't even get
lunch. Still, I wanted her to have a good time on my home turf.

The three of them were in London for an American-Soviet

co-production, on which Yelena was supposed to work as companion and dialogue coach for her friend Yelena Sofonova, the star, opposite Marcello Mastroianni, of Nikita Mikhalkov's film *Dark Eyes*. They stayed in the Park Lane Hilton Hotel, courtesy of the American producer; they had an allowance of fifty pounds a day each. They also had a chauffeur-driven car—and Yelena loved it all.

The trouble—I sensed it immediately, on the evening she arrived, with me pretending, for the benefit of the heavies, that we were just good friends—was that the film was never going to be made; the American visa she showed me proudly in her *sluzhebny pasport* was meaningless. There was something cautious and provisional about the producer when I met him the first night: something less than celebratory. The boat was not being put out in quite the right way; the visit to London, I thought, was a holding operation, while he penny-pinched and scurried for funds elsewhere. I suspected him too, for some reason, of organizing the trip just so he could spend time with Yelena. So I found myself feeling both angry and sorry for her; I set out to demonstrate how a hospitable Westerner ought to behave. During the days, they would negotiate, while I pushed forward my plans for the films on Russian culture. Then, sooner or later, I would show up at the hotel. And then, imitating some bonhomous English version of the American producer (my relationship with Yelena not, whatever it was, to be told), I would take her and the two heavies—one droopeyed, as unreadable as China; the other full of untranslatable laughter and fond of a drink—to restaurants or to a tired production of the musical *42nd Street*. I was lavish; I was helpful; I made conversation; I was friendly. It was as if I were covertly courting, in the face of the blandishments of my imagined rival, the ward of two trousered and bulldog-jawed maiden aunts.

Through all of this, Yelena played her part (of the coy, noveletish nineteenth-century ward) as if to the manner born. She was distantly alluring and secretly flirtatious. But when we were alone together, she was skittish and standoffish: she didn't want me to stay in her hotel room overnight. I never stopped to think at the time that there might be a perfectly good reason for this: that she was under the surveillance of the maiden aunts, if only to see that she did her job properly and so could be trusted to go to the West again. It never occurred to me that one of them almost certainly had a watching brief from the KGB. Instead, I was half amused and half infuriated by her behaviour; I expected, I suppose, some sort of quid pro quo. I imagined that I was once more being put through strange Russian hoops, only this time as an animal accessory: not a knight, more a performing dog. This was confirmed for me when I finally had to face, on Yelena's only day off, the worst ordeal that any Westerner at the time had to endure when dealing with a Soviet: trial by shopping.

I met Yelena in Chelsea in the afternoon. (She'd spent the morning with the American woman producer she sometimes worked for.) She was looking into a shop window, her eyes glazed, her breathing shallow. It was the first time she'd been out in the city on foot. She'd never seen shops like this; she still couldn't believe that they existed: rows on rows of them, next to each other, compet-ing with each other. It was as if she was in some crazed dream. She was almost feral with greed; she wanted to see everything, to buy everything. She wanted to buy her way out of all those years when she'd had to scrimp and swap and buy the castoffs of actresses and ballet dancers who'd travelled abroad. She was also (by now) broke: she'd spent every penny of her fifty-pound per diems and whatever else she was owed by the American woman. She'd purchased presents for her mother, her father, her uncle, her friends: everyone she knew, it seemed. But she'd gotten nothing for herself or Ksiyu-sha, and she was desperate. I, it became plain, as she took my arm and looked up at me shyly but with considerable determination, was to pick up the slack.

The afternoon was a nightmare. I was forced into the role of a millionaire john, a sugar daddy buying clothes for an avaricious teenager, out in public as a kept woman for the very first time. If I said something was too expensive, she would affectionately agree and suddenly remember something nearly like it on the other side of town. We careened across the city. I sat in narrow little boutique chairs as she scoured through racks and chattered like a sparrow to shop assistants, trying to be light. I lolled against counters in department stores, watching her indulgently as if I did this every day, and secretly longing for the earth to open up. I had heard about Russians being driven over the edge by the abundance of the West. I had even once interviewed in New York a young defector, a violinist, who said that for months she couldn't practice, so obsessed was she by the twenty different kinds of orange juice on the shelves of every supermarket. But I had never seen it closeto, and it was frightening. Yelena couldn't stop herself. She was transformed that afternoon into a sea of need, and forced by her need to become a grasping, ontherun bookkeeper, constantly having to weigh up the debit of what she could ask for against the credits of my affection for her and what she thought she could do for me later on. In the end, as the blessed cutoff of closing time came nearer, I bought her things— some costume jewellery, a suit, a blouse, some shoes, I don't remember—that matched whatever formula she'd come up with, and balanced, at some expense, our EastWest amative account.

That night, her last, I stayed in Yelena's hotel room, but it didn't give me pleasure. I felt, I think, like she did when I gave her the bottle of perfume in the Ukraina Hotel: dirtied in some way. In the morning we made love, but only perfunctorily. "Poor Jo," she said, stroking my face, as if she understood. I helped her pack, and then we went downstairs separately. And as I waved goodbye to her and the two maidenaunt heavies, both laden now with electronic goods, I thought of something Marjie had said. Boris had stayed with Marjie in London during the making of the record; and after he'd left, she'd said, laughing, throwing her hands wide: "Show me a Soviet, Jo, and I'll show you a broke Westerner."

At about the time of Yelena's visit to London, Gorbachev won the hearts of the West with a stirring speech at the United Nations in New York. A few days later, the leadership of the Communist Party met in Moscow to discuss the upgrading of surveillance on Western journalists. One of the people who signed off on the memorandum prepared for the meeting was Alexander Yakovlev, the so-called father of *perestroika*. KGB, CIA; saviour, devil; millionaire, kept woman. "Same two-step," as a Russian taxi driver once said to me in Los Angeles in another context. "Different partners, that's all."

II

A month and a half later, I went back to Moscow, bearing gifts; and everything was changed. Yelena bounced through the barrier of customs as if it didn't exist, and met us as we were looking for our baggage in the chill gloom of the arrivals hall. "Hello, Jo," she said to me, holding out her hand. And then she winked.

I'd come back to explore the films on Russian culture, which had become, via the insular wisdom of highly paid British telecrats, one film of, "say, an hour and a half." With me was the producer, a grizzled Canadian who laughed at the world when he wasn't dowsing it for political heresy and conspiracy; and the director, an Englishman whose air of earnest scepticism made me think of him as a perambulating question mark. Both had made films in the Soviet Union before. Both had loved the experience; they were up for more of the same.

Yelena fitted their mood exactly. She bubbled; she danced; she was wry; she was funny. It was as if some strange ghost had been laid and lost: outmanoeuvred. She was also hugely efficient. When I'd introduced her to the Canadian producer in London, and he'd agreed to hire her as translator and fixer for the film, I'd had no idea, for all my reading, how on earth to collapse and confine such an enormous subject as the culture of Russia into a palatable, just-so concoction for the West.

So I'd decided to try to meet in Moscow people who might help: editors, historians, writers, scholars, and so on. I'd made up a list of them, which had been revised several times on the telephone with Yelena; and on the plane I'd added a few extra names. I was astonished to find, when we sat down for a drink in the Rossiya Hotel that evening, that she'd already thought of most of my extra names and had arranged for us to talk to them. "See, I can read your mind, Jo darling," she said, and smiled serenely, like a Tartar Madonna.

The city had also changed, almost beyond recognition. People were stopping each other in the streets to talk; they had begun to take over the public spaces. Despite the cold, there were large crowds on Pushkin Square and outside the offices of *Moscow News:* fighting, talking, hectoring, arguing. In the subways, new newspapers and broadsheets were on sale. Election meetings for the new Chamber of People's Deputies were beginning to be held; voters' clubs were springing up; and the Mathematics Institute and the Aviation Engineering Institute were holding constant teach-ins and political meetings. At *Dom Kino,* the headquarters of the Union of Film Workers, there'd been recent demonstrations for Solzhenitsyn and Sakharov. On television, there were bold new programmes, "Vzglyad," "Before and After Midnight," and "600 Seconds," which seemed to dare everything. Long-banned novelists and philosophers were appearing in thick journals (now with huge subscription lists) like *Novy Mir* and *Znamya;* Freud and George Orwell were about to be published for the first time. A ferment was abroad in the city. Everything that had been promised, it seemed to me, was finally being delivered. Thanks to Gorbachev, Moscow was getting its memory, its identity back—and more.

One night, as we were wandering the streets, we stood and watched in the snow as a huge crowd came from a meeting for the disgraced Boris Yeltsin, chanting and arguing, some carrying plac-ards. And the young director we were with turned to an old man as he shuffled past us towards the Metro. "How old are you, father?" he asked.

"I'm ninety-two," said the old man, stopping. "I was born in 1896."

"So you've lived through everything: Lenin, Stalin, the Revolu-tion, everything," said the director.

"Yes."

"Tell me then: is this what a revolution feels like?"

"Yes," said the old man, looking back towards the crowd. "This is *exactly* what a revolution feels like."

12

"If I was a Martian," I said, "and I knew nothing about this country, where would you point me if I asked you what was the most important focus of its culture today?"

"The discussions at the Mathematics Institute," said Yuri Afanasyev, the co-chairman of Memorial and rector of the Institute of Historical Archives. "And rock music," he added.

"The church," said Sergei Zalygin, the editor-in-chief of *Novy Mir.* "The church is what has kept the sources and the resources of the culture alive."

"The kitchen," said Natan Eidelman, the historian. "The kitchen *kruzhok* epitomizes the fact that people here want to be independent. Historically, the kitchen is the only place where they could be free." Writer Lem Karpinsky agreed. "Kitchen life is definitely the most important focus," he said in the beer bar of the National Hotel, nodding his head, his eyes shining. "And now it's moving outwards and taking on new forms: in political clubs, palaces of youth, exhibition halls, national movements, and business cooperatives. These are all an essential part of the building of civil society here—and they come in the end from the kitchen."

We had three or four meetings like these a day, and I found myself to my surprise, as we ran from meeting to meeting, asking virtually all the questions, being the interviewer. The other two remained silent, and Yelena and I little by little became a strange double act, a partnership, almost as if they weren't there. It was an extraordinarily exciting and heady time, I think, for us both. We crouched round the table of Solzhenitsyn's editor, Vadim Borisov; we talked, through him, to Sakharov and to the dissident Slavophile mathematician Igor Shofarevich. We met people barely out of the camps; dissident priests; and powerful editors—with huge circula~ tions—like Vitaly Korotich of *Ogonyok* and Gyorgy Baklanov of *Znamya*. In the evenings we didn't stop: we went to poetry readings and to the theatre. We watched teenage poets and poets who'd been denied a public voice for twenty~five years; we saw the poet Andrei Voznesensky answer questions from the audience with the charged gravity of an oracle. We watched Yuri Lyubimov's stunning, mov~ ing return to his Taganka Theatre, and saw three of his productions, with Yelena scattering translation like ticker tape among the three of us. We went to Mikhail Bulgakov's *The Heart of a Dog* at the Theatre of Young Spectators and his *Molière* at the Art Theatre; and to the brilliant actress Marina Niyolova playing Yevgeniya Gins~ burg in *Into the Whirlwind* at the Sovremennik. Afterwards, we went to restaurants where we met filmmakers and actors; we sat with violinists and guitar players as they sang the poetry of Pasternak and impossibly sentimental romances. And then Yelena and I would go back to the apartment on Vorotnikovsky Alley, drunk on the wine and the good hope of it all, and make love—the past forgotten—with a long exploratory joy, as if we'd finally come to terms by opening up for each other this brave new world. At five in the morning, I'd walk back through the empty streets to the hotel, imagining that the brigade of street sweepers I sometimes heard in the alleys were poets and rock musicians and writers and dissidents contemptuously fulfilling their obligation to the state. I don't think I slept more than two or three hours a night the whole time we were there.

13

At the end of seven or eight days of this, with words and themes and phrases rolling around in my head, as indigestible as marbles—the Russian soul, the Russian intelligentsia, Russia's age-old argument with God, the poet as sacrificial victim, the need for some kind of collective repentance for the foul dysgenics of the past—I was taken by Yelena to see her father. Gennady's "asthma"—which is what Yelena's family called his bronchial illness—was giving him trouble, and he was a patient in a small specialist research hospital in the north of Moscow. We drove there one afternoon and waited in a deserted visitors' room until he arrived, looking tired and wan but with a certain dapperness, in a brown plaid robe, his hair slicked back off his forehead. He was very courteous; he might have been playing host in his own house. He seemed happy to be where he was, as if it was a world he knew; he seemed proud that he was included in it. And when we went to look at his room, I could see why: it was spotlessly clean and neat, with a pile of books beside the bed, a world away from the congenial chaos of the flat on Vorotnikovsky Alley. It occurred to me then that the monkish, privileged quiet of the hospital gave him more of a sense of belonging and continuity than his own noisy family, split by *perestroika* and the attractions of the West.

We talked for a while, in formal old-fashioned French, about hospitals; I told him that I'd been virtually raised in them, since both my parents were doctors. He seemed very interested. Then I left him and Yelena alone to talk, huddled together, while I wandered down the linoleumed corridors and pretended to read the notice boards like a visiting physician. It was while I was playing this part and peeping with more and more boldness into all the rooms that Gennady said to Yelena that he liked me very much, even though I was almost certainly CIA. "It doesn't matter, though," he said (perhaps wearily). "They are professionals. He is no doubt an honourable professional."

14

After that, as if some sort of permission had been given, the Canadian producer and I spent more and more time in the Vorotnikovsky Alley apartment, after the theatre or sometimes instead of it. (The question-mark director often wanted to see old friends from the Bolshoi Ballet or the circus.) We would bring wine and beer from the hard-currency *gastronom* at the Mezhdunorodnaya Hotel. And Yelena's mother, Tatiana Samoilovna—clucking welcome— would cook borshch and *goluptsy* (cabbage stuffed with spiced meat) or else giant pastry *kulibiaki* filled with cabbage, eggs, and beef. She'd bring out the tomatoes, peppers, and cucumbers she'd pickled the year before, and the fiery Georgian hot sauce *(adjika)* she'd made. She would beam over the table at the outlandish noise we made that we called language, and swoop down on tiny glasses of vodka from time to time with the watchful delicacy of a peregrine falcon. (Similes and metaphors flew around her like the birds she resembled.) It wasn't long before the Canadian producer and I took to calling her Mama.

Sometimes, when she was out or cooking and Yelena was on the telephone, I would prowl around the flat and inspect it for secrets: Gennady's room, with a huge clothes cupboard, an old forties radiogram, and biographies and memoirs of Second World War generals; Yelena's room, with what looked like framed frag-ments of tapestry on the walls, and a room-long armoire-cum-bookcase leaking cosmetics and clothes and photographs and thick journals out onto the floor; and Kseniya's room at the back, through the dining room (where Tatiana Samoilovna mostly slept), with a stand-up piano, a signed poster of Dean Reed, a massed phalanx of her childhood toys behind her sofa-bed, and everywhere, in rows and regiments and crazy ziggurats, books. Every cupboard I tenta-tively opened in the apartment seemed crammed with goods: bags of flour and macaroni and sugar in the kitchen; in the dining room, soap, boxes of chocolates, and the cut glass Tatiana Samoilovna had brought back with her from Belgium thirty-six years before. In a way, I suppose, I was the spy Gennady thought me: I wanted to know what lay behind the facade of this microcosm in which Yelena lived.

One evening, when the Canadian producer was doing some-thing else, I sat down to talk to Kseniya (or Ksiyusha, as I too started to call her). Her grandfather had said of her, I knew, that she was not of this time, but from the beginning of the century, before the Revolution. And certainly she had more than her fair share of the sort of intense, brooding high seriousness which people tended to identify with the so-called old St. Petersburg intelligentsia. But though she wrote poetry and read voraciously, in many ways she was much younger than her (sixteen-year-old) age group in the West. She was also confused—confused by what was going on in the society and by the legacy of her own background: "Stalinist" grandfather (as she put it), "rebellious" mother, and grandmother "tip-toeing between them, trying to keep the peace."

"It looks easy to be a child in the Soviet Union," she said, playing with her hair. "But it's hard, because children are the only thing that parents really possess. They can't be sure of anything else; everything else belongs to the state. And when nothing is left for them anymore, they say: 'We didn't have it. But our kids, maybe our kids . . .' So look, you know, yes, children are treated specially, and a lot of families manage to create a beautiful little world of childhood, with its own little miracles. But even then, well, the child grows up and finds out that by protecting him from the reality of the outside world, his parents were simply showing how scared of it they were themselves."

I asked her about her grandfather. "Every one of us is a product of the system," she said enigmatically. Then: "Well, I suppose he is a Stalinist. I have terrible arguments with him. But what about me? I'm very conscious of the fact that I'm not free enough. I'm too categorical, too ready to judge people. Sometimes I see only black and white. And when I argue with my grandfather, I think perhaps I'm just taking revenge on him for my own disappointment. It hasn't actually turned me into somebody else. My active 'yes' has just become an active 'no.' I'm as unforgiving as anyone else: another little Stalinist, in fact."

"Do you think that's to do with your schooling?"

"How can I know?"

"What was it like?"

"It was just . . . well, the normal Soviet education," she said. "I learned to read with Papa Ilyich and Baby Lenin"—the Soviet equivalent of Dick and Jane. "In kindergarten, I sang songs every day about Lenin and the USSR. I remember the system of inform-ing there, the permanent whispers—'I'll tell! I'll tell!'—and it wasn't the teachers who were doing it; it was us, the kids. I loved

Lenin to the bottom of my heart—it's true, Jo!—and I was angry
with my mother when she didn't seem to feel the same thing. When
I was five, I remember I read the story about Pavel Morozov, the
Young Pioneer who betrayed his own father to the KGB in the
name of the Communist Party, and I felt ashamed because I
doubted whether I'd be strong enough to do the same. And about
then, I discovered—I don't remember how—that my grandmother
was Jewish. It turned my world upside down. I screamed: 'Go back
to your Jewish country!' It had nothing to do with anti-Semitism.
It was a kind of confusion: I didn't understand how anyone could
belong to another nation. You see?" she said, looking up from
beneath the floppy cloche of her hair. "They did their job well.
Underneath, I'm the little Stalinist they wanted."

"What about after kindergarten?" I asked.

"Oh, you know. I was a Young Pioneer and then a member
of Komsomol. We were given lectures on how wonderful our life
was and some little treats from time to time to prove it. Later we were
taught about the theory of communism and all that, so that by the
time we were fourteen, we were already political animals. But school
. . . well, actually school was O.K. The first three years were like
one big birthday party because of our teacher. We were lucky: the
teacher in the class next to us would force a girl down on her knees
just for taking a look at the class journal. I don't know. What else
do you want to know?

"I remember the day of Brezhnev's death: everyone was afraid
to tell us and whispered in the corners, even though black banners
were already up on the walls of the buildings. Oh, and I remember
the way a teacher screamed when she once saw the English flag on
a girl's school bag." She laughed. "But things were a lot more
dangerous in other schools. I met two girls who told me that when
they were eleven or twelve they lived through an awful time. The
grandfather of one of them was a friend of Academician Sakharov

and he'd been put in prison. Her school found out about this and connected it with her 'non-Communist behaviour': they decided that she and her friend were dangerous for the other kids. So every week they were called to the school council and called 'prostitutes' and 'political criminals'; the teachers tried to split them up by telling one girl bad things about the other. They said: 'In 1937, we *shot* people like you!' And it was the parents of their classmates who had inspired the whole thing. The kids secretly supported them. Can you *imagine?*"

"Has all that changed?"

"I don't know. I keep living through the past again and again. I am definitely not free from it." She paused. Then: "You know, I have a private history teacher now, for my entrance to the university. He works as a night watchman. He recently told me he'd completely lost all his ideals."

"Why?"

"Because now they're being joyfully supported by all those people who in previous years either kept silence or suppressed dissidents themselves."

I asked her why she had to have a private history teacher. So she told me about the "ridiculous" history textbooks that she'd been taught from in school: books that reduced Lysenko's destruction of Soviet genetics to "theories that were not subsequently borne out by experiments and failed to find practical application," and dismissed Stalin's terror and genocide as "a series of grave mistakes that were resolutely condemned by the Party." She told me that the year before the graduate exams in history had simply been cancelled because there were no reliable textbooks available at all. "Most good teachers these days," she said, "have to use the thick journals to teach. They change their own and their pupils' minds about the history of this country and what happened to it once a month."

1 5

In the vast awfulness of the Rossiya Hotel one day, the producer, the director, and I dredged up one after the other the remarks that had struck us along the way: "After seventy years of repression and enforced isolation, we are trying to find out just who on earth we are" (Yuri Afanasyev); "The state is always trying to direct and control the culture; it is afraid of undirected activity, so its representa-tives act like religious leaders with the functions of the Inquisition" (Lem Karpinsky); and especially, "You know, 1988 was a very important year: for the first time in seventy years, no new political prisoners were taken. But don't be too optimistic about what is happening here. *Perestroika* may be a disaster; and *glasnost* is only a very small cloud. The plants of the new are very young and scrawny, and without water, they may never take root. The country may be entering a period of total chaos" (Vadim Borisov).

In the end, over many discussions, we took the line of least resistance for our film. Along the way we had met, thanks to the irresistible bustle of Yelena's charm, a philologist and mediaeval scholar called Dmitri Likhachev, an old man with a surprised graveyard face and a wonderful shy smile who'd said he no longer had time for interviews. He was an Academician and the joint chairman (with Raisa Gorbachev) of the Soviet Fund for Cul-ture—which had brought into the light the art collections of private collectors and was involved in restoring the houses and apartments of Pushkin, Gogol, and the poet Marina Tsveraeva. In the twenties, though, it had been a different story: he'd been imprisoned for his involvement in a student discussion group at Leningrad University; and he'd spent years in the camp at Solovetsky Monastery, which Solzhenitsyn called the birthplace of the Gulag. In the late forties, having watched his parents die of starvation in the siege of Leningrad, he was accused once more—this time of cosmopolitanism and of taking the wrong historical line on Ivan the Terrible and the first Russian dissident and defector, Prince Kurbsky—and was attacked and beaten by Party thugs. Today he was widely known (with Sakharov) as "the conscience of the nation." But, unlike Sakharov, he was old: his memory reached back to before the Revolution. His family had lived in St. Petersburg near the Maryinsky (now Kirov) Theatre, he said. He had known the great pre-Revolutionary balle-rina Karsavina, and had gone to the same church as the family of Vladimir Nabokov.

He also spoke English (if slowly: like an old prospector sieving a forgotten stream bed for gold). And it was this that decided us. We would try to concentrate, we agreed, on three men who spoke English, to represent three generations: Likhachev, to embody the culture that had existed before the Revolution and that had after-wards been systematically destroyed; Andrei Voznesensky, one of the sixties men *(shestidesyatniki)* who were now the most important champions of *glasnost* and *perestroika,* to speak about the post-Revolu-tionary avant-garde, the worship of Stalin, and the brief window of hope under Nikita Khrushchev; and my friend Artyom Troitsky, to address the levelling boredom of the Brezhnev years and the gradual appearance, against the odds, of an embattled, underground, alternative culture. We had lunch with Voznesensky in the subsi-dized dining room of the Writers' Union, in the hall that had been used by Tolstoy for the masonic lodge meeting in *War and Peace.* And we spent a long day (and in Yelena's and my case, a long, grateful, illegal night) with Artyom and Svetlana in the dacha at Pakhra that they'd rented after the repossession of their flat in Moscow. I idly suggested, some time after that, that perhaps Artyom and Voznesensky should meet together with Dmitri Likhachev for the purposes of the film. And the next day the idea came back from the director as a fully fledged plan. The three would form a sort of *kruzhok,* spinning out of their separate memories and knowledge the story of the culture, surrounded, as the poet Wallace Stevens said in another context, by "pages of illustrations." It was these "pages of illustrations" it would be my job to organize.

16

When the producer and the director left, I stayed on in Moscow for a few days to meet some of Yelena's friends: her Three Musketeers. There was Tomas, the tall, grave Georgian I had often met before: a man who looked like an Italian patriarch or godfather, and worked for the same film organization as Yelena and the maiden aunts. He was at that time negotiating with Greek millionaires for a joint venture to make video cassette machines and mass-produce cassettes. And it occurred to me that in another country he would have been a millionaire himself. He had the indefinable air of someone used to getting his own way, as if he had a tested and trusted reservoir of force within him that others could only guess at. There was something slightly unnerving about this. But he doted on Yelena, as if he were a favourite uncle and she his wayward, outspoken, incorrigible niece. He said to me: "You know, is very, very difficult for Westerners here, Jo. Martin Walker, he was a good boy; he understood. But most people think we are backward part of Europe, place where same rules apply, but in primitive way. They come here to make quick judgment and fast money. Moscow is full of—how you call them?—Western hustlers, who never leave home: who can't even recognize who they're dealing with, who don't know who to bribe or where real power is. If you stay here, Jo, I hope you at least try to understand." It struck me then that he was giving me a warning.

The next night, in what I began to see as a Musketeers' parade, Savva and Varya came to dinner. Savva was a feature-film director:

a restless, engaging man with a huge, thick, curved moustache like a furry half-moon or the corner eave of a thatched roof. His wife, Varya, was the daughter of the playwright Alexei Arbuzov: a stocky blonde woman with calm eyes and a determined mouth—she was definitely the gatekeeper, I thought at the time, of the house of her husband's talent (if he had any), the keeper of the keys. They were enormously friendly and—Yelena later told me—almost crazily social as a couple: they made the rounds of the embassies; they happily trawled for connections. Savva's career and his future as a director had taken the place of the child they'd never had.

First we watched a film that I'd made long before, as if to establish my credentials. And then Savva, over dinner, talked excit- edly about my new subject: Russian culture. He bristled and bustled with ideas. He talked about the barbarian Russian gods and the Old Believers; the church as the preserver of the Russian soul; and the importance, to Russians, of interior freedom. He walked the high wire of serfdom and slavery. He juggled with Tartars and stoves and bread and eternity. And he constantly threw out the names of all the places I should visit, like some professor-clown frenziedly strewing notes all over the circus-ring floor: Kiev and Novgorod, Svetogorsk and Pushkinogorya, Vladivostok, Lake Baikal, and, "but abso- lutely, Jo, the Volga River." He kept coming back to the Volga River. "In the middle, the shores are invisible, Jo," he said; "it's the huge, huge space of the Russian soul. *Prostor,* space, yearning for space—that's what's important in Russia." Then: "There are power stations and dams in the Volga, Jo: they represent the block- age of Soviet power. And by the Volga there's Stalingrad, with its memories of the war and of the way Stalin turned the bravery of the Russian spirit into concrete." It was an endearing performance; he was knowledgeable; his enthusiasm was catching. But there was something in it that reminded me uneasily of what I'd thought of in Leningrad as the strange omnipresence, the simultaneousness of all history in Russia. Savva, smiling, gesturing, never talked about developments or processes, of one thing coming after or resulting from another. He seemed not at all concerned with the massive geographical distances between the places he conjured out of his capacious clown-pockets. It suddenly occurred to me that when the subject was Russia, Russians never seemed to sift or weigh the evidence at all. It didn't matter where the evidence came from— from mediaeval battles or landscapes or writers or modern political institutions, from pre-Christian Kiev or post–Second World War Stalingrad—it all had equal force. The internal radar of Russians, in other words—when it came to their favourite subject—didn't seem to have any function that could show the size and importance of the objects and events it came across when scanning. All that mattered was the number of blips—and the intensity of the feeling of the scanner himself. (Later Ksiyusha told me that this, in the end, was what Russian poetry was all about.)

Next up was Guram, the brain surgeon whose address in California I'd got for Yelena, via the Hollywood Director, in 1988. Virtually the first thing he said to me after I took off my coat in his apartment the next night was: "I've been thinking about Jesus Christ today."

Guram was a Georgian: a swart man in his thirties with thinning hair, a slightly wolfish look, and an extraordinarily elastic face, the parts of which—eyebrows, lips, nose, ears—all seemed capable of independent motion. He was a man who appeared constantly to be assembling himself out of the raw materials of his mood and the demands of his audience. He was like a consummate character actor who could play, from moment to moment, whatever role the occasion required. What was required now, it seemed, was an intellectual quizmaster.

We went, then, into an enormous, well-appointed living room and talked for half an hour, with almost demented intensity, about

immanence and emanence, godhead and the ability of the human
individual to turn the wheel of history. Then, suddenly, it was over.
"All right, Jo," said Guram, standing, "let's go and join the girls."
I appeared to have passed some sort of test.

Guram lived with his wife, Yelena, in the smartest apartment
building I had ever seen in Moscow. It had gates and a driveway,
an imposing entrance, wide, carpeted corridors, and lifts that sighed
(rather than clanked) their way upwards. I'd stopped and gawked
at it on the way in, and asked Yelena what on earth it was. It
wouldn't have been out of place in the East Fifties or in Mayfair.

"It's *nomenklatura,*" she'd said, shrugging her shoulders. "It's
how they live. Yelena's father was a Politburo member."

Yelena was Yelena's best friend. She had a high forehead,
beautiful cat's eyes, and a certain firmness of manner which, together
with her wide shoulders and authoritative chin, suggested her background. (Her father, I found out, had been the Party boss of
Byelorussia.) She was an economist specializing in Spain and Latin
America at one of the Institutes. And she was also a fine cook. In
the kitchen/dining room, we ate borshch and veal splintered with
carrots and garlic, while Guram made long sideways toasts, loving
the English words, dwelling on them, jingling them like a poor man
with sudden coins in his pockets. We talked while the two Yelenas
leaned together, gossiping in Russian and laughing. I asked him
why he'd become a doctor.

"It was my grandmother," he said. "One day when I was in
school, she sat me down and said: 'Guri, you know that I love you.
You know that I admire everything you do. You know that when
I read what you write and when I see you acting on stage, I am full
of pride. But Guri, I have to tell you that when you act, you are not
Stanislavsky. When you write, you are not Lev Tolstoy. So my
advice to you, Guri, is: be a doctor. That way, when they come for
you and put you in the camps, you will always have bread and a

warm place by the radiator." He laughed. "She was the daughter of a duke, you see. And her husband was shot in the 1930s."

I blanched. Soviets always seemed to tell stories like this so equably, with such blithe good humour. So I asked him what it was like being a doctor in the USSR, what conditions were like where he worked.

"I'm very lucky," he said. "I work in the Burdenko Institute. My boss, Kornovalov, is world-known and well-connected, so we get all the patients from across the Soviet Union who can't be treated elsewhere. We have pretty good conditions; we have a lot of high-tech equipment, scanners and so on. But we still suffer from the same problems every other hospital has. We don't have enough drugs or bandages or surgical thread or disposable syringes, or even aspirin—basic things like that. Can you believe? And the pay, well . . . the pay is ridiculous. An anaesthetist with twenty years' experience gets about eighty roubles a month, less than a tram driver. The tram driver gets almost four times as much as a nurse. When *I* need extra money to feed my family, I have to ask to be paid for my lectures abroad in computers or something which I can sell here. Otherwise I have to use my Moscow car like a taxi and pick up passengers." He laughed. "You see, Jo, here you are unimaginably rich, you foreigners. To help me put my research together and write my thesis as a candidate of science, I'm allowed an extra thirty roubles a month—about what they charge you for two cups of coffee in one of the hard-currency hotels."

17

Before I left, Yelena and I decided we would go to Yalta together as soon as the film had been set up. We met Artyom and Svetlana in the National bar for a drink. "Too bad about the Boris project, Jo," said Artyom, who had always wanted me to opt instead for some untranslatable, unassimilable band like Zvuki Mu. (Zvuki Mu performed what they called "collective folk hallucinations," and their lead singer, Peter Mamonov, was in and out of alcohol-abuse clinics with the alarming regularity of a German town-hall clock.) "Now that you've finished with him, they're calling Boris 'the man with the American Express card.' " He laughed. " 'The American Express card—don't leave Nome without it'!"

I shrugged my shoulders. I no longer cared. Though rock music was now on television and on the face of it getting more and more political (as in DDT's "Prediction of Civil War"), I sensed that the pressure (which, after all, creates diamonds) was off; public acceptance was beginning to bleed the life from it. Besides, Yelena had just told me that ten or twelve of the people the producer, the director, and I had met were likely to be elected to the Chamber of People's Deputies in little more than a month's time. Things were on the move again. Moscow was a lot more interesting than Leningrad. People I knew, people like Tomas, Savva, and Guram, even Svetlana and Artyom—my people!—were beginning to take it over.

Chapter 7

August 1989–March 1990

"What is Russia?" I said in the museum at Repino, in what once had been Finland. "That's the first question. Is it Europe or Asia?"

"That part of Russia which is Christian," said Dmitri Likhachev, "belongs historically to Europe. The Christian church is the European face of the Russian state."

"But the Russian church has its roots in the East," said Andrei Voznesensky, leaning towards him over the table. "Not in Rome, but in Constantinople."

"And besides," said Artyom, "for two hundred and fifty years and more it's been emasculated. It's had no independent life. It's simply been an appendage of the state."

"Nevertheless . . ." I listened from behind the cameras as Dmitri Likhachev, in his old gold-prospector's English, talked patiently about Russian Christianity and the first political institutions that went hand in hand with it. He spoke about the ancient trade networks between the Baltic and the Black seas; about the mercantile settlement of Novgorod, which in the ninth century invited a Viking adventurer called Rurik and his two brothers to rule over its affairs; and about how the Rurikovichi rulers, twenty years later, took over a settlement at Kiev (in what is now the Ukraine), and established the capital of a new Slavic state, Kievan Rus. From there they extended their hegemony over other cities, and fought off the nomadic tribes threatening them from the east. They raided the outposts of the Byzantine empire, and eventually came to terms with it, in 988, by adopting Byzantine Christianity as the official state religion. Kievan Rus, said Likhachev, eventually controlled an area stretching from Poland to the Volga River; it made dynastic marriages that linked it to France, Denmark, Norway, and what is now Czechoslovakia. It was resplendent; it was full of churches and monasteries. But both pagan and Christian, it was from the beginning a much freer society than the feudal states to the west. As for Novgorod, he said, which in the twelfth century had paved streets and a high degree of literacy, it was a benign merchant republic not unlike that of Venice. "Relative freedom, then; Christianity; the Novgorod assembly of citizens: these are the first important traditions of Russia, its European inheritance."

"But what about the Tartars?" said Artyom abruptly, taking his hands away from his face. "Or the Mongols, as the West calls them?"

2

The Mongols, I thought as the three men argued quietly inside a tent of light: they must have seemed like a plague; their thirteenth-century invasion some terrible act of God. And yet they ruled here for two hundred and fifty years, and left behind them, not monuments, but an ideology, outlook, and system of state organization which lasted for five hundred more: permanent and lifelong service to the state; absolute power in the hands of one man; all other power given or withheld only inasmuch as it served the order, security, and God-guaranteed justice of the social dispensation. Whatever Russia might have been before the Mongols' arrival, by the time their power was finally broken in 1480 it had been firmly redirected into an auto-cratic, millennarian form of state socialism. The princes (later tsars) who toadied to the khans and finally defeated them simply took up where they left off.

And yet how could you explain this to a Western audience for whom history was merely long ago: a distant legacy or, at best, (in the West) a long, slow climb from barbarism towards democracy? How could you explain that what these three men were talking about was not the past—their equivalent of the Roman or Norman invasion of Britain, say—but now? Everything they discussed re-ferred in some way—because of the slowness, the interminable repetitiousness of Russian history—to the present. Which was better, they were saying in effect as they talked about the Mongols: the brutal, unifying order of the khans (the Communists) or the bitter infighting of the independent Russian city-states that had preceded them (the chaos that many feared would come with democracy)? And the creation of the nation, of a great power: did the historical result justify the means taken, or should the whole enterprise of gradual, centuries-long expansion into Asia and Europe be con-demned? Was Ivan Kalita (or Moneybags), for example—the man who began the rise of Moscow to power over the other principali-ties—a vicious lickspittle who grovelled for favour from the Mongol khans or a man with a precocious and canny vision of future empire? Was Ivan the Terrible, his descendant—was Stalin?—a brutal psychopath or a sad child of history, who knew that terror was the only way to achieve the unity of a scattered people?

All questions, all answers, as they talked and the cameras rolled, were like that. Present and past had no essential distinction. History was a succession of variations on unchanging themes, all of which were still being played out today. In their mouths there echoed the old arguments of the nineteenth-century Slavophiles and Westerniz-

ers. Was Peter the Great, the first modern tsar—or Gorbachev, for
that matter—a true European, or a traitor to old Russian (Soviet)
traditions? Was Russian culture the product of isolation or of contact
with other countries? Was there some special core of Russianness that
would be (or had been) contaminated by too much openness to the
West? Culture, politics, the Russian character, the power and prestige of the Russian state—these things were all still inseparably
yoked together, indivisible.

3

We spent the whole of an August day at the museum in Repino,
trying to recreate for the film, around the table the great painter
Repin had shared with other painters and writers like Serov and
Gorky, the intimacy of a *kruzhok*. Ksiyusha, orb-eyed, framed in
black hair, sat among the three men, to represent her generation and
to lead the conversation on. But she was tentative—at first, at any
rate—and a little overawed. And the talk, in any case, was not a
success—and not simply because, though in English, it was impenetrable. Yelena's father, Gennady, had died suddenly in June. And
Yelena had just told me that she was pregnant; she needed to know,
she'd said archly, what I intended to do about it. So I was preoccupied. There was also a problem throughout the day with Russian-
English communication. For the Canadian producer and I had
decided, when the English director had had difficulty meeting the
dates we'd set up for the shoot, to hire in his place Yelena's friend
Savva. (We wanted to make a real Russian film.) Savva—the
bubbly, ingratiating Savva—had turned overnight into a martinet.

During our discussions before the shooting had started, Savva
had talked earnestly and often about all the things which, in my
muddled way, I wanted to get at: the Russian idea, inner freedom,
the role of the intelligentsia, and so on. But when he'd met the

English cameraman on his arrival from London, he'd immediately addressed him as *ty* instead of *vuy,* as one would an underling or a child. Here in the museum, too, he was forever issuing orders, bellowing out "Motor," "Kamera," and "Stop," as if we were on a feature-film set—as, in a sense, we were. For he'd decided in his wisdom that, since the film was to be divided among the three men, their day-long talk, too, should be split into three parts, representing the spring, summer, and autumn of the culture. And for this he needed not only elaborate changes of lighting, but also the addition and subtraction, to and from the table in front of the speakers, of the necessary seasonal fruits and flowers. This took considerable time— more time than we really had available. And it also involved long periods of interruption, when the cameraman and the whole crew— electricians and researchers and photographers and set dressers— would whirl into mad, noisy action, thus destroying any continuity of mood or thought that might otherwise have been established.

"*Do* something about it!" said Yelena fiercely in the middle of one of these breaks. "*Do* something!" But there was little or nothing that I could do, and I said so. Savva, after all, had been hoisted with our conception of using the *kruzhok* as the focus of the film; and by his lights, he was doing the best he could. The problem—as I was to discover the further we went into the shoot—was that he had no experience at all of the way in which we in the West made docu- mentaries. We tended to operate, on location, as an essentially democratic little guerilla army, shuffling across the face of reality in a knotted conga line, and interfering with it as little as possible. Savva, by contrast, was always, out of habit, trying to improve reality, by speeding up the passage of clouds across townscapes or having anything that looked unsightly removed. He was, by instinct and training, if not intention, a socialist realist. He also thought of himself as something none of us would ever (for a minute) have claimed: as "an artist," an *intelligent.* (This, after all, was one of the things being a director-member of the Union of Film Workers underwrote and guaranteed.) He saw himself, moreover, from the beginning, very much as our boss, or *vozhd*. This was partly—and no doubt quite rightly—because of our ignorance. But it allowed him to try to foist off on us from time to time artists and others of his acquaintance who were part of his circle, his clientele: involved in his vision of things—not to mention his network of favours given and debts owed. (He early on angled to have Artyom removed from the film, and offered in his place a dwarfish, bespectacled young man whom I simply threw out of the apartment when he spoke scurri‑lously and suggestively about Artyom's connections with the KGB.) Savva was in the end, I realized, in his own way a victim of the past. For, for all his personal good humour and bravery (he had a reputation as a fighter for good causes within the Union of Film Workers), he was Stalin's child to a degree that could never quite be shaken off. He had no reserves of irony or self‑deprecation. (He had in their place the unstoppable, unsteerable certainty of a child's noisy windup toy.) He was never able to sit still with collective decision‑making, being merely one of the boys. He was, deep down, I thought—at least to our Western eyes—the same sort of Russian autocrat as the drama director Yuri Lyubimov, who because of his obduracy and his refusal to debate with the English cast of his *Hamlet* (among them my brother) soon became known to them collectively (and unaffectionately) as "Yuri Bugger‑off."

I pulled Ksiyusha aside. "There's nothing you can do now, Jo," she said. "He'll lose face if you interfere."

Instead of confronting Savva with his peacocking, then—which would have been useless—Ksiyusha and I took Dmitri Likhachev upstairs during the breaks to what had been Repin's studio. We sat him on a chaise longue. We gave him tea—he had come that morning from a sanatorium, where he'd been taking a rest cure—and talked to him quietly, on tape. I asked him about his arrest in the twenties.

"We had a student discussion group at the university," he said, speaking slowly and softly. "And we had an anniversary of some sort. So one of our members sent a telegram to congratulate us. It was pretended to be from the Pope. Well . . . it was enough." He laughed dryly. "Contact with a foreign power; agitating against the state. We were all arrested, every one of us. I . . . I was sent to Solovetsky Monastery, on an island in the White Sea. It was before the Gulag; and monasteries, you see, made very good prisons. They already had *keliye* . . . how do you call them? Cells."

"What was it like?" said Ksiyusha quietly.

"Oh, it was a place of death, of terrible brutality. People were frozen to death. They were put on the edge of very steep stairs and ordered not to move as they looked over this precipice. Always they fell. The propaganda, of course, said that it was a sort of holiday camp. One time, Maxim Gorky, the writer, came to Solovetsky, to inspect, to bear witness. The camp was made clean. People were even given newspapers. But no one was able to speak to Gorky alone, except for one boy. After Gorky left, he was not seen again."

"How did you survive?"

"Well, Solovetsky was in a way my university," he said. "There were many professors there, many members of the old intelligentsia. I did what I could to go on thinking. I even wrote some things. I became very interested in the criminals, for example: in their under-world slang and their games."

"But how did—"

"Ah, you mean: how did I remain alive?" he said. Then he paused for a long time, the afternoon light catching his spectacles. "I was, I think, very fortunate," he said. "One day, my parents came to visit me—this was permitted. I went to the guardhouse and I saw, by chance, a list of prisoners who were to be shooted early the next morning. My name was on the list. So I never returned to my quarters. All night I hid behind a large pile of wood, and when dawn came, I counted the number of shots they made. There was a shot for me; someone had died in my place. So, you see, ever since then I have had to live two lives: my own and the life of a man whose name I do not even know."

"What did you do when you were released?" asked Ksiyusha.

"I went back to Leningrad—as it had become by then. I tried to continue my life. But I lived with terror. For five years I did not speak to anyone outside my own family. For five years. Not anyone. Never. It was more safe that way." He paused again. "I have lived much of my life in silence."

"In inner freedom?"

He stared out at me for a moment. "It is difficult for you to understand, I know," he said, "the Russian idea of inner freedom. But yes. I have kept silence. But I have not changed my views. After Solovetsky, it was the Soviet Union which moved, not I."

During other breaks, we talked of other things, for possible use in the film: about the destruction of the churches and monasteries after the Revolution; about the collectivization of land in the late 1920s, which not only uprooted and murdered whole populations, but also destroyed forever the old continuities of the countryside and the ties that linked the people to the earth they cultivated. We talked, too, about the German siege of Leningrad—"the third time I have nearly starved to death"—when Likhachev watched his and his wife's families die, and ate soup made from wallpaper paste and the leather from furniture and books to survive.

Finally, before he left at the end of a long and trying day, to return to his sanatorium, I said: "You know, it's very hard for us in the West to imagine such a history, such continuous suffering."

He said: "As long as you do not envy it."

I said: "But look, there's one thing I want to ask you. I don't want to be impertinent. But two hundred and fifty years: it's a period of time that keeps coming up again and again in Russian history. It's come up today all the time. Two hundred and fifty years from the adoption of Byzantine Christianity to the sacking of Kiev by the Mongols. Two hundred and fifty years from the arrival of the Mongols to Ivan III's proclamation of independence from them. Then from the proclamation to the death of Peter the Great and the emergence of Russia as a great world power, *another* two hundred and fifty years. And yet what happened here in all that time except oppression and suffering? In the West, I don't know, there was from Ethelred the Unready to Magna Carta to the Crusades. From Chaucer to Cervantes to Shakespeare. From Giotto and Leonardo to Columbus and Magellan. Yet what was happening here? There's no track of it: no noise, no process, no development. It's as if everything's been muffled in the snow. We know the names of a few icon painters and a few writers who praised despotism for a living. We know of a few pretenders to the throne, maybe an explorer or two. But the rest is just a procession of tsars and soldiers and abbots and metropolitans. Even in Peter the Great's reign, only six or seven books were published."

"Yes," he said. "But something was going on nevertheless: something interior, something private. It was still . . . its own world. You must just learn to look for it somewhere else than where you would expect to find it in the West. Much of it has been destroyed. So you must learn to look at what has survived: inside the heads and hearts of Russians, in their relationship with God, the way they see their country and each other and history. Because if you don't, then you will never understand, I think, what happened here in the *last* two hundred and fifty years: why we were able to produce Pushkin and Tolstoy, Gogol and Dostoyevsky, Tchaikovsky, Mandelstam, Shostakovich—even Lenin."

4

"This," said Artyom, standing outside the little monastery of Ferapontovo, "is the most beautiful place I know in Russia. The
Kremlin, Red Square: these things, I suppose, are beautiful. But
theirs is an official beauty. This place is something else. It reminds
me . . ." He stopped, squinting up into the sun, obviously moved.
Then: "I'm sorry," he said. "Can we do this again?"

"All right. Cut," I said to the cameraman.

I was astonished. For this was Artyom: cynical, worldly, Artyom, who had grown up in Prague (where his father worked for a
socialist magazine) and had never forgiven the Soviet Union for
anything since the invasion of Czechoslovakia; Artyom, whose life
seemed to have started with the first Beach Boys record he'd ever
heard; who'd given lectures on Western bands at Moscow's first
discotheques, and was as happily at home with Derrida and deconstructionism as he was with Dire Straits. And yet his first thought,
when I'd asked him where he wanted to go for his segment of the
film (which was supposed to be about the long boredom of the
Brezhnev years and the rise of some kind of alternative culture), was
here, to this tiny gem of a monastery, standing on a hill above water
and a village, and backed by an endless stretch of northern forest. It
was indeed beautiful—the monastery grew out of the landscape
with the same sort of unassailable grace as the extraordinary Church
of the Intercession of the Virgin on the river Nerl near Vladimir.
Inside, too, it had (damaged) frescoes by one of the greatest of all
icon painters, Dionysius. But what was it to Artyom?

"All right," I said to the cameraman, "when you're ready . . ."
Savva had been detained in Moscow. I was glad.

Artyom composed himself, and then said, turning his face away
from the camera: "This place—Ferapontovo Monastery, the village

of wooden houses, and the countryside around them—reminds me
that the old Russians who were here before us knew something,
something maybe important; they have something to teach us. It
reminds me too that there are some things in this country of which
we can still be proud." He looked up. He said: "All right, Jo.
That's it."

Puzzled, I filmed the village, the frescoes, and the domes of the
monastery as they took fire at a distance from the light of the setting
sun. And then we drove back to Vologda, the nearest town. It was
another place on Artyom's odd itinerary.

Vologda was the home of Andrei, the student I'd met in
Leningrad on my first day there. It was also the home of Pushkin's
tutor, of whom there was a fine statue overlooking the river; and of
Varlam Shalamov, who had had a daily work norm of ten tons of
coal in a Gulag coal mine, and who'd survived to write bitterly:
"The experience of Russian humanist literature led to the bloody
executions of the twentieth century before my very eyes." It was the
place where Stalin had been benignly exiled by a tsarist tribunal,
even though by that time he had already escaped detention four
times. It was a sleepy provincial town, not far from the northern city
of Cherepovets, "the awful Elizabeth, New Jersey, of the Soviet
Union," said Artyom, "where the rock poet Sacha Bashlachev was
born." We were due to visit Cherepovets for the sake of Bashlachev,
who had thrown himself to his death from a window in Leningrad
the year before, and whose work Artyom had greatly admired. But
that's not why we were here.

"See, Jo, this is a *decent* town," he said in the morning as we
drove through the streets from the functional little Party hotel we
were staying at. "I wanted to show you a place where it's possible
to live a modest, decent, ordinary Russian life, with some kind of
principles."

We got out of the coach, and he introduced us to the director of the municipal gallery, which was showing an exhibition of local painters. He led us about the town's huge, ruined monastery, and then to the doors of the bell tower, where we were met by a team of young volunteer ringers, the first to play Russian bell music here since the Revolution. We climbed interminable stairs, through end-less galleries, until we reached the top, where the bells, large and small, were hung in the open air from beams, yoked together by a system of ropes and pulleys. The volunteers put on earmuffs and then played the bells as if each one was holding a pack of dogs or disciplining a team of horses, pulling on separate reins. Their breath came from their mouths like spurts of laughter into the cold air. And the music they made spilled out around us, old and metallic and clangourous, full of echoes of Mussorgsky and Rachmaninov, ring-ing out over the rooftops, the old wooden houses and the market square, now filling up with booths, below. It was a holiday. It was beautiful—as the snow came softly down around us. I wished it would never end.

We finally trudged downstairs with the camera gear. One of the young ringers said: "We've done research in Leningrad. There's enough written Russian bell music to last us until the next century." It was one of the only *kolakolniyi zvoni,* or rings of bells, operating outside the capital cities. When we came outside, we gave the ringers tea from the giant thermos we carried in the coach, and money. We rescued Yelena, who was brooding—she had no head for heights, she said—and then we walked through the booths, selling *shashlik* and *vareniki,* to the icon museum.

"Here! Here! You must film this, Jo. And this one," said Artyom in the museum. "They're wonderful!"

"I thought you said you were an atheist."

"No, I never said that," he said. "I just said that I hated the Orthodox church. All that hypocrisy and state window-dressing. They're just KGB agents and self-involved prima donnas—like the

Bolshoi Ballet. But icons . . . well, I don't know. Look! They're comforting. They're old. I think every home should have some, for contemplation."

"You mean, like the red corner in an old peasant's hut? St. Nicholas," I said, pointing, "to protect against fires. He was the patron saint of sailors, fishermen, and carpenters. And Paraskeva Pyatnitsa: patron saint of the marketplace; protected brides; was in charge of women's jobs and held against needlework done on Fridays. If you disobeyed, she'd prick you with a distaff and turn you into a frog."

"You've been reading again, Jo," Yelena murmured behind me. Actually they were the only two saints I could recognize, apart from Elijah—who wasn't a saint, and who was a stand-in for the old Russian god of thunder and lightning—and St. George, who'd once been Yarilo, the Russian god of spring.

"They're also the first strip cartoons," said Artyom, bending and pointing at the edges of an icon of St. George, where scenes from the saint's life were painted in small squares. "Birth, life, death. Time round the corners; eternity in the middle. A bit like the Soviet Union." He laughed.

I realized then, I think, for the first time, that Artyom too, for all his Western hardheadedness and cynicism, was very Russian. He never spoke—except mockingly—of those strange categories like "inner freedom" and "the Russian soul" that still inhabited the talk of many intellectuals, not to mention our conversation at Repino. He had an ascetic's horror of sentimentality and self-indulgence, both of which he identified in just such phrases; he thought of these qualities as a peculiarly Russian curse. He found it easier, he'd once told me, to write in English rather than in Russian, because in Russian it was such a constant battle to be both elegant and precise. Vagueness and beauty, for him, stalked together through the Russian language like a pair of dreadful, inseparable Siamese twins—a fact which made him more intolerant of beauty (and of his own response to it) than he might otherwise have been in everyday life. The sentimentality and self-indulgence he was most suspicious of were, of course, in other words, his own.

He also had, I thought as we walked through the icon museum, more than his fair share of "Russian soul," whether he liked it or not. For what else was "Russian soul," in the end, but a question mark that hung over the heads of all Russians, a sort of puzzled dream of belonging? Who were they? What could they point to and say: "This is us; this is it; this is who we are"? The problem was, there was so little of the country they could identify with. The people who'd built the nation had left no tracks in the landscape; there were no henges or canals, no old inns or mediaeval villages; no Glaston-burys or Stratfords, or even Manchesters or Birminghams. (Until the middle of the nineteenth century, only three percent of Russians lived in towns and cities, and almost all buildings continued to be made of wood.) Nor was there any real romance in Russian history, or sustaining myth, as there was in America. There was simply the fact that millions of Russians over hundreds of years toiled and died, leaving nothing behind but a few more square feet of earth redeemed from a harsh landscape and harsher enemies. They were the people of the frontier—"Ukraina," for example, meant exactly that—and frontiers left no lasting legacies. Yes, there were churches and monas-teries (sometimes fortified, almost all now ruined and dilapidated). There were country houses and palaces and estates. But these had been built for the greater glory of the state or its servant nobility. They were, to Artyom, the buildings of an occupying caesaropapist power, unless they were saved by some lack of presumption, some small core of independent grace. I realized that in Vologda he was—laconically, as usual; without explanation—offering us the best of Russia he'd been able to find; and that this was what he had always done with Western reporters. He'd pushed them, as far as he could, towards what was least imitative of the West—the most Russian bands and the most Russian painters and performers he'd been able to identify—and had often ended up disillusioned by the reporters' failure to understand. His kind of "Russian soul," then, was neither consolational nor self-justificatory, the kind that was forever being invoked as the spiritual distillate of Russia's long sufferings, its earned extra portion of God's special fondness. It was instead an internalized, embattled, and almost secret quest for something in the country—as he'd put it outside Ferapontovo Monastery—of which he could be proud.

We filmed in the icon museum, then; and afterwards he showed us a little crafts museum, mostly filled with kerchiefs and skirts and trimmings of linen. "Vologda was once famous for its flax crops, its linen, as well as for its beer and butter," he said. "Now there's nothing to eat, but they all know each other, work together." Then we went to see the workshop of an icon restorer, a small, shabby man with pinched eyes and hands that had the blunt declarativeness of tools. His father had been the director of the local museum, he said; he had rescued huge numbers of icons from the local villages when the churches had been destroyed, and for this he'd been arrested and sent to the camps. He showed us the letters, with little coloured drawings, that his father had sent from the Gulag; and then a few of the thousands of gathered icons that were still to be restored: blackened by smoke and grease and neglect. "It will take my lifetime to restore them, and that of my son," he said, pointing to the young man who was working with him. Artyom interviewed the older man on camera with a strange shyness and, when they were done, asked us to give him money, so that he could buy new equipment and beat the terrible vacuum of all that time.

The next morning, we drove through the countryside, then past chemical factories belching out flame and foul-smelling smoke, to Cherepovets. In the centre of the city, outside a flat blue-and-white building, amid a swirl of traffic, Artyom said into the camera: "This is Cherepovets, a big factory city, a sort of twentieth-century Soviet Inferno. It could be a thousand miles from Vologda, and in another country. But this was the place where I first met the greatest of all the Soviet Union's young rock poets. He lived in the little building behind me. His name was Sacha Bashlachev. When I met him, almost by accident, he had just stopped being a student; he had some sort of job on a local newspaper. What he played that night in Cherepovets was the most intense, concentrated, and, above all, *Russian* music that I had ever heard."

Later he said to me: "It was as if Sacha had been given this talent by—I don't know . . . God; no one knew where it came from—on condition that he use it all, all in one go. He burned— and he burned himself out until there was nothing left, only death." He paused. "I don't think I'll ever forgive myself that I didn't see it, that I didn't do more." Later still, in Leningrad, at Bashlachev's graveside, as we stopped filming and turned away, he cried inconsol-ably, in a terrible torrent of grief, for what had been lost, for what he himself might have done. On the grave in front of him were flowers, coins, cigarettes, photographs, letters, and service medals from the Afghanistan War.

5

Words aren't enough, of course. There's Artyom weeping by a grave in Leningrad for another poet who—as is usual with Russian poets—failed to die in his bed. There's Dmitri Likhachev listening, in effect, to the sound of his own murder, and then creeping his days through Leningrad in silence, too frightened to talk to anyone for fully five years. These word pictures are fine; perhaps they stagger and touch the heart (as Russia does endlessly). But they'd have to be multiplied by tens, by hundreds, by millions—beyond the power of our ordinary, orderly language—before their context could really be understood. Poets? Pushkin and Lermontov: killed in duels; Gumilyov: shot on a trumped-up charge. Mandelstam dying gibbering in a transit prison camp near Vladivostok; Yesenin hanging himself in Leningrad's Hotel Angleterre; Mayakovsky confronting the false god of the Revolution with a bullet in his brain; Marina Tsvetaeva knotting the noose that would end her life and her perpetual exile in a little village called Yelabuga in 1941. Nowhere else on earth, Mandelstam once remarked, do they take poetry as seriously as they do in Russia: "for here they kill you for it." His widow, Nadezhda, with her head echoing with his unpublished poems—they were too dangerous and precious to trust to paper—survived the war years only because she was smuggled to Tashkent by another great poet, Anna Akhmatova, who shared her daily rations with her. Akhmatova herself survived only by keeping the mouth of her muse publicly shut for forty-four years. She spent eighteen of those forty-four trying to get her (and Gumilyov's) son, Lev, out of the camps where Stalin had pitched him in order to shackle his mother's tongue. *We weep for the past.*

And Dmitri Likhachev? Yes, Likhachev was brave. But he did survive. He was beaten on the street and had his arm broken in later years for being a cosmopolitan: for being soft on Jews and hard on Ivan the Terrible and defending Sakharov; but he did survive. He was eventually made Academician; he was telephoned by Raisa Gorbachev: "Mikhail Sergeyevich has just been reading your latest book. I wonder if . . ." But what about all the millions of others who didn't survive? What about the blood and the stench of the abattoir in the Leningrad Cheka cellars in the 1920s, where men and women were hacked to death? What about the hundred thousand people in the city who were deported or exiled or shot for their "complicity" in the death of the Party boss Kirov, whom Stalin had had assassinated in 1934? And the victims from Leningrad . . . well, what were they? Only a drop in the country's vast sea of suffering. Whole villages were massacred, whole towns depopulated; children were given ten, then twenty-five years in the camps for stealing a few grains of wheat. For every Russian who was shot (and there were millions), another ten, it was said, died of exposure, exhaustion, and starvation in the Gulag. They were arrested as Trotskyists, left deviationists, nationalists, whatever: it didn't matter; it just depended on which quota needed filling up that month. There were VAT (praise of American technology), VAD (praise of American democracy), and PZ (toadyism towards the West). You could be arrested for telling an anecdote, or for not reporting one that you had heard someone else tell; for being a friend of someone on a list, or having been a student or a co-worker, years before, with somebody who was on another. You could die for the smallest slight on "the Father of the Peoples of East and West" or for praising him with something less than the prescribed level of enthusiasm. Solzhenitsyn tells the story of a district Party conference in the Moscow region where a formal tribute to the Boss was made. There was a standing ovation. The applause went on for five minutes, six. The secretary of the district Party committee was new (his predecessor had been arrested); he didn't know how to stop it. Seven minutes, eight. The predecessors of the KGB were in the audience. Nine minutes, ten . . . no one, looking around, dared stop. Finally, after eleven minutes of this madness, the director of the local paper factory sat down and the applause immediately ended. He was arrested the same night.

And that was just the half of it. (Half? A thirty-millionth.) Banners: "We shall stamp out sabotage in the trading network"; "Liquidating the effects of sabotage in industry, we resolve to exceed the norm." Newspapers were full of "arch-spies," "hostile elements," "enemies of the people," and "sentences carried out." In the courts, Prosecutor General Vishinsky screamed surreal abuse at Lenin's old comrades and the leadership of the Red Army: "hyenas and jackals," he called them; "mad dogs," "stinking carrion," and "syphilitic lice." Language and truth lost all meaning. Loyalty meant nothing; friendship, nothing. How many *stukachi* (literally "knockers," or informers) were there in Moscow or Leningrad? One million? Two million? Nobody knew. It didn't matter. All public space filled up with lies; no private space was any longer safe. Staunch Party workers were asked to sign lists "for the good of the Party"; then they were shot, along with the people they'd con-demned to death. No one was immune. Out of the 139 members of the Central Committee elected at the Party's Seventeenth Con-gress in 1934, 110 were arrested before the Eighteenth in 1939. Of the less than two thousand delegates, more than eleven hundred disappeared down the black throat of the NKVD. Stalin's secretary Poskrebyshev was given a new wife by Uncle Joe when his own was arrested. "Whole strata," according to the butcher Kaganovich, were "removed." The Leader simply signed their lives away before he went to see a film in the Kremlin cinema, while his henchman the NKVD chief Yagoda fired pistols at icons with his naked cronies in his bathhouse in the country. *We weep because we survived; we are therefore guilty.*

And yet how can any of this be communicated: this omnipres-ence of the past in Russia, this overlapping of the personal and the collective, this constant wash of sorrow and guilt? Were Artyom's tears real in the cemetery in Leningrad? Yes. But still he didn't do enough for the man whose grave he wept over. Perhaps he didn't recognize this steel-toothed, gravel-voiced young provincial for the original he was—until death made him see it. Who was he weeping for, then? The past and himself.

And Dmitri Likhachev's bravery? Was it, too, real? Yes. But on the other hand (and this wasn't my question; it was Ksiyusha's; it was, I'm sure, Likhachev's: it was a very Russian question), how could he, however unwittingly, have sent another man to die in his place? Oughtn't he, rather than that—wasn't he morally bound to—have embraced his own death?

To communicate all this (to resume), you'd need the skills of a great metaphysical novelist, and—perhaps this was the point of Likhachev's remark in Repino—of a great *Russian* novelist at that, like Dostoyevsky. At the very least—and this was nearer to such resources as I had, trying to make a television film for the West—you'd need a screen that was always split, two reels of film unfolding side by side: truth and lie, facade and background, past and present, morality and character. I remembered once seeing a television film which a famous old British journalist had made about India, which he knew well. The film had been fairly conventional, but it had ended with a long sequence of him waiting to make a telephone connection with London from his Delhi hotel room. He drank most of a bottle of Scotch while he waited, and talked to the camera. Finally he said something like: "The problem with India is that there is nothing of which you can say 'This is true,' without it also being *un*true. The problem, perhaps, lies not with India, but with us in the West: our obsessive truffling for the truth, our damned either/or." The film was one of a series called "One Pair of Eyes." And that, he seemed to be saying, was itself part of the problem: for anyone who wanted to understand India—or Russia—had to start by being (at least) bifocalized. "Either/or" should be kept at home; for "both" (not to mention "although" and "maybe") was where the truth, such as it was, seemed to be buried locally.

I tried from then on to see the "both," then, that my friend Artyom saw—and which he was. A Westernizing Russophile; "official beauty"; truthfully false tears; immoral survival; Ksiyusha's "Soviet sincere." I tried to turn what seemed like self-evident truths on their heads, to see if their opposites might also be true. I learned to see my early heroes—those whom Yelena and I had exulted over at the beginning of the year—for what they were: Yuri Afanasyev,

who was by then one of the prime movers in the so-called Interregional Group in the Chamber of People's Deputies, as the same
man who had been on the board of the Central Committee journal
Kommunist and had launched a vicious attack on Anna Akhmatova's long-imprisoned son as a "White Army bastard"; Vitaly
Korotich, the editor of *Ogonyok,* who was then the West's darling
as a sly English-speaking spokesman for *perestroika,* as the same man
who had addressed bad poems to Brezhnev's eyebrow, and had
attacked Ukrainian nationalism and Western imperialism on his
own (Kiev-based) television programme. I tried to abandon the idea
of heroes, and with it the notions of absolute good and evil that I'd
brought with me in my Western baggage. I tried to see the good that
stemmed from the bad in the Soviet Union, and the bad that
supervened so naturally—because of its defects—on the good. For
what real right did we in the West have to assign these categories?
Russia was its own place, with its own history and its own culture—as Dmitri Likhachev had said—and no amount of finger
wagging on our part would alter it one iota. All we could do was
to keep the two strips of film running side by side in our heads—and
preserve the possibilities of irony.

6

Irony. Did I believe in God? Well, no, not exactly. (What else do
you expect an Englishman to say?) Did I feel closer to this not-
exactly God in the Soviet Union? Yes, from the beginning—and
now more than ever, as we went filming from church to monastery
to cathedral and back again. But then the Russian God wasn't like
the Western one I knew, with His orderliness, His timetables, His
precise schedules of reward and punishment, His neat household
furniture. The Russian God was older and more scattered and less
interventionist; He did not seem, in fact, to be much interested in
earth at all. (Intercession, for example, He tended to leave to His

Mother and to His saints.) Eternity—where He dwelt at the focal point of the iconostasis—was a lot more important. Christmas, the beginning of His Son's redemptive adventure here, was of no great account; what mattered was Easter, His paving of the way homeward. So His Russian church, in the end, was as otherworldly and mystical as He. It concentrated on the afterlife—of which this world was but a pale and infinitely distorted reflection. It preached the equality of poverty and suffering; it offered, in the morality play of its services, a sea of salving, shriving emotion. It had little to say about the responsibility of the individual or the inherent value of his work. Instead it peddled togetherness, the mass, the collective—the losing of the self in the community of God's children. Did this make its services attractive, moving? Yes, it did: achingly so. Did the church, in this, serve the purposes of the state? Yes. For the Russian church was never in opposition. While the church of Rome may have called itself the bride of Christ (and thus the potential enemy of all sorts of temporal powers), its sister church, which had developed in Byzantium, was, after five hundred years' exposure to the East, already married to the state (much like Islam). Mother Church, Mother Russia, little Father Tsar—the church was even prepared to come to terms (out of old habit) with the monstrous exseminarist "Uncle Joe" Stalin. In 1927 its head, Metropolitan Sergei, announced: "We wish to be Orthodox believers and at the same time to acknowledge the Soviet Union as our civil motherland, whose joys and successes are our joys and successes, and whose misfortunes are our misfortunes." In return for this (historically unsurprising) concession, Uncle Joe kept alive perhaps three of the one hundred and sixtythree church bishops there'd been before the Revolution; he tore down or closed ninety percent of the churches. So much—one might say—for marriages made in an Oriental heaven. The twentieth century finally turned them sour, when the state sued for divorce.

Bad things supervening on the good. Or *did* it turn them sour? Didn't the twentieth century actually work out the kinks in this impossible arrangement? I thought. (Yes, we're still on the coach, making the film—travelling, travelling. Yelena's still here, giving me a hard time.) For what are you most likely to inherit from a powerful but played-out style of secular government, which is married (morganatically) to a totally dependent spiritual authority, but a sort of obverse of itself: a secular ideology with strong (but buried) religious overtones? By these lights, Bolshevism was the final apotheosis (is that the right word?) of Byzantine Orthodoxy, just as much as it was the bastard child of the European Enlightenment—with its "enlightened" notion that man was essentially good, only his institutions bad and correctable. The Bolsheviks, after all, now guaranteed (after 1917) the equality of poverty that the church had preached. They had their own synod of bishops—the Politburo and the Central Committee—to enforce it. They had a new iconography, of heroic revolutionaries and workers as saints. They had, in the monuments and war memorials that seemed to be everywhere, new national altars. They had a supreme patriarch, Stalin. And they even had a Holy Sepulchre, where the body of Lenin—known to Moscow intellectuals as "the smoked fish"—lay in Red Square in a mausoleum that owed much not only to Byzantium and the khans but also to another Eastern god-king: Tutankhamen, whose tomb had been discovered a few years before Lenin's death. In many ways, the Bolsheviks simply continued the Byzantine church by other means, only they left God out of the equation and made a religion directly of the state (and of themselves). Russian Orthodoxy, in this secularized form, left the churches and hit the streets, where it followed the pattern of Orthodoxy in the fifteenth century. The rival ideology of capitalism was anathematized, declared the work of the devil, with just as much horror as the reunited Catholic church had been declared (once and for all) apostate after the Council of Florence in 1439. Fourteen years later, after all, Constantinople had fallen to the

Turks—which only went to show. With capitalism—as Khrushchev was often at pains to point out—it could only be a matter of
the same sort of interval.

7

Two strips of film. Valentin Rasputin: fifties, modest, highly intelligent, Orthodox Christian; writer of so-called "village" novels;
author of the magnificent *Farewell to Matyora,* a threnody for the
passing of the old peasant life and faith. Hear him talk! Leader of
the crusade to rescue the world's largest freshwater lake, Lake
Baikal, from erosion and pollution by tree-fellers and cellulose
plants. Also a patriot and "anti-Zionist." Told the *New York
Times:* "I think the Jews here should feel responsible for the sin of
having carried out the revolution and for the shape it took. They
should feel responsible for the terror that existed during the revolution. They played a large role and their guilt is great." Number of
Jews said to have applied for permission to emigrate: one and a half
million. Number said to be joining the queue every month: sixty-five
thousand. Insert dissident mathematician Igor Shofarevich, on television: "I am not attacking Jews, you understand, merely the Jewish
cast of mind." (One of the features of "the Jewish cast of mind" is
apparently the desire of Jews to leave the country.) Lenin was a
quarter Jewish; Kamenev, Zinoviev, Yezhov, Kaganovich: all
Jews. Trotsky turned down the job of deputy leader of the Bolshevik
government (and Lenin's successor) on the grounds that he was a
Jew. Trotsky to Lenin on the day of the October Revolution: "It
would be far better if there were not a single Jew in the first Soviet
government." Chekhov in a letter to Suvorin from Nice: "When
something is wrong with us we seek the cause outside ourselves
. . . capitalism, the Masons, the Syndicate, the Jesuits—all phan-
toms, but how they do relieve our anxieties!"

Two strips of film. A cavalcade of priests at Danilovsky Monastery, one of the monastery-fortresses built to defend Moscow's southern approaches against the Mongols and the Crimean Tartars.
Watch them parade! Now it's the church's new headquarters. But
under Stalin—insert here—it was a children's prison; monks are
said to gather now at night to pray for the souls of its murdered
victims. At Novodyevichy, another of the monastery-fortresses,
where Tsar Boris Godunov was crowned, Peter the Great imprisoned his sister Sofia after an abortive coup and built a scaffold
outside her room where the bodies of her supporters could bang
against her windows before they were left to rot and stink. At
Donskoy and Novospassky monasteries, unmarked mass graves
from the 1930s. (Pan left; pan right.) At Optina Pustin Monastery,
outside Koselsk—one of the intellectual powerhouses of Russia
during the nineteenth century, on one of whose holy men Dostoyevsky based Father Zosima in *The Brothers Karamazov,* and now
being rebuilt—a prison camp for Polish officers. Over four thousand of these officers were transferred into the hands of the Smolensk
NKVD; they were last heard of at a railway station three miles from
Katyn. The church hierarchy—hear them chant!—is still appointed
and controlled by the Council for Religious Affairs, an arm of the
Central Committee and the KGB. Father Vladimir Rusak—
young, upright, on his way into emigration—was given twelve years
for daring to write a twentieth-century history of the church. And
"Look at this," said the KGB to imprisoned Christian dissidents,
waving a newspaper article in their faces. (Cut to dramatization.)
"Metropolitan Pityrim says there are no prisoners of conscience in
this country. Not one—not you, none at all. Do you hear?"

Two strips of film. Beauty, cruelty; tears, blood; Gorbachev,
Stalin; romance, death; icon, axe.

8

We filmed for six weeks. We filmed rural slums and ruined churches; singers singing pre-Christian songs recovered from forgotten villages in the northwest. We filmed the work of lost painters and gnarled, ancient craftsmen; Beatles fans, and installation artists packing up their work to go to the West. We visited the graves of Pasternak and Akhmatova; we recorded plays in Moscow that dealt with tsardom and the camps and the meaning of the Revolution; we went to towns and monasteries where they seemed never before to have seen anyone from the West. And we devilled in the Film Archives: for feature films and old documentary mate-rial—anything—that would yield up some quiddity, some image or another, of the long-fused time-and-history bomb that had destroyed the culture in the first half of the century.

The Canadian producer, a man of saintly trust, looked at all this activity—generated almost entirely by me—with, for the most part, I have to say, benign restraint. (His name was Christian, and he was immensely pleased that "Christian" and "peasant" were the same word in Russian.) The British crew were frankly irked by it: all they ever saw were long coach trips and constantly amended schedules; all they looked for, increasingly (in the absence of under-standing), was the unlikely prospect of an early arrival or a late start. As for Savva, the director, well . . . it began to seem, as time went on, as if he were merely along for my mad ride. This wasn't his fault. It was the result of a culture clash, the echoes of which kept on reverberating as I burrowed more and more wildly into what he no doubt thought of as his (easy) special subject. He saw us Westerners, I think, as brute factualists: we believed in nothing but what was happening in front of us; we didn't understand that it could either "stand for" or "symbolize" anything else—which was a tradition firmly rooted in Russian poetry and thought. And we saw him as, by our standards, both undeservedly autocratic and wilfully vague. The crew began to defer to me, even when he was there beside them. It was a Western conspiracy. Some unspecified business of his started to keep him in Moscow for longer and longer periods, while we continued to travel the countryside.

That left me and Yelena together on the coach. She was the only person I could talk to about the shape of the film, about my growing panic about all the material I wanted to get in. The problem was that she was pregnant, and our conversations—naturally enough— always came round to that. She seemed to think that my immersion in what we were doing was a sort of displacement activity, designed to help me avoid facing up to the fact.

At first, I'd brushed aside the idea of Yelena's pregnancy— which must have begun when I'd come to Moscow for Ksiyusha's high school graduation and for the ceremonies for the final passing of Gennady's spirit forty days after his death. "Why don't we just wait and see?" I'd said. But it had soon become clear that she was indeed pregnant, and I didn't know quite what to do about it. By this I don't mean that I didn't want the child. I did, probably above all other things: soon I would be too old to be a father; I'd wasted too much time, I thought, content with other people's children. I also loathed the idea of Yelena submitting herself (and our child) to an abortion destruction-line. (Thirty thousand gynaecologists in the Soviet Union, I knew, performed nothing but abortions. In the absence of any other kind of contraception, some women had as many as twenty-five or thirty.) But did I want to get married again? More: did I want to take on a whole new family, a whole unhappy country? I loved Yelena, but that was easy as things were: she was beautiful and exotic, and besides, I came and went to and from England whenever I pleased—I could relapse into bachelordom whenever I felt like it. Also—and I had almost forgotten the fact—I was still legally married to my American wife. And though I had started the process of a friendly divorce, there was something in me that hoped it would take a longer rather than a shorter time to settle. In the end I said—and I meant it—that yes, of course I would marry her; that I wanted to, I was glad to. But I hoped, in some muddled, far-off way, I think, that it could be put off until abortion was no longer an option: until I'd *really* made up my mind, until the film was finished; until I'd seen Yelena once more in England.

Yelena knew at once that I was dithering, that I was offering a half-assed commitment: on the sly, on the cheap. And she associated it with all the condescension she'd met with in other Westerners: their lack of understanding. She loved me; she said so: "You are my life now, Jo," she said. But she also said on the coach: "What are you doing? Why are you filming everything you can see? Can't you make up your *mind?* Don't you *know* what you want?" She attacked me in front of the crew; she made bitter jokes at my expense. She seemed to stand sometimes between East and West, Janus-faced, looking both ways: lost, wild. Sometimes she would defend Savva, saying: "Listen, you're a pig; you're being unfair to him. Sit down with him. Listen to him. He knows what he's talking about. He's Russian, after all—which is more than can be said for you!" Other times she would say: "Why don't you sack him? Why don't you trust yourself? Take the film over. For God's sake, be a *man!*" She became, for me, little by little, as I tried to concentrate on what I was doing, a continuation by other means of all the head-ramming difficulties we faced while on the road: the dumb obduracy of restaurant and hotel keepers, the sly vanity of some of our interviewees, the constant renegotiations, the impossibility of making any arrangement stick. I faced her—I faced the whole country, through her—with a growing exasperation that sometimes amounted to hatred. It never occurred to me to apply to her my own rule of thumb: two strips of film running side by side, in opposition to each other.

9

In London, after the filming, the rows went on. Yelena, as I'd expected, refused to go anywhere except by taxi; she spent all her money (and much of mine) on presents and clothes. Meanwhile Savva—with Yelena translating—began work with the film editor: this was where his real skills lay, he said. But it wasn't long before the Canadian producer and I started to realize that in his hands the film was bound to yaw towards disaster. Short sequences began to balloon out of all proportion; his first laborious rough cut was more than four hours long. At first, I didn't want to get more involved in the film than I already was. I had to commute twice weekly to the country to visit my increasingly ill mother (and to give my brother time off); I had divorce papers to deal with; and besides, the atmosphere in the rented house in north London that Yelena and I shared with Savva and his wife, Varya, was already difficult enough. More, by this time there was—daily—astonishing news from all over Eastern Europe as the Russian empire finally started to unravel forever. And—once again—as the Berlin Wall came down and Communist Romania went into its last brutal convulsions, I found myself buried in newspapers and racing for the television evening news like an obsessed research student. I even went briefly to Budapest—to fulfil an obligation to my New York magazine— just to keep contact with what was going on, hating to be left out.

In the end, though, after two months of mutual incomprehen-sion, during which the English film editor began to speak of things "standing for" other things and about "the Russian soul"—and with Yelena constantly accusing me of being unserious, a tourist in my own life—I was forced to take over; and the Canadian producer and I (and Yelena) left poor Savva to his own sad devices. Abruptly the rows between Yelena and me stopped—and with them, some of the spending. I was finally, in her terms, I suppose, reliable, "a man": I had now to deal with conclusions and finally come to terms, through the film, with her culture. It was the last of her strange Rubicons. We were married over the Christmas holidays, a day after we'd bought rings in a Hatton Garden store. We had a wedding breakfast, with my two brothers and sister and the Canadian produ⁄ cer and his wife, that cost twice as much as my birthday party for fifty⁄five guests was to cost in Moscow two years later. We had a honeymoon for one night in a fancy London hotel, and then I went back at nine in the morning to go on editing the film. The film was fine, I think, as good as I could have made it then: two strips running side by side; East and West; pages of illustrations. Savva and Varya never spoke willingly to either of us again. Katya, beautiful Katya, was born three months later in the birthing bath of a London clinic, just in time to meet her English grandmother for the first and last time. Throughout her long labour, Yelena kept crying out: *"Ya ne magu, ya ne magu!"*—I can't, I can't! She could. I remember thinking, as Katya's head finally came up through the water, like an otter's or a mole's, how brave Yelena was to take on the West, and what an astonishing new world little Katya was being born into.

Part Three
Being Here

Chapter 8

July–December 1990

I

It's six-thirty in the morning and the woods around me are full of the sound of guns. Next door, Katya is gurgling merrily in a borrowed pram. Yelena is asleep beside me, scrunched into a corner of a hard plank bed. It must be the beginning of the deer season, I think, though I've been told that no hunting is allowed in the cooperative village of Nikolina Gora (Nicholas's Hill). I stand up for a minute by the open window in the half-light of the misty morning, listening, and I realize that I can't tell, when I'm inside this old dacha, with its rickety furniture and unframed pre-Revolutionary family portraits, whether the sounds are scattered or come from one particular source. All noise from the outside world—the farm trucks going past on Prospekt Otto Schmidt or Katya wailing for something to eat from the clearing below the verandah—seems to travel here in anything but a straight line: it bends round the wooden house, glances off the pine trees that surround it, and then circles and reverberates across the valley of the Moskva River before being muffled to death in the woods and thick undergrowth.

Perhaps it's an escaped criminal, I think, somewhere in the woods; or the army on manoeuvres on the back road to the village of Ilinskoye; or else soldiers doing a bit of potshot target practice while waiting to go into the fields for the gathering-in of the harvest on the collective farm nearby. I decide later—when the shooting stops suddenly at around seven o'clock—to ask Seriozha, one of Nikolina Gora's little band of *militsia* men, what on earth it could have been. Seriozha has recently resigned from the Party, much to the approval of most of the local inhabitants, and he moonlights as a driver for the pianist Nikolai Petrov, who lives down the road. He once drove us into Moscow on a shopping trip in Nikolai's $34,000 Volvo, shyly accepting Yelena's congratulations for following Boris Yeltsin and Moscow mayor Gavriil Popov out of the Party, and waving gracefully to traffic cops from behind the steering wheel on his way into town.

Later, I run into him in the village, at the junction by the dilapidated telephone booth which is the only link to the outside world for *dachniki* with no telephone (like me). But he doesn't seem to know what I'm talking about, or else he's not telling. Yelena Fyodorovna, the matriarch of the family we're renting from, says in the afternoon that she heard the shots too, but doesn't know what they were, "though maybe it was [the film director] Nikita Mikhalkov, who's said to be fond of guns." All I can say is that there were a lot of shots. Maybe Mikhalkov had friends to stay, and it was the end of a perfect party. Maybe the mosquitoes in his big dacha behind a tall green fence finally drove him mad. His father, a famous poet, wrote the words to the revised Soviet national anthem, I remember, and once condemned rock music as "moral AIDS." "It's not only music," he thundered. "It's a soil where anything can grow—from drug abuse to prostitution to betraying your mother-land." Maybe the house, where the old man still lives—and where Nikita's brother, Hollywood film director Andrei Konchalovsky, is now being filmed each day, I've been told, by an Italian film crew—just has bad karma.

2

We come to Nikolina Gora for the first time in July, in the middle of the Twenty-eighth Communist Party Congress, as crusty out-of-town delegates, appalled by the wicked ways of the capital, are calling for legislation to ban pavement caricatures of Lenin and to forbid the sales on the Arbat and in Izmailovo Park of "Gorby dolls"—*matrioshkas* with Gorbachev on the outside and a tiny Lenin buried within (or vice versa). I've arrived in Moscow the day before the Congress begins (with Yegor Ligachev immediately on the offensive, accusing Gorbachev of various unmentionable heresies), and find Yelena worried about the future, but on the whole immensely sunny and happy. She's broody, though, about two things: first, that I've missed the three-month anniversary of Katya's birth; and second, that we still don't have a dacha for the summer. Katya doesn't seem to mind the first—she is huge, I think in the airport, and noisy and pays me little attention. The second is plainly more serious.

When we get back to Vorotnikovsky Alley, the subject refuses to go away. Ksiyusha bounces up and down with delight as we arrive. She is about to finish her first end-of-year exams at Moscow University, and she's begun to write poetry again, she says. She only got a four in her exam on the history of the Soviet Communist Party—the top mark is five—but she doesn't care. "It was political," she says. "I'd been making speeches about how the course was irrelevant—it absolutely has to be abolished." She's been reading Cortázar and Borges in new translations, she says, and now she wants to write short stories. The question, of course, is: Where? She hates the city, which is oppressively hot, she says.

Her best friend, Dasha, has gone to America, on a student tour that was supposed to have taken her. And everybody else she knows is scattering as fast as they can for their country dachas, or for holidays in Pitsunda or Yalta or Tbilisi or Tallinn.

Tatiana Samoilovna stands in the kitchen doorway as we talk, beaming with quiet pleasure and rubbing her clasped hands together, as if washing them. She proudly points out the *goluptsy* bubbling on the hob. And then she beckons me into what was Gennady's rather austere little room. The huge bookcase—once full of Stalin and Lenin, marshals' memoirs, detective literature, and encyclopaedias for his crossword puzzles—has gone. The sofa-bed has been moved, and in its place is a tall wooden cot for Katya, donated by one of Yelena's cousins. There's a little blue Marks and Spencer lamp beside it, and beneath it the huge stocks of Pampas we sent back with everybody we could find who was on his or her way from London to Moscow. I'm oddly surprised to see these things in place, as if I'd imagined them disappearing into a void, and astonished to see the blue-and-white bed sheets, pillows, duvet and bolsters we bought in London fitting so snugly into the slightly ungainly cot. (Still buried in me somewhere, I think, is a profound belief that the Soviet Union produces things of peculiar, unhuman dimensions, skewed away from any Western norm I know, as if it were some Galápagos Islands of style.) *"Khorosho, da?"* says Tatiana Samoilovna happily, leaning over to smooth the duvet and pillows with the flat of her hand. And I suddenly remember that now Gennady is dead; she's lost the space in the dacha in Saltykovskaya that they had for years. I'm responsible for her summer vacation, too.

While Yelena and I are bathing Katya—I trying to get back in touch with her, to make her pay attention to me, to recognize me (and failing)—Tomas calls. He once said, I remember, that all he wanted (like some Georgian Eliza Doolittle) was a dacha in a wood somewhere, with an old babushka to look after him. But there seems little hope for that this summer. He sounds exhausted. The building of his video-cassette plant is still going maddeningly slowly, he says, its construction held up by paperwork and a complicated network of permissions withheld and responsibilities dodged. The recent elections to the Moscow Soviet haven't helped, either, since— though the right side won, he says—he now has to start all over again with the new administration. (I assume that he means he'll have to issue a completely new set of bribes.) Meanwhile, his Greek partners are coming soon on a tour of inspection; he and his wife, Galya, have finally split up; and there are the inevitable rows about who's going to live in their apartment on Bolshoi Tishinski Lane with its spectacular views of five of the Seven Sisters, the Babylonian-Gothic skyscrapers that Stalin built. I don't ask him about Yelena, his model girlfriend, who constantly seems to threaten either suicide or exposure. I can hear the pressure in his voice.

After Katya's bedtime and dinner, and the distribution of the gifts I've brought with me—jeans and sneakers, records, smoked salmon, videotapes, and underwear—Artyom and Svetlana arrive to say hello. Artyom has a cold, and they both look tired, but their news is mostly good. Artyom's mother has finally managed to pull off an almost unheard-of swap: her own two-room apartment for two one-room apartments in the same building. So now they're moving their possessions across town, from Svetlana's mother's flat, where they've been camping for the past year, unable to find anywhere else to live. Their homelessness has almost been the undoing of them as a couple, I know, for Svetlana has told me. I remember Artyom saying bitterly to a visiting friend of mine: "I can't ask you to our place, because we don't have one. We have suitcases full of roubles, and no home to go to. Such is life in this great Soviet Socialist Republic."

"It's great news, about the apartment," I say.

"One room is great?" says Artyom bitterly.

"For two writers?" adds Svetlana.

Artyom says he's spent much of his time since they last came back from London plodding around Moscow trying to to find an alternative: an apartment he can buy for hard currency from a Jewish family about to emigrate. "Maybe you should buy one yourself, Jo," he says casually, looking around. "And then we could buy this one from you."

3

After they leave, the Vorotnikovsky Alley apartment, though large by Soviet standards, suddenly seems to me, newly arrived from the West, impossibly cramped and constrictive, full of ears and eyes. I make up the sofa-bed in Yelena's tiny room, and we make love almost furtively, because of the danger of being overheard. Yelena falls asleep almost immediately, holding on to my hand. But I cannot sleep. The air, as Ksiyusha said, is as hot and damp as an orchid house; and kamikaze Moscow mosquitoes, which seem to nest in the tree outside the window, are soon dive-bombing my body, cutting off their tiny outboard motors as they land. I slap and swat at them for a while; then I disengage myself from Yelena, get up, and tiptoe across the hall to look at Katya. She's jerking slightly in her cot as she sleeps, as if whole networks of synapses are independently switching themselves on and off in her brain. As I lean over to stroke her head with its straggle of silky hair, the smell she gives off is warm and woody, like mushrooms.

I leave her sleeping, and then go into the kitchen and smoke and drink tea until dawn comes up over the swings in the courtyard and the crows start squawking like bronchial patients. What should I do? Now that my mother has died, should I buy a new apartment in Moscow? Is this place big enough now that I'm here? Should I pay a lot of money for a dacha for the summer? How do I want my new family to live?

Housing, I think as I sit sipping my tea: everything in the city seems to centre on housing: on the search for a place to live, where you can work and eat and make love in comparative privacy. In Moscow, I've read, there are now one and a quarter million people on the waiting lists for new housing; an individual still has to wait an average of thirty-seven years for an apartment of his or her own. It wasn't until a few months ago that communal apartment dwellers who'd been waiting forty years or more for their own accommoda-tion were finally guaranteed it; and forty-eight thousand families were immediately registered on this new list. Meanwhile, almost one and a half million Muscovites live in intolerably cramped condi-tions, occupying a living space of between one and five square metres each, when the official allotment—small enough in itself—is supposed to be twelve (roughly nine by twelve feet). What on earth can be done about this situation nobody seems to know, though the flim-flam rhetoric of the Party still talks about "an apartment for every family by the year 2000." The new Moscow City Soviet that was elected in March appears to think the best solution is private ownership—there was a pilot experiment earlier in the year in the Leningradsky district, where two-room city-owned apartments were put up for sale to tenants for about 3,500 roubles (eighteen months' average salary); and now the Western press is full of an announce-ment that three million of Moscow's apartments are to go on sale, this year or next, to the people who live in them. I'm sceptical about this: all property in the Soviet Union belongs to the state, after all, so what right does the Moscow City Council have to start dealing in it? Besides, in its first two-month session, all the new council seemed able to do was to elect a new mayor, set up a commodities exchange, and change a few street names—despite the fact that it's dominated by the Democratic Rossiya bloc. The fact is, it has no power to decide anything, and it's packed with deputies who do nothing but endlessly parade their opinions in front of the micro-phones and cameras. It took them a week at the beginning of their deliberations even to agree about the decorations in the hall they met in (e.g., should the plaster bust of Lenin be removed or not).

I get up and make another cup of tea. We'll stay in Vorot-nikovsky Alley, I decide, until the city council or the local district makes up its mind. It's central, just off Gorky Street; and as for the lack of privacy, I'll get used to it—I'll do what I usually do: get up before everyone else, or hide out in the evenings behind a book. But what about the dacha? I've heard Yelena talking urgently about it on the phone from London; she was speaking to Andrei Voz-nesensky tonight, trying to find a place in the writers' village at Peredelkino or anywhere else he might know of. The whole family seems obsessed with the idea. In fact, everyone I know seems ob-sessed: for months, they've been trying to beg, borrow, or rent a place for a week or two, for a month, for the summer—in a dacha, or one of the so-called creative houses, or a sanatorium.

I don't really understand it, I think as I sit down again. I've never been in a place where the countryside has been so blighted and destroyed in the name of progress. Yet Russians have a persistent, passionate, individual love for it: they flock to the parks and forests, given the slightest excuse. And it's not a romantic love, love of some prettified, idealized notion of the country, like that of the English. It's something much older and wilder: an almost Gothic passion for uncultivated nature, for woods and wilderness. Maybe it has to do with the speed with which the industrial revolution took place here. When the Bolsheviks came to power, after all, eighty-four percent of the people they ruled still lived on the land as they'd always done. And though the move to the cities began immediately afterwards, it wasn't until 1928, with the crisis in the grain supply and the beginning of forced collectivization, that it really took hold. In the following decade, an astonishing twenty-seven million people moved to the cities. And in the years since 1939, the number of city dwellers has multiplied in the Soviet Union more than three times.

Nowhere else on earth has this process taken place on such an enormous scale over such a small period of time. Nowhere else in the industrialized world, therefore, are cities like Moscow a third to a half filled with people actually born in the country. One can probably overvalue the importance of this, I think; one can use it to excess, to explain everything that seems so resolutely foreign here for Westerners like me. But there's no doubt that it helps to account for the strangely intimate, parish-pump atmosphere of Moscow, which I feel again, very strongly, as I look out over the courtyard. And it may well help explain, too, the clannishness of Muscovites, their consuming love of gossip, their suspicion of strangers, and the superstitions that dictate the smallest of their actions, even among the most citified and Westernized of people. For these are the characteris-tics (for better or worse) of a people who despite the move to the cities are most at home in a village—a self-contained place in which everyone knows everyone else and ancient accommodations with fate survive. They're the products of the immense, brooding vistas of the Russian countryside, to which, every summer and autumn, it seems, they have a Gadarene urge to return—as Yelena does now.

A dacha, I think as the crows begin to flap and hawk in the trees: yes, we'd definitely better find a dacha.

4

Nobody but me seems even remotely interested in the goings-on at the Party Congress. Gorbachev is being attacked daily now for departing from socialism and forgetting about Communist ideology; the current chaos of *perestroika* is being unfavourably compared to the prosperity of the Brezhnev years; and woe to anyone who dares to stand up and talk about the Party's responsibility for what has happened in the past. (He is simply howled down from the speakers' rostrum.) Even though the Party lost its constitutional right to sole

power in March (Article 6 of the Soviet Constitution), the mood
of the Congress is chauvinist and unrepentant; it's dominated by
permanent Party officials, and every day on television they seem
endlessly to invoke "the people" in their attacks on the move towards
a Western-style market—as in "the people's forests are now being
cut down just to provide paper for pornography." (I agree with
Pasternak's Dr. Zhivago: "I can just accept that there were 'peoples'
under the Caesars—Gauls and Scythians and Illyrians and so on.
But ever since, the idea has been utter fiction, a phrase for Tsars and
kings and politicians to use in their speeches: 'The people, my
people.' ") All of this makes me nervous for Gorbachev—the
Moscow Voters' Association booed him off the podium at the May
Day parade two months ago—especially when someone called
Colonel General Makashov stands up to rail one day against democracy, *glasnost,* and Gorbachev's whole policy. What he says is eerily
reminiscent in tone of an open letter that's recently been circulated
to army units, it's said by General Rodionov, the man in charge of
the troops responsible for the Tbilisi massacre in April 1989: full of
accusations against political "scientist peacocks" and "the boulevard
press" for undermining the efficiency of the armed forces, "the
brightest symbols of the state." I wonder why on earth Gorbachev
doesn't simply turn his back on all this: resign from the general
secretaryship of the Party and put himself up for nationwide election
as president. The question, I suppose, is: Would he win? Is it already
too late?

No one else seems concerned with any of this, though, despite
the fact that there are rumours all over Moscow of troop deployments
and a coming army-led right-wing coup. The Congress is "just
something to watch late at night if you can't sleep and haven't got
anything better to do" (my friend Tolya Shevchenko). And: "It's
all a foregone conclusion; the conservatives have no place to go.
They'll end up having to back the boss, just as they've always

done" (Yuli Missitski, an ex–mathematics professor, with whom I'm trying to do some business). The famous clairvoyant and healer Dzhuna Davitashvili—who's said to have treated Brezhnev (though she didn't), and who predicted a few weeks ago that Boris Yeltsin would get 538 votes to win the presidency of the Russian Republic (he won it, in fact, with 535)—has announced, in any case, that everything will work out fine at the Congress "after some minor unrest"; and that seems to be enough to satisfy most people. Besides, they're all much more concerned with what the Western press has been calling "the crisis in the food supply"; getting food on the table.

Ever since Prime Minister Ryshkov announced last month that food prices were going to to go up, "there's been absolute chaos," says Tatiana Samoilovna. The day after his announcement, the whole of Moscow simply stopped work. "Everybody at the labora﹈ tory took the day off," she says, laughing, "and joined the queues. It was incredible. People were fighting each other for the last pack﹈ age of macaroni: *militsia,* army officers, old babushkas, young girls, everybody. In two days, they say, a month's supply of food disap﹈ peared from the shops: flour, cereals, cans of fish, salt, matches, everything there was to buy." She opens the cupboards in the kitchen to show me the results: smiling, proud. Inside there are big brown bags full of flour and buckwheat, bottles of oil, and cans of tomato sauce and condensed milk. But I don't see the thirty﹈seven pounds of sugar which every household is supposed now to be hoarding.

5

Yelena's friends come by every day now to ooh and ah over Katya. So I tell Tatiana Samoilovna one day that I'm going shopping. She grimaces: "Don't bother," she says. "There's nothing to buy. And if there is anything worth having, you have to show your internal passport, to prove you live in the city. If you're from outside, or don't have a *propiska,* you can't buy it. They've even stopped long-distance lorry drivers from stopping off to get something to eat here. It's crazy. Still, bread," she says, handing me a plastic "perhaps bag." "I suppose you could buy bread."

The bread is easy: there's a bakery on Gorky Street and only a seven-minute wait for the cashier. But then I walk down to Gastronom Number One, the other side of Pushkin Square: the huge, chandeliered food shop that's still known as Yeliseyev's, after its pre-Revolutionary owner. It's a woeful sight. The shelves and counters are almost bare; there are probably no more than about forty different items for sale, mostly in dented cans and bottles with torn labels. The milling crowd is aimless and dispirited. The only action is in a long line for *kolbasa* (sausage) and *sardelki* (thick frankfurters) produced by a a Soviet–West German joint venture called Delikates. The *kolbasa* costs a day's average pay per kilo; the *sardelki* only slightly less. Yeliseyev's was known as "the Temple of Gluttons" before the Revolution: it sold burbot livers, coconuts, and strawberries out of season.

I buy some *kolbasa,* queuing twice, once for the cashier and then for what I've purchased. People dip in and out of the line in front of me, having their places kept. There is a lot of grumbling. The whole process takes about forty-five minutes. I remember reading somewhere that when cheap goods are in short supply, there has to be some form of rationing. The form of rationing in the Soviet Union is the queue. People in the Soviet Union spend sixty billion man-hours a year in line. It's no wonder that no one does any work.

After Yeliseyev's, I traipse down to GUM (the State Universal Store), facing Red Square. It's a huge and beautiful building. I remember the Writer saying on our first visit: "You know, they should just hand the whole thing over to Bloomingdale's. A few palm trees, a bit of paint, some music: it could be the greatest store in the world." But today it's every bit as dispiriting as Yeliseyev's. Hordes of people are grinding slowly past piles of tat of every kind, without any single alleviating quality of design or pattern or material. Until this year, I remember, the Soviet Union used annually to buy from its East European satellites fifty million roubles' worth of shoddy goods *na sklad* (for the warehouse)—stuff so bad it could never be offered for sale—and that there's now a billion roubles' worth of these useless goods held in depots all over the country. It seems to me suddenly, as I walk through, that they must have opened up these entrepots of awfulness and that today is the opening day of the joke sale that's the result. But no one in GUM, so far as I can see, is laughing, or even smiling.

In any case, surely there'd be, I think, if that were true, joke razor blades and cups and teapots and footwear. But I can't see any at *all* of these, joke or otherwise. There's toothpaste, but there's no soap or shampoo; no hair spray or cologne or creams or perfumes on offer. There's literally nothing, I think, that anybody from the West could want: no socks or wristwatches or knives and forks (for our once and future dacha); nothing. There's a photo-developing service, operated by a joint venture, and, opposite it, a branch of a Finnish company selling aspirin and clothes and graceless shoes for hard currency. There are *militsia* men checking Soviet passports every now and again, to make sure that nobody's buying this tat who doesn't have a right to it. But there isn't anything worth looking at, let alone buying; there's just this hangdog crowd wandering about in the dim hope that it'll be in the right place when something desirable is brought up from a storage room at the whim of one of the managers. They'd be much better off, I think grimly, giving blood at one of the local hospitals. In Leningrad, Ksiyusha's told me, anyone willing to part with two hundred grams of the stuff gets a ticket which gives him the right to stand in line for items rare enough to be the stuff of dreams: kid gloves or subscriptions to the collected works of Mikhail Bulgakov; Chinese mohair scarves or West German tights; Italian shoes or whistling kettles. In Kazan, she says—and nearby St. Basil's Cathedral, after all, was built to celebrate a victory over the Tartars of Kazan—his blood will buy chickens.

After GUM, I simply trawl through the streets on my way homeward. I buy some Narzan mineral water at a diet shop, and batteries at TSUM, the Central Universal Store, which used to be a branch of the English Muir and Merrilea's—and where a jazz band is for some reason playing "In the Mood" on the esplanade in front. In a dairy shop on Chekhov Street I find milk and even *tvorok,* the curd-cheese that Ksiyusha eats with sugar every morning before she goes to university. But I ignore the rotten fruit and vegetables I see in the greengrocers' shops along the way, and abandon a long line at a wine shop on the Garden Ring when it gets longer in front of me than it was when I started half an hour before. By the time I get back to Vorotnikovsky Alley with my miserably slim pickings, I've been on the streets for four and a half hours. I've also seen four television crews filming the lines (and in one case me) for the evening news in the West of bad times in the city.

"Poor Jo," says Yelena, when I tell her. "I don't think you're going to be able to live like a Russian. Not unless you learn how to be in three queues at once."

"Or learn to work as a team, like Granny does with her people at the film studios," adds Ksiyusha, laughing.

"The problem, Jo," says Tolya Shevchenko later, when he comes to dinner, "is that you're starting from scratch. You have to be *born* here to be able to get by. Then you'd have your own network of people who owe you favours and your own contacts inside the shops, so you'd buy *na lyeva,* on the left, out of the back door. You'd also have a job and a history. So in some cases you wouldn't have to rely on the shops at all. Thirty percent of all canned meat and ten percent of all cheese and sausage never goes anywhere near the shops. It goes into *zakazi,* or orders, which war veterans and invalids, veterans of labour, and workers in the ministries get every month."

"Granny gets one," says Ksiyusha. "And Grandpa used to get a *good* one."

"Yeliseyev's, for example, fills about seventy thousand *zakazi* a month."

"And there are special places—there's one at Yeliseyev's and one round the corner on the Garden Ring," says Ksiyusha, "where you can buy *zakazi:* made-up packages, with maybe some sugar, some condensed milk—"

"And two kilos of rotten apples and something else you don't want," says Yelena, interrupting. "You have to buy everything in the package or nothing. It's like getting a cheap ticket for a good production at the price of having to buy three for bad ones."

"And then there are other ways of getting food outside the shops which the West doesn't know about," says Tolya. "Factories and associations, for example, buy food in bulk for their workers; they organize special invitations to closed shops; they even hold lotteries for specially rare items. Something like five billion roubles' worth of stuff is distributed this way every year: sewing machines, perfume, TV sets, furniture, all kinds of things like that."

Tolya Shevchenko is a free-lance fixer in the film business, whom I met last year in the closing stages of the shoot on Russian culture. He's a dapper, good-looking man in his early forties, with twinkling eyes and a brown brush moustache. He looks like the youngest, most recently retired wing commander in the British Royal Air Force; and since he learned much of his English translating one of Robert Ludlum's books into Russian, he knows a lot of the appropriate words, like "rocketry," "circuitry," and "dead on ar-

rival." He's also a mine of information on how things work in the
Soviet Union. "Apart from that, Jo," he says now, "well, you're
a smart man, so you'd probably have a job in a ministry or in the
Party: somewhere in the *nomenklatura*. So you'd have a subsidized
canteen you could buy from, as well as special food and other shops
like the ones in GUM you don't see, marked No Entry."

"There's one just off Kalinin Prospekt, round the corner from
Vointorg, the big military store," says Yelena. "And another one
inside the House on the Embankment." The House on the Embankment is the huge apartment building built by Stalin in the
thirties, not far from the British embassy, for military and Party
high-rankers. It later became known as "the crematorium" or "the
chicken-processing plant" after almost everyone who lived in it was
either executed or sent to the camps.

"Go on," I say to Tolya. "Is there anything else?"

"Yes," he says. "Then there are the waiting lists. You can't buy
a television set, for example, in the stores anymore. You have to do
it through your factory or office or organization. A place on *that* list
sells for a thousand roubles. Then, if you're a veteran of labour or
of war, you're now allowed to buy ten thousand roubles' worth of
consumer goods, if you register with your local communal housing
office. A place on *that* list sells for between two and two-and-a-half
thousand roubles."

"Oh, 'I am forty-first for Plisetskaya,' " says Ksiyusha, quoting
a poem of Voznesensky's " 'thirty-third for the theatre at Taganka, |
forty-fifth for the graveyard at Vagankovo. | I am fourteenth for the
eye specialist, | twenty-first for Glazunov, the artist | forty-fifth for an
abortion—when my time comes, I'll be in shape.' "

It used to be easy, I reflect after Tolya has gone: before the
Revolution, you just went to the shops, like everybody else: to
Gautier's on Kuznetsy Most, for example, where Anna Karenina
used to buy the latest books; or to the musical instrument shop a few

doors away, where Tolstoy went one day to listen to piano music on one of the first phonographs; or to the furniture shop on Stolesh-nikov Alley that used to belong to Nikolai Schmidt, who bought guns for his factory workers, died in prison in mysterious circum-stances, and left all his money to the Bolshevik Party. Now goods have become a way of keeping everyone in line. The misery of the shops is one thing: it's a fact of life, it's universal. But if you offend your boss, or your trade union, or the Party, or the KGB, then you risk everything: job, privilege, car, dacha, television, food, the future, everything.

Then: Kuznetsy Most, Stoleshnikov Alley, I suddenly think: they mean Blacksmiths' Bridge and Market Stall Alley. And for half an hour I pore over a rudimentary map of Moscow with Yelena, reconstructing out of some of the street names the old commercial face of the city. Fish Alley, Crystal Alley; Silversmiths', Capmak-ers', Printers' alleys; Tablecloth, Knives, Cups, Gatemakers' alleys; Bun Street, Carriagemakers' Street, Cannon Street; Pipemakers' Square, Cauldronmakers' Embankment, Coachmakers' Row. It's the first of the many mad lists I start making, as I try to come to terms with where I now live.

6

Never pass salt from hand to hand; never shake hands across a threshold; never leave your apartment and then return unless you look in the mirror. Wear a safety pin against the evil eye, and if you come across it in someone, wash your door handle (or your baby, three times) in holy water. Always wash your hands after leaving a cemetery. If you take an examination, put five coins in a shoe for good luck. If you have a button sewn on by someone, put a piece of thread in your mouth or you'll lose your memory. If you lose something, tie a piece of thread round a chair leg. If someone says something good about someone or something you hold dear, spit quickly over your left shoulder three times. To someone on the brink of something important, remember to say: "No down, no feather" (May you never have anything soft); the proper response being "God damn you!" If you leave on a journey, make sure to sit down together before leaving the house, with the youngest member of the family the first to stand up. Avoid black cats and (especially) people carrying two empty buckets. Pay attention to your dreams.

A dream involving *blini* means illness; cats, an enemy; vodka, unexpected happenings; lemons, betrayal; a full moon, love; shaving one's beard off, loss. Sigmund Freud was published here for the first time a year ago. Astrologers and faith healers are more trusted than physicians or psychologists. Russians say, not "I had a dream," but "I *saw* a dream," as if the dream were something real and palpable, like a rocking horse or a chair.

7

Things I see abandoned in the alleys and courtyards: planks, rods, laths, wattles, blocks, bricks, slats, wheels, cartons, crates, pipes, scaffolding, nuts, iron, wood, broken glass; slabs of reinforced concrete, sheets of zinc and aluminium, piles of bent nails and rusted screws; old bathtubs, busted radios, heaps of filthy sand and gravel; matted paper, crazed springs, oozing vegetables, dank mattresses, smashed fencing, sharded stone.

Things to avoid in apartment buildings: empty basements and blind stairwells where the faeces and the broken bottles are; the pool of urine in the elevator; rats and the mangy courtyard cats that are fed to keep them down.

Ugly company names: Giproavtotrans, Vniichrom, Tiazhmash, Informtorg . . .

8

The seven-storey apartment-building I now live in lies between the
Garden Ring and the Boulevard Ring, the two more or less circular
inner-city road systems, which make the Kremlin, at the centre, look
from the air like the bull's-eye on a dartboard. The Garden Ring
is two minutes' walk to the north, and three or four minutes' walk
from the junction is the nearest Metro station, Mayakovsky Square.
Mayakovsky Square is a huge open space just to the east of Gorky
Street (which runs north-south along its rim), where a statue of the
great revolutionary poet dominates what was once the haymarket, the
place to which, in the sixteenth century, peasants used to bring in
goods from outside the city. The Garden Ring dips into a tunnel
beneath it; and on it are the Tchaikovsky Concert Hall, the Mos-
soviet and Satire theatres, the Moscow Cinema, the Peking Hotel,
and the Sofia Restaurant. The area in the middle, around the giant
statue, was where, in the 1960s, Yevtushenko and Voznesensky used
to give poetry readings, and where SMOG, the Union of Young
Geniuses, was founded. In those days it was known simply as
"Mayak," and it was one of the great meeting places for the young
of the city.

To the south, towards Red Square along Gorky Street—past
the local bakery and the Baku Restaurant and the Minsk Hotel—is
another famous landmark and meeting place, the statue of Pushkin
on Pushkin Square, where last year's turbulent sea of arguers and
hecklers has now given way to a long, thin river of queuers for the
new McDonald's. (When I take my visa for inspection to the *militsia*
station in one of the alleys behind it, a *militsia* man says that the wait
for a Big Mac is about an hour and a half, which must make it the
slowest fast food anywhere on earth.) On Pushkin Square (which
the Boulevard Ring crosses from east to west) are the constructivist
headquarters of *Izvestia* and the offices of *Moscow News, New Times,*

and *Novy Mir,* as well as the Rossiya Cinema and the Central House of the Actors' Union, recently gutted by a fire. Underneath it is a long walkway, like the central strut of a Celtic cross, where flowers, posters of a British "Page Three" girl, and *Sex: Thirty-Seven New Positions* are for sale on makeshift stalls.

Vorotnikovsky Periulok (Gatemakers' Alley), then—running, as it does, from just behind the Minsk Hotel to the Garden Ring—is in the centre of things; and to live in number 5, next to the high school where Stalin's daughter, Svetlana, went, you have to have *blat,* or influence. ("There are no people off the street here," says Tatiana Samoilovna proudly.) Across the elevator landing from us, for example, lives Lev Fyodorovich, the head of the *militsia* for the district, a stocky man with a tiny, surprised quiff of hair, and his mother, who has recently taken to knocking on our door at all hours of the day and night—much to Yelena's horror—asking to see Gennady. (Lev Fyodorovich likes a drink or two and recently gave me a bottle of moonshine—*samogon*—which he must, I reckon, have confiscated in the line of duty.) On the second floor, with the best apartment and a circular balcony, is the executive of the local housing authority; on the third floor, the recently returned cultural attaché from the Soviet embassy in London; and somewhere else in the building, the first secretary of the district Komsomol.

Not all of the people in the building, though, are bureaucrats or Party *apparatchiki.* The ability to jump the housing queue (and land on this privileged square) takes many forms, says Yelena, as she introduces me, one by one, little by little, to the neighbours. On our fourteen-apartment stairwell (the middle one of five in the L-shaped building), there's Sergei, for example, a young man who works in a cooperative and who comes down from upstairs to mend the electrics from time to time. His privilege comes from his *mnogo dietnaya semlya* (family with many children), as does the Azerbaijani engineer Ali's and his wife the doctor's three floors below. Then there's Vladimir, the sleepy-eyed, strikingly good-looking man on the fifth floor: he works for Eastern Europe's common market, Comecon, Yelena says, and his wife for Czech radio. And then, above us, next to Sergei, there are two dancers, Rita and her husband, another Vladimir. She's a People's Artist of either the Russian Federation or the Soviet Union; he's a lead dancer at the Stanislavsky Theatre—hence their sufficiency of *blat.*

All of these people I slowly learn to recognize and to say "Good morning" to. *"Kak vy pozhivayete?"* How are you? Little by little, too, I begin to identify some of the people on the other stairwells: a professor; a script writer (who is also a People's Artist); the actor father of Yelena Sofonova; other actors and dancers from the Mos-soviet and Stanislavsky theatres. But it's not until some time later that I finally ask Yelena (over dinner one evening) how on earth her family got its apartment here. Gennady's work—whatever it was—for the KGB is something I still tend to steer clear of.

So "Was it that?" I ask, as Kseniya translates for Tatiana Samoilovna. "Was it, uh, the KGB? Did they . . . ?"

"No, Jo, *I* did it," she says. "When Papa got ill, I wrote to a man I knew, who'd been Brezhnev's foreign policy advisor and was a deputy of the Supreme Soviet under Gorbachev. He sponsored a documentary series I worked on with some Americans in the late seventies; he was our sort of godfather, the man who persuaded Brezhnev that we should be allowed to do it. Well, the Americans never met him—he was a secret—but I got to know him quite well. So I wrote to him, saying that Papa was a veteran of war and now an invalid and that he'd done, well, other services for his country. I asked him if he could help us find an apartment of our own. We lived in a communal apartment the other side of the Boulevard Ring—"

"In the courtyard behind the fish shop on Gorky Street," says Ksiyusha.

"So anyway, he wrote to the mayor's office. And they offered us a number of places—"

"But a long way away from the centre," says Tatiana Samoilovna. "And I said no, Gennady Pavlovich had spent his whole life in the middle of the city. How could he live anywhere else?"

"And finally," says Yelena, "they showed us this place, which was near Mama's work and Ksiyusha's school—"

"And listen, it's a great story, this," says Ksiyusha, interrupting, laughing. "Originally this building was built on the site of a church that the Bolsheviks destroyed; the school next door was put up over the church's cemetery. And the church people, in the twenties—whenever—said that nothing built on this site would ever stand. So, sure enough, it fell down and parts of it had to be rebuilt in the eighties, just before we moved in. The legend says that it's only standing today because they finally got a priest to bless the site and sprinkle it with holy water. You see, Jo?" she says, slapping her thighs under the dining room table. "We live on consecrated ground!"

So many bones, I think; so much blood. I remember last year filming unmarked mass graves in two Moscow cemeteries, and seeing a photograph of rows of unearthed skeletons lying on a table in front of Sakharov at a public meeting. I've just been reading about a lake bank at Moscow's Novospassky Monastery, where thousands and thousands of bodies have been recently discovered, including most of the foreign members of the thirties' Komintern: Yugoslavians, Romanians, Poles, Germans, Italians, even the delegate from the American Communist Party. The television current-affairs programmes, too, seem these days to be involved in nothing so much as competitive exhumation. On "Before and After Midnight" recently, Vladimir Molchanov interviewed old women who remembered truckloads of bodies being driven every day for four years in the thirties from the secret police's headquarters to the Church of All Sorrows near the Taganka Theatre, to be buried there in mountains by the Bird Market on Kalitnikovskaya Street. So many old bones rattling in the cupboard of *glasnost,* I think. There's no way to quiet them—especially if you live on top of them.

"So how did you get the communal apartment?" I ask on another night.

"My great-grandfather," says Ksiyusha. "He had a house in the country, but he had a heart attack and had to move into the city. So he swapped his country house for one room in this communal apartment. He was lucky," she adds. "If he hadn't had a heart attack, he would probably have been shot in one of the purges." The others are silent. "He was Cheka," she goes on, "one of Dzerzhinsky's special assistants. He investigated the Social Revolutionaries when they made a bomb attack against the Bolsheviks in Moscow—no one knows what else."

"So . . . who lived in the apartment?" I ask.

"There were five families when I was a kid," says Yelena. "The biggest number of people we ever had was thirty-three." She turns to Tatiana Samoilovna. "Yes, Mama?" Tatiana Samoilovna nods. Yelena turns back. "Thirty-three people in eight rooms: with one kitchen, one toilet, and one bathroom between them."

"Actually, it was great, Jo," says Ksiyusha. "My friends used to like it much more than here. Before the Revolution, it belonged to a rich merchant, people said; it was the servants' quarters opposite his mansion. But the merchant was supposed to have married one of his servants and to have lined the streets with carpets all the way down to the church on Nezhdanova Street on the day of the wedding."

"How many rooms did you have?"

"Two," says Yelena. "There was Mama and Papa, they had one little room. And then there was a big room divided with curtains, where my babushka Zizi and my father's brother, Sacha, slept."

"And who else lived there?"

"Well, there was the Moshinsky family, Jewish: they had two rooms, with some lovely old furniture. The old man had a stall at a village outside Moscow—he sold soap and candy, anything that was available. Then there was his wife: she was a beautiful old woman, very elegant; she had good diamonds, I remember. She'd been married before, but her husband had been shot during the Revolution—she never told us why. She had a daughter by him, and she and her granddaughter lived with them. The daughter was a typist—at one time she worked for *Worker* magazine—and the granddaughter became a student at one of the medical institutes. Now she's a doctor."

"Then there was Maria Ivanovna," says Ksiyusha. "She was an old lady who died when I was eight. She taught Mama English and she taught me how to read. She had this very ascetic, very old-lady's room, with not much more than a sofa and a bookcase, and a carpet and wooden pictures on the wall. She gave English lessons at the Diplomatic School, and one evening she said: "I'm going to be arrested, I know it. They're going to put me in the camps. Today I called Molotov's daughter a fool!""

"When she died," says Tatiana Samoilovna, "they gave her room to a *militsia* man and his wife. He'd come in from a country village to be on duty for the Olympic Games in 1980. He was a terrible drunk, drunk all the time."

"She was a wonderful woman, Maria Ivanovna," says Yelena. "She was absolutely independent: even when she was old, she'd never accept any help from anyone. She'd been married to a famous post-Revolutionary writer, and she was very proud. She refused to inform on her colleagues at the school. And when an American woman lived with her for a while—an American woman who'd emigrated to the Soviet Union in the 1930s—she absolutely refused to spy on her for the KGB when they came to ask her. She said: 'I am a Russian *intelligent*. I would never do such a thing!' She was completely unafraid. Later they came to my grandmother and said that they were going to put hidden microphones in Maria Iva-novna's room, and that she was never to tell her. She never did. I never forgave Zizi for that."

"Yes, she was brave," says Tatiana Samoilovna. "I remember once hearing a terrible screaming in the kitchen, and going out to find her confronting Klavdia. She was saying to her: 'It's all right. I know you stole it. But it's quite all right.' I asked her what on earth the matter was. She said calmly: 'I was just telling Klavdia that she's stolen my pension.'"

There's a pause at this point. Klavdia obviously has rich associ-ations. I ask who she was.

"Klavdia? She was a woman from the villages," says Yelena. "She couldn't read or write. And she was very rude, full of bravado. She used to spit on people and curse them. She and Mama used to have big rows."

"Her family were all robbers," says Ksiyusha. "Her husband had been some kind of black-market dealer. And after he died, she had her three children all living in one room, and they were all criminals."

"There was Viktor: he was a thief and a drunkard, in and out of prison all the time," says Yelena. "And then there was the daughter, Zina—"

"During the war, Klavdia put Zina in bed with men for food," says Tatiana Samoilovna.

"And by the time she was sixteen, she was the mistress of some local gang leader. She was the lookout on the armed robberies they did. She finally got caught during a raid on the chairman of a collective farm, and was sent to the Gulag as a criminal—to a work camp in Magadan, where she got tuberculosis. She had tattoos all over her body, I remember. On her arms there was a crucifix she had done when her father died, and 'Sleep in Peace.'"

"And then there was the other brother, Yurka," says Tatiana Samoilovna. "Yurka was a real bandit! He was born with a knife in his hand."

"He used to go after his mother with an axe, and babushka would have to stop him."

"He was a psychopath. When he was angry, he could do anything," says Yelena. "The police finally got him for something terrible: hacking open his girlfriend's stomach. But it was funny. He was always very nice to us. He would never steal from anyone in the apartment. His gang people were told to be on their best behaviour when they came. And I remember he was furious when I was a little girl and I had my skates stolen at the skating rink."

"He could have *been* somebody—Maria Ivanovna used to say that," says Kseniya. "You know? He had the most beautiful handwriting, and he was in some ways rather shy. Once, I remember, it was a very bright, shiny morning, all the kids were playing; and I went into the kitchen and Yurka was making *shchefir*—you know, the unbelievably strong tea that criminals make when they want to get high. He was standing there, just in his vest, and I could see that he had all these tattoos all over him. I asked him what they were. He told me that he'd been walking down the street and had leaned on something with wet paint on it. I've always been ashamed that I embarrassed him like that—even though I suppose he was a terrible man."

I listen with my mouth open as they talk into the night. I had no idea. And a day or two later, on one of my shopping forays, I walk to the building and stand in the courtyard behind the Okean fish shop on Gorky Street, looking up at the third floor, trying to imagine what it must have been like: sixty or more years of a family's history, four generations of people being born and living and dying in one or two rooms, enmeshed with the lives and deaths of intimate strangers, vulnerable to the secret police, unable ever to escape from the eyes of others. I think of the other families I've been told about who lived in those eight rooms. The Sabanadzes: Viktor, the driver; his wife, Anna, the KGB calligrapher; his mother; and their two children—who could reach their tiny room only by running the gauntlet of Klavdia's family. And the Bashilovys: accountant father, mother, and two children—who had to split their room in two after their son died and their medical-student daughter married a psychol-ogist. I think too of the ones who remain today: of the drunken *militsia* man and his wife and new baby; and of the late arrivals, Emma Stroganova and her daughter Natasha. The Stroganovas still live, Ksiyusha says, in the rooms that the Moshinsky family had; they arrived to replace it as the result of some hugely elaborate, many-partnered room-and-apartment swap that involved several cities.

"Emma was strange, interesting, always very closed," says Ksiyusha. "She worked as a laboratory technician at a secret KGB plant, and she never quarrelled with anyone. Natasha, well, she was mysterious too; she was a student at some technical medical institute; then she married and got divorced; she had a baby daughter, Katya. But she was very talented: she used to make dolls for me and read Robert Burns aloud. She taught me to love poetry."

"I'd like to go and see the apartment," I say.

"No," says Yelena. "It would be too sad. There's nobody left there from the old days: just the *militsia* man, and the people who made a swap with Klavdia for her room: relatives of hers, drunks, with huge numbers of children."

"What about the Stroganovas?"

"I once heard Emma and Natasha arguing," Ksiyusha says slowly. "Emma wanted to marry again, but Natasha said that if she did, she'd throw herself out of a window. Now both their lives, I think, have been ruined. Natasha got married again, and her hus-band lived in the apartment for a while, but now he's gone. The last time I saw her, she had lost all her teeth."

9

Through all these days, the search for the dacha continues. In the end, though, we're saved by Alexander Lipnitsky. For the founding father of Zvuki Mu, whom I met at the *Assa* première, has a dacha at Nikolina Gora. And he tells us that a neighbour of his, a geologist, is anxious to rent off half his house. The house has no phone, he says, and we'll have to share a bathroom with the other members of his family. But it's probably the best offer we're going to get this late in the season.

The next day, the geologist—a shy, bearded man in his late thirties called Fyodor—appears with a car and drives us west out of the city, past the new apartment blocks in Krylatskoye (Wingville) and the road to the popular beach at Serebrianny Bor (Silver Woods), where, in *Doctor Zhivago,* the industrialist Koligrivov, "fond of shooting and a good marksman, spent his Sundays in the winter of 1905 . . . giving rifle-training to insurgents." Then, after we pass a huge, three-quarters-finished heart clinic (on which I never see anyone working in the months that follow), the city quite suddenly comes to an end. The verges fill up with pink, white, and yellow wildflowers. The air becomes clearer, and Fyodor becomes animated for the first time. He tells a joke in halting English. A coachload of city dwellers, he says, comes out this way for a little mushrooming, but after they've been let off at the side of the road one of them begins gasping for breath and turning blue. The others rush him back to the coach and lay him down on the verge with his mouth towards the exhaust pipe. "It's the air," they say to the coach driver, "the country air! Quick, turn the engine on! A few puffs of carbon monoxide and he'll be as right as rain!"

It feels like an adventure, driving into the countryside like this: illegal, somehow. For all around us, in the villages either side of us, are big government compounds, the dachas of the high *nomenklatura.*

Fyodor points them out to us as we go: the Executive Committee of the Moscow Soviet in Barvikha; Gorbachev down a side lane further on; Mikoyan and Stalin by the side of the road; Ryshkov over there; Andropov down here; Khrushchev to the right, past a big cattle farm. The road we're on has obviously been kept up to ease and accommodate all these past and present bigwigs; it's the best-surfaced and most heavily policed I've ever seen in the Soviet Union. Every few kilometres, at every important intersection, there's a GAI post, with traffic cops wheeling about, twirling thonged batons as if they were six-guns, under towering wooden lookout posts like a swimming guard's at Bondi Beach. There are statues of bear and deer by the side of the road; a signal box at a level crossing delicately carved like an old peasant's house; and neat passenger shelters and litter bins shaped like penguins at virtually every bus stop. It's definitely a Potemkin road, this: there's not a pothole in sight. And even the village shop at Zhukovka, when we pass it, is neat and bright, as if the getting of food were pleasurable and ordinary, and not, as it is for most people, a prolonged daily nightmare.

"This is where Brezhnev's daughter, Galya, has a dacha," says Yelena, pointing.

"And his grandson Andrei," says Fyodor. "And Sakharov's family too, because of what he did for the nuclear bomb. They say that Andrei Brezhnev and Sakharov's son, Dmitri, have always been friends. When Sakharov was in disgrace, Andrei Brezhnev simply went on talking to him; and when the same thing happened to Brezhnev's family, Dima Sakharov did the same."

"And isn't this where Rostropovich had a dacha too?" I ask. "Where Solzhenitsyn lived in a little cottage while putting together *The Gulag Archipelago*?"

"Yes," says Fyodor. "They couldn't find him. They never thought to look right in the heart of the *nomenklatura*."

Twenty minutes later, after a string of little villages—Usovo,

Kalchuga, Gorky II, and Buzaevo, where old women are selling flowers and vegetables in front of painted *izby*—we turn off the main road and cross a narrow bridge with a pitted, buckled roadbed. "This," says Fyodor, "is where Boris Yeltsin said he was thrown into the river." A jerk of the thumb. "Down there." (Yeltsin was said last year to have turned up at dead of night at the local *militsia* station, bruised and soaking wet, saying he'd been attacked and hurled into the Moscow River by mysterious assailants—presumably the KGB or Party hardliners.) I look at the water below us. It doesn't look deep; it's a long way down; and Yeltsin is supposed to have been still carrying a bedraggled bouquet of flowers when he arrived at the *militsia* station to complain of the attack.

"But wasn't he carrying . . . ?" I begin.

"Yes," says Fyodor. "Flowers." And he taps his head and drains an imaginary glass of vodka.

Fyodor's house, when we reach it, is off the main road through Nikolina Gora, behind a pair of green wooden gates. It's a ramshackle building, patched with planks, with a scatter of outhouses, a decaying shed-cum-garage, and an air of being about to collapse back into the forest which surrounds it. The grass by the driveway up to the house is tall and unkempt. A pair of black-and-white kittens, half-wild, are playing in a patch of sunlight on the house's stoop.

We get out of the car and go in through the front door, into a down-at-heels kitchen with an ancient refrigerator and a large, pocked table; then along a short corridor into the rooms Fyodor wants to let to us for the summer. There are two of them, musty from disuse; and, the other side of them, a long, windowed terrace looking out over the woods. To me, it's all faintly dispiriting. The furniture is battered and rickety; it has the air of a junk shop. But Yelena seems delighted. "Here," she says, pointing into the smaller of the two rooms. "We can sleep here, and you can work at the desk.

Ksiyusha can sleep in the small bed in the other room, and Mama on the pullout sofa the other side of the table. It'll be fine," she says, clapping her hands. "We can cook and eat on the terrace."

I hardly know what to say to her. I wander about the house as she busily talks to Fyodor about curtains and sheets, and take inventory of what's on offer: a small, shared bathroom below the stairs the other side of the family kitchen; a grimy stove, a refrigerator, a tiny table, and a sink with no water on the terrace; two narrow sofa-beds, a table, some chairs, and two chests of drawers in the bigger of the rooms; an armoire, a large, hard bed, and a desk in the smaller. The atmosphere of these downstairs rooms is broody and dark; scrub bushes and trees scratch and clatter at their windows; the sunlight can't reach them. Their only saving grace is two large, unframed portraits high up on the walls that must have been painted before the Revolution: one of a stern, whiskered and bearded pater-familias sitting behind a cluttered desk, and the other of a younger woman with beautiful eyes and a clear, sad look, as if she can see the future. Perhaps Yelena, I think, has found something here that I don't know how to look for. Perhaps this is what she had in mind all along. But I can't help feeling surprised to hear her making plans with Fyodor: surprised because, like most Russians who've had contact with the West, she only seems interested in the best that can be found there—and I've always assumed that this attitude, now she's married to a Westerner, has inevitably spilled over to what-ever's available at home.

But then, while Fyodor unloads his car, refusing all help, we wander for a while in the thick, tangled garden—which is not really a garden but a staked-out patch of wilderness, though a plot for vegetables has been dug at the side of the house. And then we walk down a steep path, blocked by a fallen tree, towards the Moskva River. After a three-or-four-minute scramble through brambles and tree roots, we come out onto a narrow back road. To

the left is a concrete structure, like a large bandstand, where a
cooperative, Yelena says, sells *shashlik* at the weekends. And to the
right, along a short, puddled path, is the beach, called Diplomats',
because, although it's outside the permitted travel limit for foreigners,
the embassy community is allowed to swim here.

It's not much of a beach: just a scoop of sand in a curve of the
sluggish river. But the banks opposite and either side of it are wild
with reeds and tufted grass. And people are scattered everywhere on
it, even on this, a weekday. There are the usual matrons bulging like
great hernias out of their brief bikinis as they lay themselves out for
the sun; and little children dipping their toes into the water before
retreating back with a series of surprised small steps like a sand-
piper's. There's a competition of beat boxes and a German family
playing a raucous game of netless volleyball beside a carefully laid
picnic table. Yelena sniffs the air and takes my arm. "Wonderful,"
she says. "Isn't it wonderful, Jo?" And then she squints into the sun
to see if she knows anyone. It seems an entirely natural thing to do.
(Moscow is a city of nine million or a village of a few hundred,
depending on who and where you are.) Suddenly she waves and
shouts: "Nika! Nika!" It's one of Ksiyusha's ex–school friends,
who's sitting and talking earnestly to two boys at the water's edge:
a long-limbed, pretty girl in a T-shirt and culottes. She gets up and
comes over to us, carrying her sneakers in one hand by the laces.
And though she seems pleased enough to see us, there is, I sense, a
peculiar reticence in her: she talks only desultorily and reluctantly
about her plans for the summer. At first I think it's because she's
uneasy with Yelena. (Ksiyusha once told me that her friends were
scared of Yelena: her hugs, her moods, her hurricane generosity.)
And then I think, no: she's just become with age a snobbish, spoiled
brat, the product of her good looks and the *blat* of her parents. But
I remember that her older sister left recently for Boston with her
illustrator husband to settle for good, and that Nika is going to join

them as soon as it can be arranged. And I realize that she's simply bored, bored with everything that can possibly happen to her here: it's become dull and provincial. It's as if she has already left, or is now merely a tourist. They say that when the borders are finally opened—as they're supposed to be within the next few months— between three million and eight million people like her will leave, though where they will go or who will have them, God only knows. Meanwhile they wait like her and endlessly talk of the West, as if it were Moscow in a Chekhov play.

We say goodbye, and then struggle back up the steep, over-grown path to the house, where Fyodor makes us Turkish coffee in a long-handled pot in the kitchen. The house settles in around us like a mantle as we talk and come to terms. And I begin to realize why Yelena loves it on sight. It's like something that's been salvaged against the odds from the past, in which the past has somehow managed to stay alive. Everything here—the cracked double sink, the wooden dresser, the old upright piano in a side room, the glass-fronted cabinet stacked with books and papers in the corri-dor—is a survivor, mended and remended, until it's become the fabric and the history of the family that lives here, in a place where outside, in the city, no public history that can be trusted remains. I try to remember a passage in Turgenev that I was reading before we set out, while we were waiting for Fyodor. And I look it up when we get back (in *Sketches from a Hunter's Album*): "He lives," it says, "does Mardary Apollonych, completely in the old style. Even his house is of antiquated construction: the entrance hall, as one might expect, smells of *kvas,* tallow candles and leather; on the right stands a side-board with pipes and hand-towels; the dining-room contains family portraits, flies, a large pot of geraniums and a down-in-the-mouth piano; the drawing-room has three divans, three tables, two mirrors and a wheezy clock . . . the study has a table piled with papers, a bluish draught-screen . . . cupboards filled with stinking books . . . a stuffed armchair and an Italian window and a door into the garden that has been nailed up. . . . In a word, everything is quite appropriate." In Yelena's eyes—to ignore for the moment Turgenev's irony—we are, in the kitchen of the house in Nikolina Gora, somewhere quite appropriate.

I ask Fyodor about the history of the house. It was built, he says, like most of the rest of the village, in the late 1920s, when a cooperative was set up here by a group of composers and actors and academicians. A famous explorer, Otto Schmidt, was on the cooperative's founding council; so was the first People's Commissar for Health; the composer Prokofiev lived round the corner until his death in the 1950s. As for his own house, he says, it was built by his grandfather, who was a professor at the Tsarevich Alexei (later Plekhanov) Commercial Institute. "He lost his job in the 1920s, which probably saved his life. If he'd still been a professor, he would have been purged by Stalin." He laughs. His grandmother ran a music school in the city—which spilled over into the house here—where she employed people who would otherwise have been declared bourgeois parasites. A great-aunt, one of the first pre-Revolutionary silent film stars, lived in the back rooms; one of the tsar's last ministers was later (after imprisonment) a frequent visitor. Now Fyodor's mother lives here for most of the summer—she was a singer, then a translator and teacher, but now she's retired and works as a cloakroom attendant in a school. Fyodor himself teaches and works at Moscow University, he says, but prefers to do field work. He longs to go to Australia to work there; he longs to get out. "Things will be very bad here soon," he says.

We make a deal—for almost no money—for the two rooms for the next three months. He gives me the keys to the back of the house and promises to help us move. In the meantime, he says, he will mend the terrace floor and ceiling and hitch up the sink to the water supply. "I could make more money as a carpenter or plumber," he

says, shrugging. "But what can I do? I like to be a geologist." As
we walk back to the car, I ask why he thinks it will be bad in the
Soviet Union before very long. "Because soon there will be no
food," he says. "And that means civil war."

On the way out of the village, Yelena asks if we can stop for
a moment to see the pianist Nikolai Petrov, whom she met last year
working on a programme about Mussorgsky for the BBC. We drive
back down the hill, past the public tennis and volleyball courts,
with Fyodor pointing out the little shop "for sour cream, bread, and
milk and not much more. Three or four years ago, it used to have
everything: five different kinds of vodka, twelve different kinds of
brandy. . . ." We turn left at the bottom of the hill and then go
through open gates into a garden of thinned trees and flowerbeds,
with piles of lumber standing either side of the driveway. The
contrast with Fyodor's house couldn't be greater. The house is wide
and expansive, with a long windowed terrace like the captain's
quarters on an Elizabethan ship. Half of it seems to be new, and the
top storeys are being decorated with new wooden fretwork like a
peasant *izba*'s. Behind the house, near where we park, there's even
a hardtop tennis court with chairs and benches along the side and
a banner advertising a Moscow family tennis tournament stretched
along the back, pinned up on the wire meshing.

Yelena, as usual on these occasions, gets out of the car and walks
straight into the house, ignoring the slowly unravelling piles of dogs
and cats who've been sunning themselves on the steps to the back
door. By the time I catch up with her, she's embracing Nikolai and
Larisa Petrov in the kitchen, and chattering about films and music
and her husband and the new baby. Larisa looks as if she's on her
way out: a handsome, dark-haired woman in her forties, she's
formally dressed, as if got up for an important meeting in Moscow;
while Kolya, bespectacled and smoking a cigarette in an elaborate
filter-holder, is in a T-shirt and a pair of shorts—he looks like her

chubby, impish son, resolutely on holiday. I've seen him not long ago on a British television programme, talking gravely about the predicament of the Soviet Union's Jews, and I've read about him in music reviews in British newspapers—he's said to have a formidable technique and an enormous repertoire. But in person there's not a hint in him either of solemnity or of the virtuoso. He brims over, instead, with a kind of glee, like a boy in the middle of a surprise birthday party, and welcomes us as if we're merely late guests he's been especially looking forward to. He leads us round the house, showing off his gadgets—his TVs, his refrigerators, his telephones, his dishwasher, and his fax machine—with an air of surprise, as if they were presents that had recently appeared out of nowhere. And then, without pausing for breath in his pell-mell, idiosyncratic English, he launches into a plan he has for a meeting with the minister of culture, Nikolai Gubienko, to discuss the fate of Russian intellectuals. I am, apparently, to have a role in this.

Nikolina Gora, he says, is a "real centre for intellectuals." There's Sviatoslav Richter, the pianist, up the road; Sergei Mikhalkov and his film director sons; Lem Karpinsky, the writer; Edik Rodzinsky, the playwright; Yuri Bashmet, the viola player. "There are composers, critics, painters, everything. There are also, of course, some terrible people—the prosecutor Vishinsky got a house here from one of the men he destroyed in the thirties. Then there's Nikolai Baibakov, who was the minister in charge of Gosplan, and the family of the minister of the interior who suicided himself, Shchelokov. But anyhow—what we must have is a meeting with Gubienko immediately, and we can have it here in Nikolina Gora. Because all the intellectuals are leaving: they're being driven out. They're being taxed ridiculous on what they earn abroad, so that by the time they pay their expenses they don't have anything left. The only thing they can do is go abroad all the time just to get ahead. So now we have whole orchestras who don't play here anymore; quartets, the best dancers leaving; musicians—"

"Doctors, mathematicians, physicists," I add. "And, soon enough, geologists," I say, pointing to Fyodor, who's joined us. I tell Kolya about the mathematicians and theoretical physicists from the Soviet Union who are being snapped up by American universi-ties, and the painters who are leaving the country because they can't get studio space or exhibitions here.

"Is a national crisis," says Kolya, before we drain our coffee and are assured by Larisa of the use of the tennis court, the fax, the telephone, the washing machine, "anything." "We will have a meeting here," he booms merrily as he stands up. "You shall tell the West."

10

As Yelena packs—and Tatiana Samoilovna brings down from the cupboards hidden high up in the apartment walls bedding and cutlery, towels and pots and extension cords—I walk down Gorky Street to a massive anti-Party demonstration. It's two days since the end of the Twenty-eighth Congress and the resignation from the Party both of Boris Yeltsin and of Popov and Sobchak, the mayors of Moscow and Leningrad. The Democratic Platform has an-nounced that it now intends to break away from the Communists and found its own party. So there's an air of celebration in the crowd, a collective confidence that now anything may be possible. I see for the first time in Moscow black anarchist flags, even the Monarchist Party's tricolor. There are chants all round me of "Down with the CPSU!"

It's impossible to tell how many people there are in Manege Square, but it seems at first very peaceful: it has a holiday feeling, unlike the demonstration in February, when there were trucks loaded with sand standing in nearby lanes and helmeted policemen in bulletproof vests, carrying riot shields and truncheons, every-where. This time, there has been no prior speech from Prime

Minister Ryshkov warning of agents provocateurs; there's been no rumor-mongering in *Pravda*. Such police as there are seem affable enough; the people are simply out and about in their own streets.

When I arrive, they're still trooping into the square after the long walk from the rallying point in Gorky Park: old and young, some in jeans, some suited and wearing chestfuls of medals, waving banners proclaiming "CPSU to the Dust Heap of History!" and "Fellow Citizens, Let's Cure Russia of Bolshevism!" It should be thrilling, of course. After all, this is a historic moment: the opposi- tion—the people of the Democratic Russia bloc, of Memorial, the Moscow Association of Electors, and the new army union, Shield—are demonstrating their strength right at the edge of Red Square, right under the walls of the Kremlin. But when the speeches start, there's something in me that begins to find it not thrilling at all, but foreign: as if a form I'm used to in the West is being filled here with a kind of aimless, destructive energy that I don't fully understand. The energy doesn't come from the speakers—they spend an unconscionable amount of time jostling and arguing with each other on the podium before they even start. (I think I can see Kashpirovsky, the TV hypnotist, among them.) And when they *do* start, they seem unorchestrated and unfocussed, as if the organizers hadn't bothered to work out either the programme or the purpose of the meeting. Speaker after speaker solemnly announces his resigna- tion from the Party, intoning more or less the same drab litany of complaint against the Twenty-eighth Congress. There are repeated demands for the resignation of the government, the curbing of the KGB, and a new constitution. There are attacks on Gorbachev and endless dark warnings of a right-wing, army-led coup. There are a few lighter moments, it's true—as when the writer Ales Adamo- vich suggests that Lenin's mausoleum be turned into a museum of returned Party cards, and when director Yuri Lyubimov (with that mad seriousness of his) says that the statue of the founder of the

KGB, Felix Dzerzhinsky, should be locked up forever in the Lubyanka and that the whole building should then be painted an uncompromising black. But these few moments only serve to show up the inexperience and self-absorption of most of the speakers and the way in which almost all of them fail to channel or give any direction to the energy of the crowd. At first it's not clear what it is the crowd wants—for a while, it's content simply to celebrate itself and the fact that it's here, at the center of Soviet power. (It applauds, at first, good-naturedly.) But then it becomes bored: it wants an enemy, after all, someone to blame, a scapegoat—not vague denun-ciations. It wants someone to follow, a leader, a direction, an action—not the complicated gestures of liberals in colloquy with their own consciences. So little by little it begins to gear itself up: it responds more and more forcefully to the strident tone, the authori-tarian posture, the grandiloquent threat. Oleg Kalugin, the KGB general who resigned, spoke out, and was then stripped of his medals and privileges by Gorbachev, receives a huge welcome— with no thought at all of what he was doing for all those years at the top of the organization at which he now yells defiance. And a Kuzbas miner gets another enormous ovation when he promises an action he can't possibly deliver: a permanent political strike if the government doesn't resign immediately.

This is not Boris Yeltsin's crowd—the worshipping crowd of working-class men and women who stretched out their hands to him, as if to a god, at the meeting at Luzhniki that I went to a year ago. The people in the square today are largely middle-class, I'd guess: better off, more various, more politically committed. But they're infected, I think, by the same restless need to find simple solutions to the complex legacies of the past: someone to hate and blame and yell out against; someone to admire and love without reserve. They should, after all, be Gorbachev's natural allies, after his freeing of Eastern Europe and his attempts to lop the tentacles off the octopus power of the Soviet Communist Party. But today they bay out against his name whenever it is mentioned. They should be suspicious about the political ambitions of men like Kalugin (who no doubt will now have a fine alternative career as a "people's champion"). But it's enough for them that he's been singled out for punishment by the state and that he now adds his (however compro-mised) voice to the general decrial. Perhaps you can't expect political realism from a mass meeting like this. Perhaps, after years of forced silence, you can't expect anything from voices, once they're freed, but passionate, pent-up resentment. But I find myself remembering, as the speakers come and go, a line from Edmund Burke: "Men must have a certain fund of moderation to qualify themselves for freedom; else it becomes noxious to themselves and a perfect nuisance to everyone else." There is simply no moderation here in the Soviet Union anymore; no longer any centre. The centre (which Gorba-chev and his beleaguered government now hold in the middle of a massive taking of sides) is too difficult, too complicated, too full of compromise. Gorbachev is a general in charge of a retreat: from empire, from ideology, from conviction, from certainties. And here, in this country of gathering certainties on both left and right, he is getting no praise for trying to hold the country together. His name, instead, is slowly becoming anathema: denounced on the one hand for betraying the Communist Party to the forces of chaos, and on the other hand for being simply another Party apparatchik in disguise.

All around these days, above all, is the notion that he is weak. For old habits in Russia and the Soviet Union are a long time dying: people are still nostalgic, however liberal they may seem to Western eyes, for a strong man, a boss, someone who will force the state in some prescribed direction and at the same time enshrine in his person its full power and glory. To Westerners like me, Gorbachev seems as a politician almost astonishingly adroit. But this is not a Western country; it's not a democracy. And the babushkas in the food

queues are not the only ones who think yearningly of the days of
Stalin and Brezhnev, "when there was a strong man in the Kremlin
and at least some food in the shops."

As the speakers in the square drone on, my attention wanders.
And I wonder whether what Fyodor said two days ago about the
Soviet Union being on the brink of a civil war might be true;
whether the country is now in what we used to call in the sixties "a
revolutionary situation." Burke, after all, was writing about the
revolution in France, at a time when, as he put it, "the compromise
that is the basis of all successful politics" had been thrown out the
window in the name of "limitless and illimitable power" claimed
on behalf of "the people." But Russia, I think, has never been a
place of Burke's compromise politics. Now in a sense, for the first
time—with Gorbachev—it's become one. The problem is that "the
people"—like the ones in the square here today—have no real
stomach for it. They want, not manoeuvrings or negotiated consen-
suses, but quick solutions, an overturning of the Revolution, which
can only be achieved, in the end, by government-by-fiat. To be
capable of this sort of government, however, Gorbachev would
have to turn himself into a virtual dictator, by gathering to himself
special executive powers and acting over the heads of the Chamber
of People's Deputies and the Supreme Soviet—which he is now,
in effect, beginning to do. And to make his authority stick, he'd
have to secure the loyalty of the army and the KGB (which are
mostly, perhaps rightly, seen as right-wing forces, the enemy). He's
being forced, in other words, by the demands of the leftists who
should be his allies into a position that's foreign to everything he's
been trying to do, it seems to me. They're pushing him back towards
what he's been trying to escape from: strong central control and the
dead hand of the Party.

I don't know whether this makes what's happening in the
Soviet Union a "revolutionary situation." Perhaps it does—poten-

tially, at any rate. For if Gorbachev is indeed reluctantly pushed back towards dictatorship, and becomes as a result both a half-hearted and a supremely unpopular dictator (as seems likely); and if at the same time the alternative democrats who now rule Moscow and Leningrad are totally unable to solve their cities' problems, and so lose *their* appeal as an alternative to Gorbachev—then the chances are there'll be a real power vacuum. And the stage will be set for a third force to enter the arena: either the army and the KGB in the name of national unity, or else an alliance between the neo-Stalinists on the right wing of the Party and the rabid chauvinists of organiza-tions like Pamyat. I remember suddenly something that Boris Gidas-pov, the Party boss of Leningrad, is supposed to have said in a recent interview: "Do you know what I would do now if I were the Party and the KGB?" he's supposed to have asked. "I would be quiet, go sort of underground. . . . The people, when they get sick and tired of the democrats, will crave a strong hand. For in the final analysis the people don't make any distinction between democracy and authoritarianism. All they want is goods in the shops."

With this thought in mind, I turn away from the gathering, and walk slowly home up Gorky Street. And later, behind Tatiana Samoilovna's elaborate door locks, brought from England, I watch the demonstration on the evening news. The organizers, Yelena tells me, have claimed that there were four hundred thousand people in Manege Square today; but Central Television sniffily puts the figure at a mere fifty thousand. I wonder who will be believed. In this strange city, the truth is immaterial; it's simply dependent on what you want to believe: it depends which side you're on in the battle of rumours and official pronouncements.

I I

A few days later, we begin the move to Nikolina Gora. A few days more, and what seems like half the Moscow apartment is scattered about the three small rooms of the dacha. Yelena busily rearranges the furniture and makes the beds, while Fyodor rigs up a cold-water line to the terrace sink and puts in new electrical points. He brings in a battered old refrigerator from one of the outhouses, and in-troduces us to his mother, Yelena Fyodorovna, a stolid old woman who moves slowly around the house like a ship, and has a gaze as penetrating as its captain's telescope. Katya, meanwhile, sleeps soundlessly outside among the pine trees, in a grand Zil of a pram on loan from Guram and his wife, Yelena.

As we settle into the house, Moscow begins to recede. The days are long and slow; time seems to stand still. I take exploratory walks in the woods behind Prokofiev's house, where there are said to be wild pigs and wolves in winter, and wave small, self-conscious greetings to the people I see wandering in the lanes. I sit on the beach and read Dostoyevsky, and try to make sense of the notes and journals I've kept ever since I first came to the Soviet Union. Yelena is as happy as I've ever seen her. She coos over Katya, and clutches at her, and lies next to her pram in the garden like a lizard in the sun. One night, as Katya bunches her tiny fists and struggles to turn herself over, rocking slowly from side to side, she calls me to watch her and sits there entranced. And when Katya finally, in a concen-trated agony of effort, plops over onto her front on the dining room table, we applaud her as happily as children at the circus.

The three of us spend the first week or so alone together, with Katya sleeping contentedly twelve hours a night, and Yelena and I slowly rediscovering each other after the nervous, high-wire appren-ticeship of birth and new parenthood. (We seem to have been in crowds—of doctors, of family, of friends—for months.) And though for some reason I've been apprehensive about this moment, I realize, as the days come and go, how much I love her: not for some seizeable inner steadiness of grace, but for the bottomless, unfathomable drama of her. She is by (rapid) turns loving and catty, coquettish, stony, and as innocent as a child. There seems to be no gap in her, in other words—no intervening, filtering gauze of (what we call) civilization—between emotion and expression, private and public, inside and outside. Her moods come and go across her face like the weather. She's instinctive and primitive and foxy and cunning. Beside her Chanel makeup on a shelf in the bedroom, she keeps a bottle of holy water against the evil eye; she has books of astrology next to her Russian translations of Rex Stout and Alexandre Dumas. I have no doubt that, after all we have been through together, she finally loves and trusts me; and now that that battle is over, I have no desire at all to change her (the besetting sin-againstitself of love). Instead, I realize happily that I'll never be able to predict her or fully to understand her; and that is enough to keep (whatever it is we call) love alive. ("Give me your poetry," says a lover in a story of Isak Dinesen's. "When you have done with your poetry, *then* you can give me your prose.") I realize too that along the way she has done something for me: she has begun to tear away the carapace of private restraint and reticence that passes for good manners and self-respect in the West; and I am secretly glad. From time to time now we fight, yelling at each other without mercy, indifferent to the other people in the wooden house, wondering what it will lead to, entering some unknown territory of the heart. During one of these rows, she screams: "You didn't want to marry *me*, Jo! You wanted to marry *Russia!*" And then she laughs, as if she's said something funny. Perhaps, I think as I embrace her, it's true.

12

At first I think that her contentedness lies in the fact that we are now a family, that we finally have in Russia, for however short a time, a home of our own: a place she can run and dispose and shop for, without the intervention of Tatiana Samoilovna. But then I begin to realize that it stems, at least in part, from the fact that we're here in Nikolina Gora. The village doesn't look much from the outside: the dachas that I see from the alleys and walkways are for the most part faded and weathered, with irregular fences, overgrown gardens, and outbuildings that jut out of the scrub like abandoned hulks in a shipyard cemetery. But then, when she persuades me to take tennis lessons on the Petrovs' court, I find that my coach, a young Byelorussian, is married to the granddaughter of one of Lenin's comrades, a onetime editor of *Pravda*. And little by little I discover that I am surrounded by Soviet stars and their descendants. On a side road, Yelena stops to introduce me to a hale old man walking in the opposite direction: it is Mikhail Botvinnik, the former chess champion. She points out the houses of the head of the Union of Composers, the family of the aircraft designer Tupolev, the scientist Kapitsa, the mathematician Vinogradov, of writers and dancers and painters and composers. It no longer surprises me, when another old man drops by Fyodor's dacha in the middle of a ramble through the woods, to learn later that it was Andrei Mikhailovich Alexandrov-Agentov, the man whose *blat* got Yelena the apartment on Vorotnikovsky Alley, the Soviet foreign-policy equivalent of Henry Kissinger for a total of twenty-three years.

I learn none of this immediately. For I realize that I am an anomaly here, an unknown, a foreigner; and though I may be Yelena's *laissez-passer* to this place, there is a tacit understanding between us that I mustn't be too pushy or investigative. She has caught wind, too, of the fact that like most Westerners I tend to evaluate (and appreciate) people in terms of what they do, whereas in the Soviet Union this may be a sensitive area or out-of-bounds in some way or beside the point. Often, then, she doesn't so much withhold information about the people we meet as leave me to my own devices to find it out for myself; to allow people to reveal themselves to me as and when they wish. This often has surprising results (I play tennis with a man who turns out to be a playwright I've long wanted to meet), but I soon see the point. One night over dinner at the Petrovs' house, one of the confusing (to me) mass of Sachas and Seriozhas and Nikolais and Natashas leans across to me and says suddenly: "You know, I work in the space programme and I'm breaking the law—I'm not allowed even to be in the same house as a foreigner."

We spend many evenings at the Petrovs' house, which seems always open; the front gates are never closed. The tennis court, before the light fades, bustles with an assortment of pickup foursomes, often dominated by the huge bulk and steely right wrist of Kolya. (He rarely moves; he swats at the ball—the racket looks like a tiny impertinence in his enormous hand.) And afterwards, there seems always to be food and drink for all comers, produced without the slightest semblance of effort by the carefully coiffed and immaculately dressed Larisa.

At the long table on the terrace, the talk is more or less always about politics. Kolya trumpets his disgust for the whole business. "Whatever happens, is same old Communist horseshit! Gorbachev make pretty little cosmetic changes for the West, but we live with exactly the same shit as always. You know the old joke? A man comes out from his apartment building in the morning, and it's raining. He look up and says: 'God! See? They do whatever they want!' The next day, when he gets up, there's enormous rainbow in the sky. He says: 'God! And they can even afford *that!*' It's same story now. They still run things. They'll never give up power. They've just changed the weather a little."

Kolya, I later learn from Yelena, was for five years denied the right to travel and play abroad, despite medals in the Van Cliburn and Queen Elisabeth competitions; and he is still filled with contemptuous resentment. "Five best years of my life!" he bellows. "They simply take them away, destroy them!" The reason was simple. When his friend the conductor Rozhdestvensky was told to "Russianize" the State Symphony Orchestra—i.e., to remove the preponderance of Jews—Rozhdestvensky said no and promptly resigned. Kolya took his part: he refused from then on to play for Rozhdestvensky's more malleable successor. And for this, he was outlawed, cast into oblivion. Whenever a Western impresario asked for him, the state concert organization, Goskontsert, would simply announce: "Petrov is busy. He is not available."

Kolya, then, has set his face against any politician who benefited, even remotely, from the system which blighted his own career. "You lie down in the shit," he says in his idiosyncratic English, "and you don't stand up smelling with roses, like they say now." Yeltsin he thinks is a fraud—"Who pulled down house in Sverdlovsk where tsar's family was murdered?" he says. "He was just errand boy for the big bosses, doing whatever he was told. You believe him now when he say he is just ordinary person, he never travel in big Zil again?" Gorbachev, too, he has little time for. "He is just trying to save the Bolsheviks' asses." Kolya is a natural anarchist. But buried in his attitude to Gorbachev, I think, is a certain snobbery. Moscow's intelligentsia, I've noticed, tends to look down on Gorbachev much as Washington society once looked down on Jimmy Carter: as a rube, an outsider, however educated a man he may be. His southern accent, his mispronunciation and misstressing of words, his longwindedness and circumlocutions—all the things that never appear in English translations—make him fair game.

The rest of the people who come and go at the Petrovs' table seem about equally divided between Gorbachev and Yeltsin, though the women—Yelena and Larisa among them—are almost all staunch Gorbachevites. (It's as if they have a better instinct for the complicated political manoeuvring that Gorbachev's had to do to survive. The men are usually more urgent and extreme: bossier.) But everyone seems mystified by the two men's plain antipathy for one another. "I don't understand at all," says Larisa one night. "Every-one knows, now that Russia has been declared a sovereign state, that one can't survive without the other. If Gorbachev goes, then Yeltsin will go down. If Yeltsin is removed, then Gorbachev will sink. Why don't they come to terms?" I say: "Because Yeltsin can't afford to. He's the people's champion; he's 'us.' Once he comes to terms with Gorbachev, he'll be finished: he'll be one of 'them' again." One night on television, the two leaders do appear together; they announce that they are willing to work together for the good of the country. But Gorbachev looks wary, and Yeltsin looks as if he has just swallowed unpleasant medicine; he has the secretly defiant air of a small boy ordered by a teacher to shake hands with his worst enemy. I wonder suddenly if what one of the Petrovs' guests told me a few evenings before might be true. He was a cadaverous man called Sacha; and he drew me aside after dinner as if he had a great secret to tell. "What you say about Yeltsin is interesting," he said. "But there is a simple reason why they will never come to terms. When Yeltsin was thrown in the river at the bottom of Nikolina Gora, he said that unknown enemies, political enemies, had done it. Then later there were rumors that it was the lover of one of his mistresses: maybe some KGB people were involved. None of this is true. What happened was that it was Prime Minister Ryshkov's birthday; he had a dacha not far from here. And Yeltsin was staying at his dacha at Arkhangelskoye. He decided to go over to Ryshkov's dacha to make peace with him, take him a peace offering—that's why he was carrying a bunch of flowers. Well, there was a party going on there, a lot of drinking. Yeltsin got through all the outer guards; he got as far as the front door. But when the front door guards came to Ryshkov and said that Yeltsin was outside, unin⁄ vited, he told them to throw him off the property, give him a cold bath, throw him in the river. It's said that Gorbachev was at the party, that he was part of it. It's said too that Ryshkov and the others threatened Yeltsin; they said that his family would be hurt if he ever told anyone about what had happened. So now," he said, shrugging his shoulders, "it's war between them, on Yeltsin's part at any rate: war to the end."

I don't know how to react. Is this just a rumour? Or does he actually know? It's impossible to tell. In the absence of any solid political news, Moscow and Nikolina Gora are full of rumours— the people's alternative news broadcasts, as I begin to call them. Tatiana Samoilovna, when she comes at weekends, is a rich source. She asks me whether it's true, for example, as they are saying in the courtyards, that there are two huge rooms in the Soviet embassy in London entirely filled with copies of the book Gorbachev published in the West, bought up with hard currency to keep it in the best⁄seller lists; and if I know whether Gorbachev is building a palace, filled with gold and precious stones, on the Black Sea. This palace—from which Gorbachev is said to commute to Moscow daily on a plane that can make the trip in forty⁄five minutes—has, she says, a private bay big enough to accommodate five ships, including a submarine. If anything goes wrong with the Soviet Union—if there's a right⁄wing putsch or a popular uprising—he's supposed to have a secret deal with President Bush by which he'll be snatched up and taken underwater to Turkey.

I ask her what else is being said about Gorbachev. "That he made millions of dollars selling off Eastern Europe to the Ameri⁄ cans," she says. "And that whatever he does, we have to keep him."

"Why?"

"Because the Bible says that the last kingdom of the earth will be ruled by a man called Mikhail, with the mark of the beast on his forehead. After him comes Armageddon."

13

Apocalypse. It's in the air everywhere this summer. There's talk of horrible diseases creeping across the country and of a green slime growing on the walls of the underground of some Far Eastern city that can kill you faster than Lassa fever. UFOs are being constantly sighted now in the area around Voronezh, while in Moscow there's diphtheria, and a pair of serial killers painstakingly stalking female victims. Monarchist flags are waving in the streets; cigarettes are being rationed. There are riots and constant rumours of pogroms. Spokesmen for Pamyat have announced that Nicholas II was killed in a Jewish ritual sacrifice; that Zionists caused the Revolution, starvation in the Ukraine, and the Second World War—not to mention Chernobyl. (Jews were warned to get away from the reactors by a pentagram published in local newspapers.) Membership in Pamyat is now said to cost the names and addresses of at least five Jews; mysterious chalk marks are supposed to have started appearing in downtown apartment buildings; a cooperative is making a fortune selling reinforced steel doors. Tatiana Samoilovna stays home on the days set for the pogroms—which never eventualize— and tells me about a new faith healer offering his services to the nation. A documentary on him has arrived at her film laboratory, and he has already been by, she says, to offer the graders a laying-on of hands. One day, in one of the lanes, I meet the wife of the Soviet Kissinger. "It's a very bad day today," she says in English, as she hobbles into view. "*Izvestia* says so."

As the rains come, day after day now, even Fyodor, my

Nikolina Gora landlord, seems touched with this millennarian gloom. When I drive with him into the city, he talks again about the prospects for civil war—and about the water supply in Moscow, which is said to carry all kinds of diseases, including some new form of water-borne AIDS. He tells me that the vegetables and fruit in all the markets contain stratospheric levels of nitrates, and advises me to stay away from the free market near the Kiev station, where the produce is supposed to come directly from around Chernobyl. He suggests that when I next travel to London I should buy a Geiger counter and a nitrate detector, for secure shopping.

Some time in the middle of all this, Yelena and I see the hot film of the year: Stanislav Govorukhin's *We Can't Go On Living Like This*. It makes depressing viewing. Murder, rape, alcoholism, rotting corpses, and complaints from underpaid policemen are intercut with pictures of dogs being trained to attack and kill. It's a documentary bill of attainder against the Revolution and the Communist Party: for genocide, corruption, and the destruction both of Russian culture and of the entire economy. It rails at the constant humiliations of everyday life; it compares the Communist Party to psychopaths. "Society is immoral," Govorukhin says in his commentary. "There's no law, no morality, and it deserves to drown in crime. . . . It doesn't matter who you ask: anyone who isn't a total idiot will tell you the same thing. Tomorrow will only be worse, not better." His film is making a fortune at the city's box offices.

In the papers, meanwhile, I read strange and astonishing things. An Interregional Association of Astrologists is being set up, its name an echo of the democratic alliance in Parliament. An Academy of Astrology is to be formed at the Higher Party School, as well as a devil's fan club at the House of Culture of the Moscow Aviation Institute. For twenty dollars a ticket, I read, you can watch soft porn movies in the apartment of a KGB general on Kutuzovsky Prospekt.

14

In the middle of August, news comes from Artyom that Viktor Tsoy, the lead singer of Kino, has died in a car crash. In the two years since I first saw him in *Assa,* he's become the country's leading youth-cult figure, taking Boris's place. "It's over," says Ksiyusha (who's now staying with us) when I tell her. "Rock music is over. Perhaps all it needed was a death to tell us." There's a wake for Tsoy, with candles, on the beach below us. But the finals of the volleyball competition, held on the court by the cooperative's little meeting hall, take place on time.

Later, when she goes back to university in September, Father Alexander Men, Solzhenitsyn's priest and friend, is killed by an axeman on his way to his little church outside Moscow. Ksiyusha and I walk in the lanes one Sunday. She says: "You remember what I said about Viktor Tsoy's death? It's strange, but it was true. At university, everything's changed. My friends have stopped wearing black. The whole rock-and-roll style has disappeared. It's as if the outside world no longer has anything to do with them. They've become very private."

"But they always were," I say. "It's one of the things that's always surprised me. Last year and this year, for example, in the East—in Prague and Warsaw, in Berlin and Budapest, even in Kiev—the students were out on the streets. . . ."

"Yes, but it's easier for them. They have someone to hate."

"Who?"

"Us. Russians."

"Maybe," I say. "But look, astonishing things are happening here. There are debates about what the country should be called."

She shrugs her shoulders. "Marlboro Country," she says.

"There's Solzhenitsyn's manifesto being published in *Kom-*

somolskaya Pravda. There are plans to turn the country into a market economy in five hundred days. There's the first church service at the Cathedral of the Assumption. There's Father Men's death. There are demonstrations—"

"And never any young people at any of them. Yes, Jo, I know, I know."

"Why?"

"Oh, it's so hard to explain. Look," she says, stopping. "Who are we supposed to demonstrate *against?* Our parents? Ourselves? My generation has had to face the problem of this country's history at the level of our own families. And yet at the same time we're living after the Flood: everything we were told to believe in has been de-stroyed—our whole civilization has been destroyed—and nothing has come to take its place. We're standing on the ruins; and we're not interested in revolutions, because we know from our own experi-ence that they bring nothing but suffering and disaster. We're not interested in improving state organizations, because we already know that they're the enemy. All we want to do is to have a private life for the first time; to be independent, to be free to think and love and care for our friends—all the things that our parents weren't allowed."

"You want a holiday from reality."

"Yes. Everyone tries to find his own way out, his own form of holiday. But all the people I talk to have the same attitude: they don't want anything to do with the state. They're not interested in social success or a career. We're the first generation, I suppose, to be able to declare our unwillingness to conform openly and without embarrassment. Our parents didn't have any choice."

"It all sounds pretty self-absorbed," I say.

"Yes!" Ksiyusha says fiercely. "But what *else* is there?"

"And not very healthy."

"Of *course* it isn't! That's *exactly* what I'm trying to tell you, Jo.

People like me have been trapped by the past—we've been crippled by it—and the only thing we can do is find a private way of escaping. My friend Polina escapes to the Middle Ages—her credo is 'What a lovely man Henry VIII was' or something like that. Another girl told me: 'Nineteen thirty-seven? Oh, that doesn't bother me. They all died—I didn't know them, so why should *I* suffer?' Half her family was destroyed in the thirties. 'The people I love: *they're* the important thing.' Some escape through whatever entertainment they can find—which isn't much. Some go through terrible depressions trying to escape into God. Some use drugs or drink vodka—most working-class kids drink vodka. Some think about suicide or invent new religions, building whole worlds out of words. And then there's crime, Jo. The percentage of crimes among the young, even among children, is incredibly high."

"And you think that's all part of the same thing?"

"Yes. Looking for a holiday."

As we walk on, I think of a poll I've heard about, taken at a technical high school in Moscow recently. When asked what they wanted to become when they left school, a majority of the boys said they wanted to become black-market entrepreneurs; over half the girls said hard-currency hookers. Is *that* looking for a holiday, as Ksiyusha says? Or isn't it just one more sign that the West and its money are now taking over?

15

At the end of the year, two months after we've decamped from Nikolina Gora—promising the increasingly pessimistic Fyodor that we'll be back in the spring—Yelena, Katya, and I take Tatiana Samoilovna to England. It is her first trip to the West in almost forty years. In Moscow, Gorbachev has announced direct presidential rule, and Foreign Minister Shevardnadze has resigned, tense and red-faced, bellowing out a warning of dictatorship to come. The harvest has been a disaster. The nine agricultural regions of the country have simultaneously stopped delivery of all dairy products to the city. So there's no milk, no cheese—and virtually no meat—anywhere to be found. In the Oxfordshire cottage where my mother lived until she died in May, I find Tatiana Samoilovna on the first day standing at the living room window, looking out at the little butcher's shop opposite, amazed, almost in tears, at the food on display, the absence of any queue. Later she learns her own form of communication with Malcolm, the butcher. She walks across the street, and while Malcolm, staggering, holds up a whole side of meat, she laughingly stabs a finger at whatever it is that she wants. It is, I think as I watch her sometimes from the window across the road, the high point of her day.

Before Christmas, we go to London to stay in my apartment. Tatiana Samoilovna has money of her own: two hundred pounds—all the hard currency a Soviet citizen is allowed to take out of the country each year. And Yelena, Katya, and she walk to the shops daily to work out how to spend it. But I go out little. I hate the advertisements, the noise, the fake jollity, and the richness of London. I realize that I have more friends in the Soviet Union than I do now in England. So I work on a film script for the BBC about an Englishman caught up in a coup in Russia; and when people ask me where I am living these days, I say: "Moscow, Moscow." When we go back to the Soviet Union in the New Year, her friends at the laboratory take one look at Tatiana Samoilovna in her new Western finery and start to call her Margaret Thatcher. One night, Martin Walker, back on a visit from his new post in Washington, offers me in a restaurant, holding up a glass, "the first annual Martin Walker Award, for the most obsessed foreigner in the city." I—just like Tatiana Samoilovna, I think—feel ridiculously proud. I have at least, as Tomas once said of Martin, begun to try to understand.

Chapter 9

August–December 1991

Turkey, the Sublime Porte, the Great Divan, the Padishah: Ivan Peresvetov to Ivan the Terrible: "Should [Russians] but combine that Turkish rule with the Christian faith, and the very angels would descend amongst them"; Catherine the Great giving away a million serfs to her favourites; Stalin and the janissaries of the Communist Party; equality without freedom; the cheapness of human life; the crescent and the sickle.

Constantinople, the Second Rome, Caesar (tsar), the Lord's anointed, the Vicar of Christ; Joseph of Volok to Ivan III: "In his mortal form [the tsar] resembles all men; but in his power he is like unto Almighty God"; Russia as the last repository of the only true form of Christianity; the iconoclasm and heresy-hunting of the Bolsheviks; empire as crusade; the hammer and the cross.

Secret police: Oprichniki, Office of the Sovereign's Word and Deed, Third Section of the Imperial Chancellery, Special Board, Okhrana, KGB. Ivan the Terrible to Prince Kurbsky: "The rule of a tsar. . . . calls for fear and . . . bridling and extreme oppression." Peter Verkhovensky in Dostoyevsky's *The Possessed:* "Every member of society spies on the others, and it's his duty to inform against them. Everyone belongs to all and all to everyone." Products of the

tsarist secret police: workers' unions, terrorist organizations, pogroms, the Protocols of the Elders of Zion, Bloody Sunday, the
assassination of the minister of the interior and Grand Duke Sergei
Alexandrovich. Products of the Cheka and its children: murder,
assassination, concentration camps, surveillance of the whole society,
coups d'état. "Work well and you too will be buried in a wooden
coffin." Among the thousands of people bugged by the KGB in
1991: Gorbachev and Yeltsin's wife's hairdresser. Number of KGB
agents needed to cover an open-air conversation between Alexander
Yakovlev and General Kalugin: seventy-two.

2

On the morning of August 19, we were in the old dacha in
Nikolina Gora. I was reading and Yelena was beginning to stir in
her bed. In the next room Tatiana Samoilovna turned on the radio.
(Ksiyusha was in England.) She gave a little screech. "Jo, Yelena,
come here quickly," she said. "Something's happened."

Yelena scrambled up. We went into the little dining room
where Tatiana Samoilovna slept. We listened to a sonorous male
voice reading a statement. Yelena began to cry. "Oh, no," she said.
"No!"

". . . due to the president's indisposition . . ."

"What have they done? Oh, my God!"

". . . a committee of national salvation . . ."

"What have they *done?*"

Tatiana Samoilovna turned on the television. There was nothing except a performance of *Swan Lake*. We listened some more to
the radio. "Our country is under threat of extinction. . . . Abroad
our Soviet people are facing humiliation. . . . Our economy is near
collapse."

Tatiana Samoilovna began to move around the room, wringing her hands nervously, compulsively tidying. "I don't know, I don't know," she said, almost under her breath. "Things have been very bad. Perhaps it's for the best."

Katya tottered into the room, attracted by the noise. Yelena clutched at her. "Mama, how can you say that?" Yelena screamed. "It's a *coup!* They'll intern foreigners. They'll close the borders. What will we do?"

"We'll wait," I said.

I went down the corridor to Fyodor's kitchen. He was sitting at the round table, his head in his hands. His mother, Yelena Fyodorovna, was standing behind him, holding a saucepan, her mouth open. The radio was on.

He looked up as I came in. "They've taken their country back," he said. "It's finished."

"Who has?"

"The army and the KGB. Yanayev and Kryuchkov. What does it matter? It was bound to happen sooner or later."

"We have to try and get into the city," I said. I was due to leave the next day for the Edinburgh Festival, to chair a discussion on Soviet television. Fyodor was supposed to drive us in.

"Moscow will be closed," he said. "They'll put tanks on the roads, stop everyone who tries to get there, arrest them."

"Then at least we have to find out what's going on. Do you know if the telephones are working?"

"No."

"Then why don't you go to the Simashkos' and find out. I'll walk across to Sacha [Alexander] Lipnitky's."

Sacha was out when Yelena and I got there. His wife Ina said he'd gone to church, to pray.

"Is the telephone working?"

"Yes," she said. "People have been calling. We've heard there are tanks round Red Square, and the television building's been occupied."

I picked up the phone. I tried to call Kolya Petrov down the road; Artyom, Tomas, Guram, anyone. Their lines were all busy—Moscow's bush telegraph was working overtime. I finally got through to an English television executive I knew who had an office in the city. I could hear the sound of crying in the background.

"What's happening there?"

"Nobody seems to know. There are tanks on the Garden Ring and round the Kremlin. Someone's just told me that people are arguing with the tank drivers, telling them to leave."

"Are the international telephone lines working?"

"Yes. I can't believe it. Why? What on earth are they thinking of?"

"And Yeltsin, Yakovlev, Shevardnadze—what's happened to them? Have they been arrested?"

"Beats me. Are you going to try and get in?"

"Yes."

When we got back to his dacha, Fyodor had more news. "I called my friends," he said. "They say there are tanks on Kutuzovsky Prospekt—they're turning back traffic coming in to the city. There've been shootings. There are fires all over Moscow, they say."

"Have they *seen* them?"

He shrugged his shoulders. "I don't know."

"So what about making a run for the city?"

"Jo," he said, "you don't understand. This is the Soviet Union. It's not a game. They're going to take the country back to Brezhnev's times. Arrests, camps, everything like it was. There aren't enough dollars in the world to get me to go to Moscow."

"Let's go and see Nikita Mikhalkov," Yelena said, "and ask him what he thinks we should do."

We walked with Katya across the road to the Mikhalkovs' compound, with Yelena clinging to me. Nikita, wearing a kimono, was on the phone in one of the houses, trying to get through to Russian Prime Minister Ivan Silayev, to whom he was an advisor.

He gestured us inside. I heard later that his brother, Andrei Kon-chalovsky, when he'd heard the news of the coup, had made immediately for Sheremetyevo Airport. "I have a family in the West to think of," he'd said. Nikita had stayed home.

We sat on a sofa opposite him as he talked and waited, then dialled and redialled. His daughters, who were very quiet and well-behaved, came to take Katya into the garden to play. Then he finally hung up.

"What's happening?" I said.

"I don't know exactly," he said, turning. "But Yeltsin doesn't seem to have been arrested. As far as I can find out, he's driven in from his dacha, and he's now in the Russian Government Building, holding as much of a parliamentary session as he can. He's issued some kind of proclamation, which they're going to take to the streets."

"Perhaps they want to make a deal with him," I said. "A coalition of some kind."

"What about Gorbachev?" interrupted Yelena. "Where *is* he? What's happened?"

"He's supposed to be at his dacha in the Crimea. But no one can get through. He must be under arrest."

"Then why not Yeltsin? It doesn't make any sense."

"Who said that the Communists had to make sense?"

I told Mikhalkov what Fyodor had reported about the ap-proaches to the city, and asked him whether he was going to try to make it in to Moscow that day. "Yes, probably," he said. "But first I have to go to Arkhangelskoye: they're holding a meeting of some kind."

"That's no good," said Yelena, crying. "We have to decide whether to leave the country tomorrow or not. And if we do leave, then I have to pick up my ticket today."

We walked through the garden together, then waved goodbye

at the gate. We went down the hill, past the tennis court, towards the Petrovs' house. "Do you think we should go?" I said, pushing Katya's pram.

"We have to, Jo," Yelena said fiercely. "Ksiyusha's in London, and there's Katya to think of. If we don't go tomorrow, we may never be able to get out. She has to come with us."

At the Petrovs', three of four of their *dachniki* friends were in the dining room with Kolya, gathered round the telephone and a radio. Kolya was trying to tune in the BBC World Service. "Welcome to old-style Soviet Union!" he said, waving cheerily. "These bastards! Who they think they are, for Christ's sake? Yanayev is simply foolish drunk. He was head of Komsomol; he spent all his time drinking himself stupid and fondling the behinds of all the girls! As for the others, they have penis for brain! Here," he said, leaning over the radio, getting the signal. "Here."

"You mean they haven't jammed foreign broadcasts?" I said, as the voice of a BBC announcer came crackling through.

"No. I am telling you. They are schmucks. CNN is even still broadcasting in the city. Here." He picked up a piece of paper. "Listen. They are reading this on the BBC now."

I looked at it. It was a copy of Yeltsin's proclamation, calling the action of the so-called Committee of National Salvation an illegal and anticonstitutional coup d'état.

"How on earth did you get this?" I said.

"On my fax machine," he said. "All faxes in the Russian Government Building do nothing but send it out. It is now all over the world. 'Come here to the White House to defend democracy.' Yeltsin says this apparently on CNN."

While we talked and the others listened to the radio, Yelena huddled in a corner with Larisa. "I understand," said Larisa. "Of course, of course."

"What 'of course'?" I said, going over.

"Larisa says we can take one of their cars."

"Yes, but who'll drive us?"

"I'll call the *militsia* man, Seriozha," Larisa said, standing.

An hour later, Seriozha arrived at Fyodor's dacha: neat, mous-tached, in a windcheater, smiling. "We'll see how far we can get," he said, gunning the engine of the Petrovs' Moskvich.

Fyodor helped us carry our bags. "Good luck," he said. I asked him if he needed anything: money, perhaps. "No," he said. "Money can't do anything now," he added bleakly. "Except maybe for you."

We drove down the hill through the eerily empty village, then out over the bridge where Yeltsin was supposed to have been thrown into the water. Straight on was Arkhangelskoye, where the Russian government dachas were, and where Yeltsin's aides, I heard later, had broken into an empty house that morning for a typewriter to write up the proclamation that was being broadcast; to the left, in Buzayevo, were Politburo houses, then the dacha that Khrushchev, then Andropov, then Ryshkov had had. Slowly they unfolded on either side of the road as we travelled into the city—all those lanes with No Entry signs, all those dachas and meeting places, all that Soviet history: Stalin's dacha, then Mikoyan's, which had passed to Alexander Yakovlev; New Ogaryevo, where the new Union Treaty, which the coup was presumably designed to quash, had recently been hammered out; old Ogaryevo, which had belonged to Grand Duke Sergei as the governor of Moscow and then to Khrushchev; Pugo's dacha; Gorbachev's dacha. Whatever was happening today in Moscow, I thought, had its roots deep in this road, had even perhaps been planned along it, with the KGB listening in, goading it forward.

Seriozha stopped once, near Gorbachev's dacha, to talk to a group of *militsia* men. "They don't know any more than we do," he said when he came back. "But I think we'd better avoid Kutuzovsky Prospekt. Let's see if we can get into the city from the north."

We turned left, then, on the Outer Ring Road, and then drove into Moscow down Prospekt Mira, past the Exhibition of Economic Achievements and the Kosmos Hotel. We didn't see a single soldier or a single tank along the way. The journey took precisely what it would have on any other ordinary day. Nothing, in fact, seemed out of the ordinary, as we craned through the windows. The Rishky Market was crowded with the usual shoppers. There was the usual long line at McDonald's on Pushkin Square. "It's weird," I said to Yelena. "It's as if nothing's happened at all."

We dropped Katya and Tatiana Samoilovna off at the Vorot-nikovsky Alley apartment, and then went to see Tomas at his office in the Union Film Service Building. He was watching CNN in a packed side room. There were pictures of people arguing with tank crews, and then of Yeltsin clambering onto a tank outside the White House. Everybody was talking at once: speculating, drowning out the commentary. I pulled Tomas out into the corridor.

"What the hell's happening?" I said.

"Yeltsin's issued a ukase. He wants a defence force outside the White House. He also demands to talk to Gorbachev: he wants proof that he's really ill."

"Why haven't they arrested him, for Christ's sake?"

"I don't know. But soon they will have to go and get him. You know, Jo, the West should never have sent Gorbachev back from the G-7 meeting with empty hands. Now they say more tanks are coming into the city. Paratroopers, Spetsnats, OMON, I don't know."

"Is there *any* kind of opposition?"

"Only some businessmen, I think. I hear they have taken food and money, drink, girls, I don't know, to try to get the tanks to turn back."

"I'm supposed to leave tomorrow for Edinburgh, Tomas."

"I know."

"Should I go?"

"Jo, you are not a bachelor anymore. You have family. If the airport is open and you have tickets, then you must go."

"And Katya? We were only supposed to go for five or six days. Should we take her with us?"

"Jo, I am her godfather. I don't know what will happen. I say yes, you have to."

I picked up Yelena from a conclave of some of her old women-friends in the building. They were in a huddle on one of the landings, clutching at each other, some of them crying. "All right," I said to her. "I'm going to take you home, and then I'm going to have a look round the city."

"No, Jo," she said. "First we have to pick up my air ticket from Aeroflot. It's there. It's waiting. We have to go."

Aeroflot was the other side of Moscow. To get there and back, we had to circle the whole city on the Garden Ring—so I got my tour. The first tanks we saw were waiting for a traffic light to change. But after that there were many more—and they were more menacing, parked in side streets, their cannon pointing out onto the highway, or else gathered in knots outside the Foreign Ministry, the Armoury, the Press Club. The Aeroflot office, when we got there, was packed with people, waving money and documents. But Yelena, as usual, just walked to the head of the line and handed over the usual shopping bag full of Scotch or perfume to someone she knew. After a few minutes, she turned back to me, standing on tiptoe, looking over the heads of the crowd. "It's all right, Jo," she shouted. "They're still flying."

After that, we drove back to Guram's apartment on Alexei Tolstoy Street. "I'll only go back alone to Vorotnikovsky Alley if I know you're with somebody," Yelena said. This suited me well enough, for I knew that two members of the Committee of National

Salvation lived in Guram's *nomenklatura* building—Pavlov and Baklanov—and I was curious to see what kind of security they'd put on their front door.

The answer was, virtually none. There was just one nervous KGB man loitering by the steps: in a blue windbreaker, not much more than a boy. Apart from the concierge, there was no one at all in the lobby. "What are they thinking of?" I said to Guram, who was standing on the balcony of his apartment with a pair of binoculars. "They're taking over a sixth of the earth's surface. It's as if they don't expect anyone to notice."

"Well, you think they're noticing?"

"Not much."

"Let's go and see."

We went downstairs, then walked up to the Garden Ring, just in time to see tanks disappearing down Kachalev Street. "The radio building," Guram said. "Let's follow them." When we got there, the tanks were lining up in front, with one guarding their rear, backed into a side street. Some of the tank drivers got out and lit cigarettes, their goggles pushed back over their foreheads, submachine guns slung over their shoulders. A TV cameraman ran down the street and began filming them. One of the drivers waved and shouted out a message to his mother. Another was berated by a finger-wagging old woman, who stood in the street below him. "What do you think you're doing here?" she shouted. "Do you mean to kill your own people?"

"Ask the bosses," he said, shrugging.

"It's all right, babushka," said an officer. "We'll just be here for a day or two. Now get along home."

We walked back to the Garden Ring—through crowds of pedestrians who seemed to think that the presence of tanks in their street was the most ordinary thing in the world—then crossed in the direction of the White House. At the Metro station near the Ukraina Hotel, a large crowd was gathered around a copy of Yeltsin's proclamation. People were arguing with each other in knots, gesturing. "Anything's better than Gorbachev—anything!" said one man. "What about democracy?" "Can you *eat* democracy, comrade?" There was no sign of any soldiers.

I said: "It's as if this coup's been taken from some old 1930s textbook: Arrest the president; take the radio station, the post and telegraph offices, and the press club; and then put up a notice: 'We have a new president; everything will be back to normal in a few days' time.'"

"Maybe it's enough," said Guram.

Below the White House, there were trams abandoned at the side of the road and a few makeshift barricades, across which people were clambering, carrying briefcases and "perhaps bags," on their way back from offices and shops. We climbed the steps to where a crowd was listening to a speech by Vice-President Rutskoi from the balcony above. Beside him were assorted dignitaries, looking uncomfortable. Next to him was a man carrying a loudspeaker, pointing it downward. There were scattered shouts of "Yeltsin! Yeltsin!" from the crowd. It was not a rousing speech. The crowd bled at the edges. There were as many people going as coming.

"There aren't enough people here," I said, looking around. "Maybe a thousand, maybe two."

"Yes," said Guram. "And it looks like most of them have just come to take a look, to see what's happening."

There was the sound of another speech being made at the other end of the building, an echo of applause. So we went round the side, where ten or eleven men and women, grim-faced, were pulling up pieces of fencing and scaffolding and piling up saplings and sheets of insulation material against one of the entrances.

"Jesus," I said, "and they're up against tanks! How long do you think it would take the army to secure this place?"

"About ten minutes," Guram said. "Unless there were fifty thousand people standing in the way."

At the other end of the building, there was more of the same: an uninspired speech about the defence of democracy; a huge space filled with not enough people; and more leaving than arriving.

We stayed for an hour, peering into faces to see if there was anyone we knew, and then trudged back through a thin rain to Vorotnikovsky Alley to see what might be on the evening news.

"What's it like out there?" said Yelena as we came in.

"Depressing," said Guram.

After we arrived, the phone began to ring. There were calls from England, Germany, and America. The people on the other end were insanely cheerful. How were we? Wasn't it amazing that they could get through? What was the mood in Moscow like?

"I don't know. You tell *me*," I said.

"They're running it virtually live on all channels here," said one friend. "They reckon the coup must have started at short notice. More troops are on their way. They're likely to go in and get Yeltsin tonight."

"Thanks for the tip," I said.

"Maggie Thatcher's condemned the coup, and says she hopes the Soviet people will fight it," said another.

"Oh well, that's a comfort," I said.

"Are you going to leave if you can?" asked my brother Richard.

"Everyone keeps telling me I have to. I have no press credentials. I have a fixed-flight ticket."

"How do you feel?"

"Isn't that what they always ask accident victims? Shell-shocked, like everyone else, I suppose. I didn't realize what a stake I have in this place. Depressed."

But the evening news, when it finally came on, was anything but depressing. What it was was immensely puzzling. There was a

report from the White House, made earlier in the day, which—
impossibly—began with the reporter saying, "Well, they'll never
show this, but I might as well do it anyway," and which went on
to show everything we'd seen or heard about: Yeltsin atop a tank,
his defiant proclamation, people building barricades. (I later heard
the reporter was advised that night to take an immediate holiday by
his stunned colleagues in the newsroom.) And then came the press
conference, in which the Committee of National Salvation met the
world's press. ("Who did you get this idea from? General Pinochet
in Chile?") They were an extraordinary-looking set of men: surprised and slightly shifty, like a group of schoolyard bullies caught
out on a binge and now up in front of a board of prefects. Whatever
they said, however hard they groped towards the right dignified
note, all one could see was Acting President Yanayev's hands
shaking, shaking, as if they belonged to somebody else. After he'd
fielded the final question, another friend called me from London to
congratulate me, as if the Soviet Union had finally produced something truly comic. I reminded him that Stalin had webbed fingers,
and Hitler a very silly moustache. I reminded him too that the Soviet
Union was a very big and powerful place, and that the members of
the Committee of National Salvation hadn't got where they were by
playing footsie with each other under the table.

3

The next morning, early, I walked down again to the White House.
Nothing had happened in the night, though there'd been false
alarms, the sound of tanks nearby, sudden panics, I was told. There
was talk, too, of tanks having changed sides, though I didn't see
any. All I saw, again, was not enough people—though a lot of the
people I did see were young, which was vaguely encouraging.

I went back and called all the television people who were
supposed to be appearing on the Edinburgh Festival panel with me.

I could only reach one of them, who said that yes, he'd be on the afternoon Aeroflot plane with Yelena, as planned. (I had a fixed flight ticket with British Airways.) Then I called Artyom.

"Hi, Jo," he said. "I've just come back to change my clothes. You should be at the White House. It's real *tusovka"*—the place to be; what's happening. "Most of the people I know are there."

"I can't," I said. "I have to get the plane back to London today. I have to go to Edinburgh."

"Well," he said, "I don't think you're going to get anybody to go with you. Bella Kurkova was making a big fiery speech at the White House last night, and the last thing I heard, Volodya Molchanov was planning a demonstration along Tverskaya Street. They've got other things on their minds, Jo."

"What about you? Would *you* come?" He'd recently been made head of music at the new Russian Television.

"No, Jo. Come *on!"*

In the afternoon, after packing, Yelena and I took Katya to the airport and bought her an infant's ticket. I queued for my British Airways flight behind some English businessmen who talked about what was happening in the city as if it was some kind of bizarre entertainment. They were impressed, I remember, with how cheap the local prostitutes were.

Just before my plane was called, I telephoned Tomas. "Some tanks have gone over to the Russian side," he said. "CNN is in the White House, and an independent radio station, Radio Echo, is on the air, telling people to go there. They say the taxi drivers are spreading the word."

"Will you go?"

"Yes. Everyone I know is going. Maybe if there are enough people, the tanks won't come."

"Good luck," I said, before hanging up. "I'm sorry I'm not with you."

On the plane, I sat next to a Brazilian woman who had been

attending a congress of "compatriots in emigration." She had left Russia at the age of two and had never been back. She'd been to a beautiful church service in the Kremlin, but then she'd woken up in the morning to reality, to tanks. She'd bought a seat on the first plane available: she was terrified; she'd never, ever go back, she said.

At London's Heathrow Airport, I was met by a friend—and by a crew from the BBC: I was to give my impressions for breakfast television. I said that people in the West knew a lot more about what was going on than most Muscovites did; and that Muscovites seemed for the most part more bothered with finding food than finding out. Had the news finally reached them? And if it had, would they go to the White House—and in enough numbers? "I think the jour-nalists are already there," I said. "The filmmakers, the writers, the painters, even the businessmen—all the people who have most to lose from a return to the censorship and cynicism of the Brezhnev years. But will ordinary people go—the man in the street who has no time for Gorbachev and a profound nostalgia for the power and glory of Stalin?" I said I thought that this was critical. For if there were enough people there, then the army might not choose to move against them. If there weren't . . . well, it was simply a question of how much blood the army was willing to spill. "The irony is that whatever happens tonight in one block of Moscow may well dictate what happens to the entire country."

4

I was right, in one sense—more right than I knew at the time. But little of what I said survived to grace the nation's breakfasts. For by that time, of course, three young men had been killed in the small hours in the Garden Ring underpass under Kalinin Prospekt, and it was beginning to be clear which was the winning side—not because a hundred thousand defenders had gone to defend the White

House (which they hadn't), but because the coup plotters had really lost on the first day, when they failed to arrest Yeltsin, when they failed to secure the White House, when they failed to do all those things, like spilling blood and strutting like *vozhdi,* in which the Soviet Union historically specialized. By the time Yelena and I got to Edinburgh two days later—with Katya and Ksiyusha in tow— the whole thing was over. Gorbachev had returned from the Crimea and had immediately destroyed his political future by trying to absolve the Communist Party of responsibility for the coup. Then he had been publicly and brutally humiliated by Yeltsin in a session of the Russian Parliament. Gorbachev, it was already becoming clear, was yesterday's man: incapable of change. Yeltsin—and he played the part much more convincingly than any of the putsch/ ists—was definitely now the Boss.

5

"What happened was the final triumph of democracy in our coun/ try," said Galina Storovoitova, on the panel in Edinburgh.

"What happened was just a little local disturbance," countered Alexander Nevzorov, "a halfhearted battle between soldiers who didn't know what they were supposed to be doing there, and maybe thirty thousand demonstrators who never really had to take them on. So I have an unpopular question: Where was the *rest* of Moscow in all this? And what about the millions of other people elsewhere in the Soviet Union? They did nothing; they were silent. They have yet to be given a voice."

"Boris Nikolayevich Yeltsin was their voice," said Storo/ voitova. "He's the Russian people's president, their democratically elected representative—which is more than can be said for *you!*"

"It may interest you to know," said Nevzorov, "that when the Leningrad television building was occupied by the army, they sent five or six soldiers—yet it was enough to face down all those so-called freedom-loving democrats. And yet what do we see now on television? Crowds of these same democrats—most of them drunk—pulling down statues in Moscow that are our history. I speak for the silent majority, the disenfranchised. And what they want to know is this: Wasn't the failed coup followed immediately, unnoticed, by another coup—a coup of democrats this time? And aren't we to expect from them what always happens after coups: sackings, censorship, the promotion of favourites, arrests?"

"No. We are more principled than your side. We represent all views. We stand for pluralism."

"I've been told that I'll be arrested if I go back to Leningrad."

"As a criminal journalist," said Storovoitova, "you have only yourself to blame."

There was a question from the audience. "Ms. Storovoitova, you talk about pluralism. But if you were in charge of Soviet television, would you give Alexander Nevzorov a voice, his own programme?"

"It is unlikely to be my responsibility," said Storovoitova.

"But *would* you? That's the point. *Would* you?"

She shrugged her shoulders. She smiled. She never answered the question.

6

Galina Storovoitova was a last-minute addition to the panel. She was a member of both the Russian and Soviet Parliaments. She was also President Yeltsin's advisor on ethnic minorities. And during the days of the coup, she'd become both his plenipotentiary in England and the chief spokesperson for the Russian cause. She was brisk, highly intelligent, right-minded, and very self-assured. And though I agreed with most of what she had to say, I found—in common with a lot of the audience that day—that I didn't like her very much at all.

Alexander Nevzorov, an unexpected arrival, was a very different—and very odd—kettle of fish. In one of his many peculiar manifestations, he was an investigative journalist: the main producer-presenter of a muckraking, crime-busting daily TV show (based in Leningrad) called "600 Seconds." But he was also a romantic, even a Byronic, nationalist and patriot, who'd accused both Yeltsin and Gorbachev of treason and who was said to have very good connections inside the KGB and the Ministry of Defence. Whatever the truth was, he was widely seen by his audience as the champion of the little man against the hoods of both crime and politics—he was known as Nash Sacha (Our Sacha), and as such he was the most famous and popular man on Soviet television. (There was a waxwork of him—sitting with Catherine the Great—in Moscow's tiny Theatre of History to prove it.) He was in some ways a slightly absurd figure: he showed up in Edinburgh dressed like a tank driver or a paratrooper, in leather and boots and pop-up sunglasses. But he was also sincere and, in his own strange way, brave. He'd made a film called *Nashi* (Our Guys) about the Black Berets in Lithuania, who'd been responsible for the deaths of a dozen people in January 1991, and he'd gone against every kind of liberal tide by portraying them as men doing an impossible job, performing as patriots, obeying their orders. The problem was—and he was cordially hated for it by the left—that he couldn't resist romanticizing them, spangling them with sainthood. It was in his nature: he was a little-boy hero worshipper who'd grown up to become, as somebody had described him, a cross between Dmitri Karamazov and the Grand Inquisitor. It was a very Russian combination. And though he was often described as a semifascist, an extreme-right-wing Slavophile, I found, like the audience, that I liked him a lot.

So, we discovered later, did Ksiyusha. After the panel was over, she, Yelena, and I spent time with him (Storovoitova spoke English; in Britain, *she* was the big media star, and she had plenty of interviews); and it didn't take long to recognize that there was a strong—almost sexual—current between Ksiyusha and Nevzorov. At first, both Yelena and I were amused by this. But then, when over dinner in a restaurant Ksiyusha hung her head and then abruptly left the table, I was concerned; I went out into the street after her, leaving Yelena with Nevzorov.

I found Ksiyusha leaning over a canal. "What's the matter?" I said.

She didn't say anything.

"All right," I said, "I'll tell you what I think it is, and then you can tell me if I'm right. Let's imagine that there are these two Russians. One of them says all the things that you basically believe in; she's good, she's right, but somewhere deep down, there's an intransigence in her. She smells a little of the 'correct' line. Even though she's you, you find yourself not liking her much. Then there's the second Russian, who's neither reasonable nor right. Instead he's full of old hatreds and myths and dreams of glory. He praises killers. He says terrible things. You're not supposed to like him a bit, he's not like you—and yet you feel incredibly drawn to him."

She nodded slowly. "Something like that," she said.

"Well, welcome to the real world," I said. "Things don't always match up neatly in the way we want them to. Come on, let's go back and eat."

"No," she said. "Wait a minute, Jo. It's more complicated than that. Yes, you're right: there are two kinds of Russians. One is like Storovoitova; very active, full of enthusiasm for democracy and the market, the way things are in other countries, the way we'd like them to be. But then there's the other one, a dark one: who doesn't do much or say much, who broods and dreams and knows that it's impossible. He's the really Russian one, the one the West doesn't know about. And he's . . . dangerous."

"Which kind of Russian are you?"

"I don't know. Maybe both."

"All right," I said, "I'll tell you a true story. The two kinds of Russians meet at Heathrow Airport on their way up to a panel at the Edinburgh Festival. One says: 'Good morning.' And the other says: '*You!* I thought you'd have had the decency to commit suicide by now!' Which Russian was that?"

"That's easy," she said. "The active Russian: Storovoitova."

"So the question is: Which one is more dangerous in the end? The active one or the dreamer?"

She laughed. "In Russia, both," she said. Then we went back into the restaurant and finished the meal.

When we got back to the hotel that night, we said goodnight and goodbye—Nevzorov was leaving early the next morning. He took Yelena aside. "Your daughter," he said, "she is very intelligent and very beautiful: very Russian. Promise me one thing. Don't ever give her to a democrat."

The next day, he disappeared. The woman who was supposed to be meeting him at Sheremetyevo Airport off the plane from London couldn't find him. He wasn't with friends or at any of his known numbers. Calls began to flow back and forth across Europe. Then, suddenly, a few days later, he reappeared in Leningrad. He said that he'd expected to be arrested at Sheremetyevo, so he'd got off the plane on the tarmac and had then simply walked across the fields to the city. He said, too—and for a while it was the talk of the Soviet Union—that he'd turned down huge offers from Western television companies, and that he'd become engaged in Scotland to "the Princess of Edinburgh."

7

We went back to Moscow two weeks later (in time for the start of
"the Princess" 's university term) to find everybody buoyed up and
cheered by the defence of the White House. Tomas and Guram had
been there; had met Artyom. Sacha Lipnitsky had taken his video
camera, and we watched once more on his TV set the gathering of
the motley people's militia: uniformed Cossacks and priests and
Afghan veterans, painters and writers and old men wearing their
medals; tanks and soldiers; makeshift tents and canteens; and the
wild euphoria of final victory. "It was great!" said Kolya Petrov.
"We finally shoved it up the ass of those goddamned Bolsheviks!"
"It was good, Jo. It was sort of a Russian Woodstock," said
Artyom. "In a year's time, everybody in the country will say that
they were there."

Only Fyodor, our Nikolina Gora landlord, seemed less than
optimistic about the future. "Yes, I went there, to see," he said.
"What happened was good. But what has it produced? So far,
nothing at all. Oh yes, they say that we will now have a new
economic commonwealth, a union of free states. But already people
are coming from the city to steal the cabbages and potatoes from out
of the fields. Prices are impossible. It will be a very hard winter. And
what are they doing about it? Are they privatizing the land? Are they
setting up the market? No. They say that Gorbachev and Yeltsin are
now both at their dachas writing their memoirs about what happened. They compete now for history and international attention.
There is a big power struggle going on between them, which will
not stop until the whole country has been destroyed."

As the weeks passed—and we moved to Andrei Alexandrov-
Agentov's dacha a few doors away (which was better heated)—it
was hard not to see what Fyodor meant. I worked on my television

script, which had predicted the coup; we had Sacha Lipnitsky and his wife, Artyom and Svetlana, Boris Grebenshchikov, Tomas, and Guram for occasional company. But I went into Moscow often enough to see that everything had more or less broken down in the city. No one seemed to know or care what the laws were anymore. The "bulls" of the black market were operating openly; the traffic police and the *militsia* were more and more aggressively on the take. Guns were for sale in the markets, which had taken on a raw and sinister edge. Commercial shops and kiosks were proliferating all over Moscow. And everyone seemed obsessed with the turn, the deal, the acquisition of dollars that would somehow help to see them through the winter.

The mayor of Moscow, Gavriil Popov, was too busy, by all accounts, dealing with his own personal activities. (Around this time, he was named by the newspaper *Kommersant,* without comment, as one of the seven richest men in Russia.) And Yeltsin and his entourage (known as "the Sverdlovsk Mafia") had bigger fish to fry. They were preoccupied with gathering enough power to marginalize Gorbachev and shunt him finally from the stage. At the end of October, the Chamber of People's Deputies convened and almost immediately voted away its power to approve government ministers and call them to account. It banned the use of referenda and virtually all elections for more than a year, and it gave Yeltsin the right to rule by presidential decree. Russian funding for most of the ministries of the Soviet Union was subsequently cut off. And on November 6, Yeltsin announced (using the powers that had been given him) that the activities on Russian territory of the Communist Party—Gorbachev's only real remaining power base—were from that time simply illegal.

The play was almost played out. Gorbachev did what he could to ensure the survival of the Union in some form or another. But a month later, Yeltsin completed the coup d'état that (according to

Nevzorov) he'd begun on August 21. A week after Kravchuk of
the Ukraine and Nazurbayev of Kazakhstan had been elected
presidents—and the Ukraine had voted overwhelmingly for independence—he announced, from a hunting lodge in Belarus, the
dissolution of the Soviet Union and the birth of something called
the Commonwealth of Independent States. Yeltsin's first telephone
call was to George Bush, not to Gorbachev. Mikhail Sergeyevich
no longer ruled over anything but his Kremlin office.

On December 21, at a meeting in Alma Ata, eleven new
nations agreed to join the Commonwealth. And three days later,
Yelena took over the restaurant at the Taganka Theatre for a party
for my fiftieth birthday. Artyom, Guram, Tomas, and my friend the
actor Boris Khmelnitsky made speeches. There was Gipsy music
and romances and an impossible amount of food and drink. I
caroused with the Gipsies; I had the first dance with Katya before
she had to go home to bed. And when it came time for me to make
a toast, I climbed up the stairs to a little gallery and looked down
at all the upturned faces in the candlelight below me. There were
more than fifty of them: friends from Nikolina Gora and Vorotnikovsky Alley; friends in film and television and the theatre, from
the thick journals and business and politics and the KGB. I realized
in some profound way, I think, that I finally lived there, that I was
no longer just a tourist.

I began by talking about how my journey had started, in the
Moscow Club in London, with Artyom, "my first fully paid-up
Russian." I raised a glass to Boris Grebenshchikov, "who managed
to persuade everyone in the West how Western he was, only to
discover in the process—and me with him—how deeply Russian he
was, after all." I talked about Dmitri Likhachev, who "told me that
I should look at history and literature if I wanted to understand who
Russians were"; and Vadim Borisov, Solzhenitsyn's editor, "sitting
down there," who "once told me to leave as much of my Western

intellectual baggage as I could behind me at the frontier. I've tried, Vadim, I've tried," I said. "I've now turned into the only Western Slavophile I know!" I toasted Ksiyusha, "who taught me about the great swimming pool of Russian emotions, and my beautiful Yelena, who taught me that the only way to negotiate it is to jump in at the deep end." And then I said: "I think I've been very lucky. Four or five years ago, it wouldn't have been possible for us to be sitting here today. I wouldn't have been able to live here as I do. The Iron Curtain may have kept you in, but it also kept people like me out, locked up in enclaves, kept in quarantine, spied on, with almost no access to ordinary people and ordinary life. Today, the Iron Curtain is down; the Cold War, we hope, is over; the West believes that it has won. But I don't think it yet knows exactly *what* it has won. I hope that, in a small way, I'll be able to tell it."

I looked down over the balcony and raised my glass to the "brave new world that has such people in it." I said that I loved them all. The next day, Christmas Day, Gorbachev, the West's champion, resigned. And Russia, impossible Russia, took over.

Chapter 10

April 1992

I

Russia. You have to start by imagining things. Imagine, for instance, that there's a bomb scare at Harrods or Bloomingdale's. The police arrive and order everybody out, but the customers simply refuse to leave—they'll lose their places in line. The police then fetch their metal detectors and sound the place out. They don't find a bomb, but they do find the best stuff the store ever had on offer hidden in the walls by the staff.

Once you've imagined this—a secret store within the store, with the staff as customers—then the next step is to imagine a whole city, using the same inside-out logic. The first thing to picture is that most of the ads on the buses are in a language you can't understand, and offer goods it's either impossible or actually illegal for you to buy. The television commercials offer up technologies that won't be available for another ten or twenty years. At the farmers' markets, empty cans of Japanese beer are on sale, for prestige home decoration; and there's also a flourishing trade in broken light bulbs. Meanwhile, outside every supermarket, there are people selling the goods inside at four times the price. At the zoo, there's an art student trying to kill a polar bear with a kitchen knife for its skin and meat. At the commodities exchange, brokers in sneakers are exchanging cars for piglets, and Bibles for wheat that doesn't exist. And at one of the city's main breweries, a tape of recorded silence is playing full-blast on a cassette machine to a tank full of tap water. In the subways, vendors are selling astrology charts and Xeroxes of eighty-year-old dream books stolen from the public library. In their safe houses, Mafia chieftains are poring over *The Godfather* for tips on criminal deportment. And in the streets, gang battles are breaking up promptly at the same time every evening, so that everyone can go home to watch their favourite Mexican soap opera.

If you can imagine all this, then all you have to do now is to go on: imagine outwards. For the dream city you now inhabit is in a dream country so big and so strange that none of its citizens can grasp it with a single thought. No one is even sure what its name is—its Congress meets seldom and keeps changing its mind, and no one seems to know which of its contradictory decisions ended up becoming law. It hasn't got a proper constitution: its parliament can't decide on a new one, so for the moment it lives under the terms of an old one which no one with any power ever paid the slightest attention to. The main political principles of this country—which was established by an illegal coup d'état—are autocracy, paranoia, and the magical efficacy of words; and the main language of political criticism is rumour. The current ruler is rumoured to spend most of his time at sanitaria recovering from drinking bouts; and his predecessor is rumoured to have been either a Japanese or a German spy—or the last emperor on earth before the coming of the Antichrist.

Welcome, if you've done all this, to the Russian Federation, and to its capital, Moscow-Macondo, the theatre of the absurd on the Moskva River—where the fast food is slow (it takes an hour or more in line to get to), and where the Temperance Council—which employed five and a half thousand people until recently—used to be one of the best places in town to get a drink. For this is the city where everything one thinks is true becomes untrue; where everything we take for granted in the West is turned back to front and upside down. Taxis with their lights on for a fare won't stop, but private cars are usually willing. High-school students dream, not of becoming president, but of joining the Mafia or becoming hard-currency hookers. Our crime is their freedom; our freedom, their disorder. Where we believe in truth and progress, they believe in saints and demons, portents and demigods. Instead of "the news that's fit to print," the newspapers publish lists of upcoming "bad days" at the beginning of every month; and the news is anything from gossip to paid advertisement to a wild idea that simply occurred to the writer the day before. This is not the land of "before and after," cause and effect; this is the land of "maybe." A paper called *Russian Newsman* recently announced that Gorbachev had been appointed general secretary by George Bush at a secret meeting in Switzerland, and that, because he fulfilled the Nazi dream of breaking up the Soviet Union, there are streets and squares named after him all over Germany. Another newspaper not long ago broke the news that Brezhnev is alive and well and living with a sex bomb and two beautiful young children in Western Samoa. Well, maybe . . . maybe. Maybe Stalin's hatchet man Lavrenty Beria *did* escape to Brazil and leave a fortune in disposable hypodermic syringes to his native Georgia. Maybe Shevardnadze *did* sell off the Bering Sea to the Americans for his private profit. Maybe Yuri Gagarin survived his plane crash; maybe Yeltsin is a CIA spy; maybe the Moscow Metro is built in the shape of a star of David. It's possible; it's possible . . . and in any case the local rule applies: "The authorities lie—so the more they deny it, the higher the percentage of truth it must contain."

If Moscow was a city in fiction, we'd take all this as read, I suppose. ("Ah, this magical realism is wonderful stuff!") But it isn't. And most Western observers—with their well-brought-up notions of truth and falsehood, news and fact, and the orderly march of political events—totally fail to see it for what it is. Instead, they insist on grafting onto it, and onto Russia (or the Russian Federation) as a whole, not only their preconceived, ready-for-packaging back-home notions, but also their vision of the place as a (large) part of Europe which just happens to have had a nasty time of it for the past seventy-five years. Is this all we can say of the country of Yuri Long Arms, Ivan Moneybags, Vsevolod Big Nest, and Basil the Squint-Eyed—not to mention Ivan the Terrible and Uncle Joe Stalin? Is this all we can manage to summon up for a city flown over by UFOs and pregnant with apocalypse—a city where an edition of an evening newspaper sells out in minutes after it's announced that a faith healer has infused the whole print run with his healing energy?

To leave these things out of the picture that's painted for us is . . . well, to speak frankly, racist. The problem, to put it another way, is that Russians are white. If they were black, yellow, or brown, then Western reporters and other panjandrums would take it for granted that they just weren't in Kansas anymore. If Russians were South Americans, then the experts would no doubt be reading Gabriel García Márquez's *One Hundred Years of Solitude* as a completely factual guide to the flora and fauna of the indigenous mindset. But they're white—so that must mean that they've inherited, by definition, what all righteous whites have: reason and moderation and everything that goes with them, all the way down to an innate love for democracy. Democracy (so runs this argument) may be hard to achieve in Russia; it may take a while a-coming—but only because the Bolsheviks interrupted its natural development, subverted the basic industriousness and (white) decency of the Russian people, and buried what had been until 1917 an up-and-coming Western-style economy.

The truth is that virtually everything in this postulation is false: in fact, preposterous. And the best way to recognize this is to invoke the local rule: turn logic upside down and inside out, and accept that yes, Russians are black—for at least this way you'll get near to some understanding of the local reality. We're all used, these days, to the notion that America was a good, even a great idea—except, that is (and perhaps), for slavery. But the number of black slaves in the United States never rose above twenty-five percent of the whole population. In Russia, on the other hand, white slaves, at the time of their emancipation in 1861, numbered fully ninety percent of the population—and they had fewer rights and more obligations that their equivalents in the United States. They could be tortured, starved, and killed without redress. They had to pay taxes and were liable to military service of up to twenty-five years. And this was their lot, roughly speaking, for at least three hundred years.

Russians may look white, in other words, but what difference does that make? They lived, from the beginning of the Russian state, under an Oriental despotism (inherited in large part from Mongol conquerors) that had little or nothing in common with the forms of society evolved in other parts of Europe. While European cities to the west and south were beginning to bustle with all those guilds, processions, assemblies, and associations that shaped the drive to-wards municipal self-expression, Muscovite Russia was either kow-towing to Oriental overlords or else fighting for its life to protect and slowly extend an endlessly long defensive frontier. While the Renais-sance, the Reformation, the Counter-Reformation, and the Enlight-enment were shaping the character of most future Europeans, Russians—harried on all sides—were too busy with the vast na-tional projects of war and expansion to pay them any mind. By the time they emerged onto the world stage, blinking, the shape of their state had been fixed by its experience: it was a totalitarian monarchy in which all power was vested in the semidivine person of the absolute ruler, to whom everybody in the nation owed life, service, property, and labour. The Revolution of 1917 may have deposed the head of this state, but it didn't create any sort of fire break in its history; it was, as it turned out, merely its culmination, its logical conclusion. Witness the early foundation of some of the Soviet Union's most individual institutions: submission to the unlimited power of the ruler (thirteenth century); nationalization of all land, the establishment of a secret police, terror as a policy of the state (sixteenth century); secret agents accompanying Russian embassies, families held hostage while relatives travelled abroad (seventeenth century); state monopoly of industry, internal passports, rigged elec-tions, censorship, two-thirds of the national budget spent on defence (eighteenth century).

It's no use, then—given all this—trying to hijack Russia (and Moscow) into conformity with the West and the Europe we know. It simply won't fit there. This is not any kind of Europe we know. It's China. It's the moon; it's Byzantium; it's the fourteenth century. It's a place of myths and omens, of shell shock, torpor, and sudden, inexplicable upheavals. Nothing ever seems to happen by halves here. The minister for security stands up and says that the KGB only ever arrested 3.8 million people; it's had a bad press. A hypnotist goes on television to tell the nation that all its ills can be cured, and attracts a weekly audience of 200 million people. Meanwhile, solid Communists become capitalists and democrats overnight, since that's what's required of them. Party *apparatchiki* start swapping blocks of St. Petersburg for condos in Florida as if to the manner born. Inflation runs at more than one percent a day. In two years boots go up in price by eleven hundred percent; poultry by twenty-six hundred; sweaters and pullovers by thirty-seven hundred. Even vodka, which costs next to nothing to make, becomes astronomi-cally expensive—but everyone continues to drink to oblivion, whenever there's the slightest occasion. There is something tidal, awesome about this Russian consumption of alcohol. After the storming of the Winter Palace in 1917, for example, everybody in what was then Petrograd got drunk for a month. Two different regiments, then mixed guards, the revolutionary leaders of the garrison, and then armoured brigades, were all sent to the palace; they all, without exception, got drunk. An order was sent out to wall up the palace's cellars; the crowds came in through the windows. The fire brigade were sent in to flood the cellars; they, too, got drunk. By the time the binge ended, the city garrison and the army had evaporated. There were no soldiers left to guard the Revolution.

2

The tale of this demented spree is not widely known in Moscow-Macondo. (It was written out of the official histories: it didn't offer the sort of past the rulers wanted.) And this is another of the problems that Westerners have to try to come to terms with when dealing with this peculiar dream country. For it has virtually no history: no history, that's to say, that hasn't been written and then rewritten, suppressed, glossed, invented, raised from the dead, glorified, or else buried without honour in some forgotten corner. It has no *agreed* history, no *sure* history, as nations tend to have in the West: no popular consensus (however dimly felt or expressed) that takes it for granted that the past shaped the present; that such-and-such happened and led to so-and-so; that X development resulted in Y institution; or that this or that individual performed works and deeds that should be looked back on fondly, with respect, today. The whole of Russia's history has been so misted over by ideology, in other words, that everything in its past remains both forever in doubt and forever in the present, batting around in people's heads as a result of their ideological force-feeding—and at the same time simply waiting in the wings of the here and now for the next rediscovery, the next reinterpretation. Russians, it's been said often enough, have no reliable memory. (It was cauterized and sent wool-gathering by tsars and Bolsheviks alike.) But what they actually have is no sequential memory. What they have instead are (a) opinions about the past masquerading as convictions, and (b) collective folk hallucinations.

(a) In the Congress in Moscow-Macondo, deputies scream at each other, using names from Famous Long Ago. "Biron!" shouts one, invoking the corrupt favourite of an empress dead for two hundred and fifty years. "Suslov!" yells another, summoning up the ghost of the grim grand vizier of the Communist Party. "Dan and Martov!" counter the newspapers in shorthand; "Trotsky and Yagoda! Lenin was only one-third Russian!" "Yes, but Nicholas II was a saint," says one journal, "killed by the Jews." "And Solzhenitsyn was a KGB spy," announces another. Truth and falsehood have nothing to do with any of these outpourings, of course; right and wrong aren't even invited. They're merely rival incantations—competitive ritual insults—rooted in a waking dream of the past. "Vikings!" "Byzantines!" "Greeks!" "False Dmitris!" "Teutonic Knights!" "Tartars!" "February 1917!" At public meet-ings and conferences, the invasions and betrayals of the past addle the heads and spill out of the mouths of the living. "Many of the country's past presidents were agents of the West," says "Black Colonel" Alksnis sombrely at a rally in Red Square. *"Perestroika* was obviously invented in America," says "Red Duchess" Trubet-skaya, "because none of the American newspapers ever bothered to translate the word." "Lenin was the Antichrist!" announce people over the kitchen table. "No, it was Peter, who opened up the country to the West." "The Mongols did it!" "No, the Black Hundreds!" "The Jews!" "The Reds!" "The Browns!" "Ivan the Terrible!" All this in a country where the eyes of teddy bears fall out as soon as they are bought; where shoe soles disintegrate when they hit the sidewalk; and where television sets explode during the eve-ning news. Where the present is a nightmare, only the past contains reality: only it can deliver the right ideological goods.

Ah, but there's a problem. For no one in Moscow-Macondo

really knows what the past actually looks like. Was the storming of the Winter Palace, for example, a triumphant victory or a tawdry sideshow, with more victims of rape than victims of the people's wrath? Was the shot fired by the battleship *Aurora,* the shot heard around the world, a live round or a blank? Did it fall into the tsar's bedroom, or did it hit an orphanage and kill children and nurses? No one knows which story is myth, which truth. What, too, can be said about men like Bukharin and Khrushchev, public mention of whom a few years ago, if approving, would have bought a spell in the camps? And what about all those on whom the Bolsheviks cast a retrospective mantle of Communist sainthood? Were the icon painter Andrei Ryublev and the composer Pyotr Tchaikovsky really champions of the people? Was Ivan the Terrible really a psychopath, or the sad forger, in blood and steel, of the unity of the nation? These are weighty and difficult matters. For in Macondo—as in the case of Dmitri Likhachev—you could be attacked on the street and have your arm broken for taking the wrong line.

(b) When in doubt in Moscow-Macondo (and doubt is actu-ally a commodity in rather short supply), most follow the path of least resistance. The country may be fiftieth in the nation table for infant mortality, seventy-seventh in consumption per head, and fifty-eighth in standard of living, but it is still the greatest country on earth. This buried conviction is the most important of what I (West-biased) call Russians' "collective folk hallucinations"—a conviction that, whatever has happened to them in the past (and perhaps because of it), they live on a higher plane than the rest of us, with a special burden and mission from God. This has been called (by both Russians and Westerners) "the Russian idea" and, even though God may not inhabit the country quite as He once did, it's still absolutely fundamental in coming to terms with the sheer foreignness of this place.

The "Russian idea" goes something like this: A thousand years ago, before time and history began, God laid His finger on the Russian people. He made them the last protectors of His only true church, and gave them the responsibility of creating, as His servants, the only just form of society on earth: in which the people and the state would become indivisible, joined in a communion of absolute equality for His greater glory. This form of society, of course, was the Russian autocracy: in which each individual was guaranteed (by force) to serve equally; in which individualism (as we call it) was both a crime and a sin. It was coercive, antimaterialist, and in essence metaphysical: a state system in which the autocrat alone embodied the aspirations of the Russian people: the all-powerful hierarch through whom they channelled their fealty to God.

Now this makes little or no sense at all to us Westerners, with our baggage of democracy, rationalism, individualism, et cetera. Apart from anything else, once God is taken out of this system of relations, it looks remarkably like Stalinism. But in a sense that's exactly the point. For Stalin was merely the latest and most ruthless embodiment (and manipulator) of this "folk hallucination." And so firmly rooted does it remain in Russians (in part because of him) that it's again spreading across the country even now, as I write this—and not only among nationalist groups and neo-Stalinists, but also among those who would have called themselves liberals or democrats a year or two ago. And it's no use invoking against it, by way of argument, slavery, the camps, the torture chambers, the hecatombs of victims: the deaths of all those who stood in the way of Stalin's (and the tsars') vision of the state. For suffering itself is an important part of the vision, of the "Russian idea": it is what anoints it with special righteousness. For suffering shrives and makes pure; it is a cleansing wind sent from God. It is yet another proof—if one were needed—of Russia's superior spirituality and capacity for self-sacrifice, a demonstration of its unique destiny on earth.

This is our kind of history turned upside down and back to

front, to say the least. (It is history without lessons, without any kind of idea of progress: just a series of divagations on one central theme. It's theocratic history.) And yet it's a view of history that's subscribed to, one way or another, despite all the awful evidence of the twentieth century, by organizations like Pamyat, Russian monarchists, and army generals—not to mention writers and filmmakers like Valentin Rasputin, Govorukhin, Mikhalkov, and Solzhenitsyn—so we should pay attention. (I've encountered it—with and without helpmeets, anti-Semitism and pan-Slavism—in everyone from clinical psychologists to art restorers to taxi drivers.) In part, of course, it's the product of propaganda: of the persistent glorification of the state, which was as active under the tsars as it was under their Bolshevik successors. (The French Marquis de Custine, for example, wrote after his visit to Russia in 1839: "Nor in this country is historical truth any better respected . . . even the dead are exposed to the fantasies of him who rules the living.") But it goes deeper than this: it goes into folk memory, into the strange secret cupboard where Russians keep their sense of their place in the world, their embattled patriotism. It goes back, above all, into the backwaters of the countryside, from which most Russians emerged, only recently literate, in the past seventy years. Our kind of history, whether we like it or not, is essentially secular: it's the product of clocks and cities. But in Russia history has never been citified or made subject to time, as it has in the West. It remains sacral history, peasant history, full of saints and demons: the record of an ongoing crusade, a long argument with God: a struggle, if you like, towards some sort of New Jerusalem. And the personal (historical) character of Russia's rulers along the way—their psychoses or their appetites for reform— is simply of no great account in any of this. (*Facts* are of no account; *glory* is what matters.) Alexander I, for example, was historically a harsh reactionary who surrounded himself with mystagogues and sadistic disciplinarians; but it was he who saved the nation from defeat by Napoleon—so he remains a folk hero. So does Dmitri Donskoy, the victor over the Tartars; so does Alexander Nevsky, who beat back the Swedes and the Teutonic Knights. There is, by contrast, not even a statue in Russia of Alexander II, the emperor who ended slavery nine years before Lenin's birth—and was killed by revolutionaries for his pains.

"In the West," historian Natan Eidelman once said to me, "you have this vision of the Soviet Union as a uniquely oppressive state, a reactionary government holding down a population which is hungry for freedom and democracy. The fact, though—the tragedy, if you like—is that Gorbachev's government—the liberal faction in it, at any rate—is much more left-wing than the society in general. All right, yes, you could say that Russians are in one sense in favour of democracy, because it may help them work more efficiently. But at the same time, and much more importantly, they're fiercely against it, because it equals disorder. What the West doesn't understand, you see, is that Russians have inherited a number of superstitions rooted deeply in their history. First, there's the authoritarian superstition: the idea that autocracy is best; the love for Big Brother. Then, the equalitarian superstition: the conviction that it's better in the end to be poor and equal rather than well-off and unequal. And last, the alien superstition: the fear of foreigners, the belief that all they have to offer is contamination or the work of the devil. So when the West comes here and calls for full democracy right now . . . well, all I can say is that it could be very dangerous. A large part of the people would already be very pleased to see Gorbachev removed. Not one living leader has been genuinely popular here since Stalin."

Natan Eidelman, who died at the end of 1989, long before the attempted coup and Yeltsin's rise to power, knew his Macondo well. So, of course, did Joseph Stalin. He ruled it, from his monk's cell in the Kremlin, the way it understood—like a tsar. And the people loved him for it. When he was seventy, in 1949, *Pravda* spent five days listing the organizations which had sent him greetings, then two years publishing all the tributes paid. When he died, there were scenes of unbelievable mass hysteria; at his funeral, unknown num- bers of people died in the crush.

I like to think I can guess what Natan Eidelman would have said about Boris Yeltsin's accession to Macondo's Kremlin. "Now Yeltsin, you see, is much closer than Gorbachev ever was to the country's idea of a real ruler, a real Boss. He's big, he's tough: he stood up to Gorbachev and Ligachev; he faced down the coup plotters; he stood up there on the tank. He's also very Russian. He's not wily, as Gorbachev was: a political manoeuverer; he doesn't have that kind of lawyer's mind. He's straightforward, simple, brutal, and he likes to drink. He has the sort of instinctive feeling for the country that Gorbachev never had. The problem with Gorbachev, paradoxically, was that he really was a democrat, in a way a European: he was always talking about 'our common Euro- pean home.' But he was so blinded by his popularity abroad that he never saw that every time he went to the West, with Raisa in tow, or talked about Western-style democracy, he was simply seen as a weak-kneed antipatriot, almost a foreigner. Yeltsin will never make the same mistake. He will look to the West, but he will never agree to be dictated to by it. When he goes abroad, he will insist on the full panoply due a mighty head of state. And he will never be the sort of democrat the West wants him to be. When push comes to shove, he will rule by decree, because that's the way it's always been done here. If he doesn't, then someone else will, taking his place. Democracy—well, I've said it before—is not popular here. It's simply another word for disorder."

Paradox Number One: In order to get help from the West, Yeltsin must be seen to be a popular democrat. In order to maintain his popularity at home, he must be seen to be a powerful autocrat, and defiant of the West.

3

The one foreigner I can think of who got Moscow-Macondo exactly right in a phrase was an Englishman, Lord Curzon. On a visit to the city in the middle of the nineteenth century, he called it, *tout court,* "a Christian Cairo."

It doesn't look much like Cairo these days, of course. However ramshackle and rundown and full of food queues it may be, it conforms, roughly speaking, to the picture we have of a European city: urbanized and urbane; public; international; like us. Its appear- ance, though, (once more) misleads; its public face is really a front. For, despite its high-rise apartment buildings and mass transit sys- tems, it's a string of villages, half European, half Asiatic, held together by an underground communications network composed of private tips, superstition, bribery, gossip, and rumour. From the babushkas huddling together in the courtyards to the gaggles of office workers comparing notes during summer lunch breaks in the squares and along the boulevards, Moscow is a vast Oriental trading bazaar, a souk, in which the local currencies are *blat,* or influence, and inside, "unofficial" information.

Much of this alternative information is crucial to survival, of course—or at least to survival with some kind of grace. When there's little or no food in the shops, for example—or when what's there is outrageously expensive—it's vital to know someone who knows someone who's selling food out of the back door, or else bringing it into the city from their plots or dachas to sell to private buyers. To secure this—or indeed any other commodity you need (all of which are in equally short supply)—you have to mobilize your own resources, in the form of money or information or skill, or of the privileges or goods or services that your job entails. If you're a goods handler at a food store, say, or an usher at the Bolshoi

Theatre, with access to tickets, you'll have a strong position inside your own network. If you're a district housing officer or a doctor or a passport clerk, you don't really need to have a network at all, since goods (as bribes) will come your way without your having to ask for them. Sooner or later, though, of course, you too will need to find an electrician or a carpenter or a place in a sanitarium or a dacha, and your money or goods or skills will have, in turn, to be recycled. A lot of this recycling takes the form of vodka, which is known as "liquid money," so if you work in a distillery or a vodka shop, you're living in effect in a poorly policed mint—your network position is (once more) extremely good. If you have a car, you're ahead of the game—you can offer lifts and deliveries, or work on the streets as a taxi. If you work in a factory, you can steal what you make and sell it outside the factory walls. If you're a motor mechanic, then you're in huge demand—though if you need garage equipment to deal with your private jobs, then you'll probably need to bribe your boss to let it happen. And if you're the garage boss . . . Well, the permutations of all this are endless. The worst thing that can happen to you is if you have nothing to steal, no influence to peddle, and no skill or inside tips to offer. Then—in the words of a famous Georgian curse—"May you have to live on your salary alone!"

This is the first, or civilian, level of Moscow-Macondo's souk culture, which has preserved in the city many of the characteristics—gossip, secrecy, mutual interdependence, and barter—of village life before the Revolution. And though it's changing to a degree, as goods become more available and more expensive (as the economy, in other words, become more geared to cash), it's still a basic condition of the local way of life, and as such responsible for the distorted shape economic reform has tended to take on in the country. The first thing to be noticed is that it is, of course, strictly speaking, illegal; everybody involved in it—which is everyone who can be (perhaps eighty percent of the population)—is, technically, a criminal, since he or she is diverting (to say the least) time, goods, services, or tools that belong to the state. It's worth noticing, too (by Western observers), that it already contains—in a primitive and twisted form—the rudiments of concepts so beloved by Western economists: the free market and privatization. This market of the so-called "second economy" is "free" inasmuch as the state has chosen (by and large) not to interfere in it. And privatization in it happens on a daily basis: everyone "privatizes"—i.e., steals or makes private use of—everything that hasn't been firmly nailed down. (An important principle of Soviet, and Russian, life is that if it belongs to the state, then it belongs to no one—or to everyone: i.e., me.)

The same is true of the next, "corporate" level of the souk economy, though on a much larger scale, of course. Here, before the reforms of Gorbachev and Yeltsin, the high management of the official economy—the command-administrative system—and the operators of the black market were virtually indistinguishable from each other (and on this fact, again, depends the strange—to Western eyes—directions the economy has travelled over the past few years). Shortages of every kind of commodity were endemic in the system, and therefore literally everything it produced was subject to specula-tion, bribery, and manipulation of trade, at every stage in a product's life, from manufacture to delivery to distribution. What was not produced by the system was often made by underground (black market or Mafia) factories, to which raw materials were diverted by Ministry officials and plant managers, and which routinely paid protection money to *militsia* and Party bosses. The corruption which enshrouded the Soviet Union at every level (especially in the Brezh-nev years) simply beggars the Western imagination. Take the case of Sharaf Rashidov, for example. Rashidov was, under Brezhnev, the head of the Party in Uzbekistan, a warlord who offered up for sale everything in his domain: from government awards to ministe-

rial posts, from literary prizes to Party membership cards to spaces
in cemeteries (a school directorship under Rashidov cost ten thousand roubles; a place on the Central Committee, several million).
He annually cooked the books on the amount of cotton being grown
in Uzbekistan, and he simply pocketed the difference between his
fantasy figure and the reality of the harvests. The result was personal
wealth almost beyond understanding. Rashidov commanded a
Praetorian Guard of several thousand men and a network of secret
jails. His dachas contained life-size statues of himself in solid gold;
and he scattered around his various palaces gold-embroidered fur
coats and literally thousands of trunks full of gold watches, jewellery,
and coins. All this came to light with the death of Brezhnev (who
was too strung out on pills, in his later years, to notice)—as did
Rashidov's partners-in-crime in Moscow. After the death of Rashidov (still a hero in Uzbekistan), the minister of the interior and
his wife, Nikolai and Svetlana Shchelokov, both committed suicide
rather than face trial for corruption. Brezhnev's son-in-law, Yuri
Churbanov (Shchelokov's number two at the Ministry), got twelve
years in a labour camp. And Churbanov's wife, Galina, a *high-life-
itsa* with ties to organized crime and a taste for circus performers, only
narrowly escaped prosecution. (She was said to have used circus
animals as a way of smuggling precious stones abroad—hiding
diamonds, for example, in the rectums of elephants.)

The Rashidov-Schelokov-Churbanov affair—for which
Churbanov shares barracks space in the Ural Mountains with the
chief of the Ministry of the Interior's economics department, the
minister's chief aide, and an assortment of *militsia* generals—may be
an extreme case, but it is certainly not an isolated one. For the
principle was the same everywhere in the Soviet Union. Where there
is unlimited power, there are unlimited opportunities for corruption,
for turning the state's resources into private cash. And there was
unlimited power at every level of the command system, from the

market administrations of Moscow to the collective farms of the Crimea to the mediaeval fiefdoms of the Soviet Far East (all of them a mirror image of the feudal structure at the centre). An example: When journalist Yuri Belyavsky went to expose the exploitation of a group of workers on a collective farm in Georgia, he was first cajoled, then threatened, and then finally told that whatever he wrote would make absolutely no difference. "You don't begin to under' stand, fool!" said the farm's chief. "There is too much money, too many people involved. We send a hundred thousand roubles a year to the district secretary, and we're just one of fifty farms in the district. Multiply that by all the districts (and that's only the farms): the money goes into Tbilisi, to the bosses, and from there upwards towards the centre in Moscow. If you expose what took place here, all that'll happen is that some junior agronomist will lose his job." That, in fact, is exactly what happened as a result of Belyavsky's article in *Krokodil*.

This was the background, then, in Moscow'Macondo when the first steps towards the market were taken, when cooperatives and joint ventures were first set up. And it should come as no surprise that they were met with bristling hostility for the most part by the system's managers, by their semidependent Mafias, and by the gen' eral public, all of whom saw them as disrupting the arrangements they'd made, in their different ways, to secure for themselves a tolerable (or profitable) existence. The public continues to hate them, of course—they're seen by most people as "bloodsuckers" and "profiteers," getting rich (and therefore unequal) at their expense. But it wasn't long before the industrial, Party, and Mafia bosses actually changed their minds. For they realized that they were in fact an extremely good mechanism for doing precisely what the old system of corruption, underground manufacture, and profiteering had done, with a lot less bother: they were a (more or less) legal means of turning cashless state resources into money.

This is how it worked. The head of an industrial plant, let us say, would make a deal with a new private cooperative for factory repairs costing two million roubles (which could be taken for this purpose—for the first time—from the plant's notional, state-controlled, and otherwise unuseable bank account or reserve fund). But the actual cost of the repairs, as everyone agreed in advance, would be only five hundred thousand, four times less than the original "estimate." One and a half million roubles, in other words, would be liberated from the state by a simple stroke, to be shared (among others) by the cooperative, the plant chief, the factory's bookkeeper, and the representative of the appropriate ministry. An operation of the reverse (or negative) kind was also now possible—and this is what seems to have taken place in those early halcyon days of the cooperative movement at the USSR State Depository of Valuables. The depository (with the encouragement of a deputy minister of finance) set up a foreign-relations department (in effect a cooperative linked to the depository), which after a series of eight transactions abroad posted a loss of $22 million. No one was fired, since the loss was no one's—it belonged to the state. The personal profits made along the way—the bribes, the trips abroad—are not, of course, on record. Eighty percent of cooperatives and a large number of joint ventures were said to be of these two (positive and negative) types.

In the end, then, seeing how useful they were, the old Mafias simply took them over—working hand-in-glove with their allies inside the command system (whose children and relatives were to be found in large numbers in the cooperative movement). Such organizations as they didn't control—like the first private restaurants in Moscow—they bought a piece of in the old, time-honoured way: via extortion and protection. Others they brought into their orbit of bribery and *na lyevo* fairly rapidly—as was inevitable, given the fact that the distribution channels and wholesale markets that the new movement really needed simply didn't exist. If a new cooperative wanted to make fur jackets, for example, there was no open market on which it could buy its fur; it was forced to acquire it on the black market—which meant, as one such owner said at the time, that "at the end of the year, the mob is going to collect." And even where a necessary commodity was available from state sources, it was impossible to get hold of it without having to pay huge bribes (to the director of a factory, the head of the planning department, and the bookkeeper, for example). Under these circumstances, if a coop⁄ erative's books were to be balanced at the end of the year (as was required), then the owners really had only two options: they could either sell their goods under the counter, at massive—and undis⁄ closed—markups; or they could buy their basic raw material (cot⁄ ton, for instance) without entering it on the books at all, and have it made up into finished goods underground. Either way, of course—whichever option they were forced to take—they became, willy⁄nilly, black marketeers themselves.

All that the first steps to the market really achieved, then, in this upside⁄down country was a huge burgeoning of the black market, a spreading of the *blat* system, and a universalizing of bribery—for registrations, permissions, premises, protection, and goods. And the only locally available solution to the chaos of peculation, specula⁄ tion, and book rigging that was the result was (this being Macondo) to compound it and make it official. It wasn't long, in other words, before the system's high management—as well as Party, municipal, and district bosses—simply jumped on the bandwagon: joined their children and relatives, cut out the other middlemen, and joined the game themselves.

This process began, roughly speaking, around the time of the local elections in 1990, when the Party lost control of the Moscow and Leningrad city councils; and when the outgoing administra⁄ tions voted to hand over to themselves large amounts of what were on paper the cities' own assets: newspapers, dachas, office and apartment buildings, printing plants, and so on. From that point on, managers, directors, and bosses began progressively to strip and privatize whatever lay within their domain. Trucks were sold off by garages to their own chiefs; funeral-service cooperatives were founded by cemetery managements; specialist metal workshops were set up by the directors of metal plants. Shops and businesses were bought at token prices by trade administrators; and goods and services were siphoned off from state concerns for private profit. This, though, was small beer compared to what took place in 1991 and 1992, with the rise of Russia, the demise of the Communist Party, and the dissolution of the Soviet Union. Then a real bonanza began.

It's hard to describe in moderate terms the feeding frenzy that took hold of the old *nomenklatura* as well as so-called democrats in those years. A country, an empire, a whole system of state organiza- tion was in danger of simply disappearing. Then—my God—it had! The Supreme Soviet, the Politburo—dumped, gone, at a stroke of a pen! The Council of Ministers, the Central Committee, the Party—vanished into history! And with them all their People's Thises and People's Thats: their organizations, their institutes and academies, their hotels, sanitaria, office buildings, dachas, ministries, limousines, bank accounts (who knew?); their state businesses, their garages, their industries, their perks and their apartments, their special shops, their newspapers, their gold! All bets were off; every hand was untied. The mayor of Moscow sent people rushing off to claim dachas and presidential palaces on behalf of the city and himself, only for them to meet guards sent from the Russian govern- ment at the front door. Whole ministries were dismantled overnight to become "corporations," "trust concerns," and "associations" belonging to those who had enough power of the pen to create them. Office buildings became "free" universities; dacha compounds be- came "holiday homes" for hard currency; the city's state-owned hotels became just another profitable international business. The

KGB went into banking; the church into computers. Cashless roubles were turned into dollars on the exchanges and poured out of the country. Every kind of favour was called in along the way. (These were people who knew each other, after all, had always known each other; so how could they deny each other their support?) Committees on property and privatization funds were set up, making sure that whatever money was raised or property sold went into the right (the same old) hands. Export licences? No problem: "Here, you can fill it in yourself." Preferential bank credit? "Here's my number; just give me a call." Dachas, holiday resorts: everything was available. Newspaper puffs and television tributes: anything could be had for cash on the nail. And now, of course—bliss!— that the political situation had been finally "stabilized," there were more dollars pouring into the country to help the "new" economy. (Marks, pounds, and the rest . . . well, they were simply "geography": everything had to be in dollars from now on.) "You want real estate, Mr. Foreigner? Here, sign this consultancy agreement." "You want oil and timber and aluminum? A little something in my account in the Cayman Islands would do." To the victors went the spoils—and the spoils were huge. By the time the dust settled, and the free market the West had demanded had more or less emerged, the economy had been effectively filched. What had emerged was not capitalism, or even cooperative socialism, but Macondo's own special domestic variant: *nomenklaturism*—socialism for the already powerful and capitalism for the rest. The ruling class and its attendant Mafias had simply taken over everything that was available, that wasn't (again) nailed solidly down.

And what about the people in all this, the ordinary man in the street? Well, Western economists, in their infinite wisdom, had demanded, as a precondition for aid from the West, that street prices should be "liberalized." And so, in January 1992, they were. But what the economists had forgotten was that some degree of genuine

privatization might perhaps have come first; that some extra production capacity or stockpiling of goods would have been a good idea.
They might even have remembered that a degree of competition is
necessary to the workings of a free market. But they didn't. So all
that happened on the ground as a result—as the prices for basic
commodities soared overnight and inflation set in in earnest—was
that people's savings were progressively wiped out—confiscated in
effect—and handed over either to still hugely inefficient state industries or to the Mafias, the black marketeers, who busily cornered such
market as there was. This might have been the intention, of course,
of the Western economists; one can put nothing past them. They
might have thought that it was time to give a boost to the Mafias,
since they were the only groups—apart from the *nomenklatura*—who
understood the nature of capitalism. They might have thought that
once the general population was stony broke, it would immediately
turn to honest entrepreneurship, helped out by laws against monopo-
lies and against public officials' involvement in commerce.

This might have worked in Geneva or Duluth, Minnesota—or
wherever it is these days that law-abiding White Anglo-Saxon
Protestants, with their fine Christian work ethic, foregather. But it
flew smack in the face of all tradition and history in Russia. Who
was to enforce these perfectly modulated laws, for example, when
everyone (by long habit) was on the take—the *militsia*, the traffic
police, the fraud squad, everyone? Getting the smallest business
started in Moscow in late 1992 cost hundreds of thousands of
roubles, since the local prefecture, the city architect's office, the
power utility, the health inspector, and the fire brigade (among
others) all had to be paid off. So honest entrepreneurship was, for
most people, out of the question. All they could hope to do was sell
what they possessed or horn in on a piece of some already existing
action—*any* action at all. This quickly became a national obsession.

The slightest glance at a history book might have tipped the wink to the Western economists. "In Russia, there has never been a tradition of popular entrepreneurship. Towns were never commer⁄ cial centres, merely administrative centres of the state. Before the Revolution, in fact, there was little experience of private ownership" (Natan Eidelman). Or perhaps a small nod might have been made in the direction of the New Economic Policy of the 1920s, the last time a free market was permitted. "During the New Economic Policy, a one⁄party authoritarian system mixed with free enterprise tended to unleash the worst aspects of both. It was an age of rampant corruption and speculation. Brothels and opium dens flourished in Moscow. People made fortunes buying and selling food, some of it donated by the American Relief Administration. Inflation was so high that the government annually lopped several zeros off the value of the rouble." Or this: "The ban on private enterprise had been lifted [by the New Economic Policy] and trade within certain narrow limits was allowed. Deals were made on the scale of the turnover of a rag and bone merchant in a flea market and their pettiness led to profiteering and speculation. No new wealth was created by these transactions and they did nothing to relieve the squalor of the town, but fortunes were made out of the futile selling and reselling of goods already sold a dozen times over."

These last words come from Pasternak's *Doctor Zhivago*—not exactly prescribed reading, I suppose, among Western economists. And I think of them whenever I go to the markets in Moscow and see the sad bundles of possessions on sale outside, and then compare their prices with the astronomical (Mafia⁄fixed) costs of the meat and vegetables on the counters inside. I think of them too whenever the phone rings with news of some new harebrained transaction that one of my friends has got wind of and wants to get involved in: buying up surplus Red Army gas masks, for example, or selling Korean electronics to Iceland. "Business in Russia," someone I know said recently, "now consists in a meeting between one person with no

goods and another one with no money. When the deal is made, they
rush off to see whether they can actually get what they've promised."
It's called "trading in air" *(torgovlya vozdukhom),* and it's now more
or less universal. Nobody today seems to be producing any new
goods. Everyone I know is either broke or a hood or is dealing in
dreams. I wonder how long it can possibly last.

Paradox Number Two: Everything imported into Russia has a
tendency to turn into the opposite of itself. European socialism
becomes Oriental despotism. Capitalism turns into *nomenklatura*
socialism with an individual face. The well-meaning efforts of
Western economists will soon be seen as a plot to enmire the great
Russian nation.

                                4

Perhaps in Boris Yeltsin's Kremlin they understand something of all
this. But I doubt it. Russians, after all, are no better at their own
(sequential, exemplary) history than we are. And the country is still
so huge that laws and edicts, unless backed by force, emanate from
its centre only to disappear into the outlands, leaving barely an echo.
Besides, those who occupy the Kremlin these days are busy: they're
involved in a struggle for power, say insiders, as intense as any in the
past. "It's the Kremlin's legacy," said a friend of mine, a television
producer and People's Deputy, recently. "Once men take office
there, they sooner or later succumb to the spirit of intrigue and
paranoid power-jockeying that's been sucked over the years into its
walls. Nothing at all has changed today, except perhaps for the
names on the doors. In some ways you could say it's actually worse.
In Gorbachev's time, you could simply walk in if you had an
appointment. Now you have to be met at the gates."

"Yeltsin is no Gorbachev," another deputy told me. "Gorbachev was very much his own man. He didn't listen to advice much;

he tended to make up his own mind about things. But even he, when the going got tough, was in the end ruled by the people who got his ear—particularly by Kryuchkov, the KGB chief, who convinced him at the beginning of 1991, for example, that demon-strators were going to use hooks and grapnels to invade the Kremlin. Well, times have changed, of course; the KGB is perhaps not quite so powerful. But Yeltsin relies much more on advice than Gorba-chev ever did. And there are any number of competitors for his ear. The stakes are very high. For whoever has his ear in the end runs the country."

Paradox Number Three: Yeltsin is by instinct a boss, but he's a weak boss. The power increasingly belongs to those who always had it, the new business *nomenklatura*.

Chapter II

May–October 1992

I

In the spring of 1992, I took a walk through the Nikolina Gora woods with Andrei Alexandrov-Agentov, the slight, sparrow-boned Siberian who had been chief foreign-policy advisor to four Soviet heads of state. He was on the point of retiring from his job in the archives of the Foreign Ministry; he was beginning to write his memoirs, he said. As we walked, the buds were bursting out of the trees overhead; the fiddle ferns were pushing out of the exhausted mulch of last year's leaves so fast that you could almost see them grow. Spring in Russia comes each year like an impossible victory.

He was in retrospective mood that day. We talked, as we walked, about the people he'd worked for: first about Alexandra Kollontai, the legendary Bolshevik agitator and proselytizer for free sex who'd become the commissar for social welfare in Lenin's first government. He had met her in 1940 in Stockholm, where she was ambassador, and where he'd been sent, straight out of university, as a second-string correspondent for TASS. A couple of years later, he'd joined her staff. "She was a very interesting woman, of noble family," he said in his odd, careful, high-pitched voice. "But after the Revolution she became one of the leaders of what was called the

Workers' Opposition, which wanted to give economic power to the trade unions, and thus take it away from the Party. There was a terrible battle, with Trotsky and Bukharin against her, on the opposite side, and Lenin and Zinoviev somewhere in the middle. It almost broke the Party apart. So after it was over, Lenin sent her off to Scandinavia in 1923, and Stalin chose to keep her there. I think she was glad to go—her husband of that time was having affairs with his secretaries and so on. And perhaps it was just as well. When she finally came back to Moscow as an old woman, she was able to die in her bed. I still go to her grave on her anniversary every year. There are few of us left."

"When did you come back to Moscow yourself?"

"In 1947. It was the first time I'd ever set foot in the Foreign Ministry Building. I became a secretary of the Department of North-ern European Affairs; then assistant to the chief; then vice-chief. Then I was Gromyko's foreign-policy advisor for four years."

"So you knew Prosecutor General Vishinsky after he became Foreign Minister?"

"Yes. He was one of the most loathsome people I've ever known."

"And Khrushchev?"

"A little." He stopped. "You know, he made many mistakes, Nikita Khrushchev, especially perhaps in agriculture. But he made one remarkable decision that he doesn't get enough credit for: He decided that you didn't have to kill your political enemies in order to hold on to power." He laughed, then walked on. "He was a very . . . bluff man. I remember that he was suspicious of his son-in-law's drinking. [His son-in-law was Alexei Adjubei, the editor of *Iz-vestia*.] Once, when we were travelling by ship to the United States in a huge delegation, he stopped at the table where his son-in-law was sitting and picked up the bottle of mineral water in front of him to sniff it, to see if it was vodka!"

We walked on towards the architects' village, Builders of Cities, in the woods in front of us. Children were playing war games in the trees around us. "And then you worked for Leonid Brezhnev," I said.

"Yes. When I began, I was his only foreign-policy advisor, but then I was joined by two others, both from the Foreign Ministry. I kept America and Canada, part of Europe, and the Near East. I used to have to read about six hundred documents a day: KGB and military-intelligence analyses, dispatches from TASS, briefings from ambassadors and residents, papers from the ministries. I had to reduce all these, and for the first ten years I reported to Leonid Ilyich every day. After that, well, briefings were less regular; different factors came into play. His health, you see, had been ruined by sleeping pills; he was insomniac and moody. He was depressed about his family: his son and daughter were both alcoholics; Galina, particularly, was going to the bad. At weekends he stayed in the Kremlin and slept in order to avoid them. The door to him during that time was guarded by Konstantin Chernenko, who was the only man who knew how to present material to him in this state."

"What was he like?"

"Brezhnev? Oh, very personable, very charming in many ways. And I think that if he'd been in charge for only ten years, he'd have been an excellent leader. He was always trying to improve the life of ordinary people. He was, after all, an ordinary man himself: he came from a simple worker's family; he'd worked in a metal plant for a number of years; and he was basically a good man. He and Nixon got along very well together; they were never aggressive with one another. And they achieved a great many things: the first SALT agreement, new terms of trade, the doctrine of peaceful coexistence. Watergate put an end to much of this, of course. I remember when Nixon came for the last time; there was a feeling that he was finished. There was a cruise on the Black Sea, and when he stood up to make a toast, he could only just keep his feet. He was very drunk."

We came out of the trees past piles of building materials, and went through the gate into Builders of Cities. Inside the fence, the houses leaned up against each other across tiny gardens; it was like a ramshackle toy town. Everywhere there was the sound of hammer- ing and sawing. People were patching and mending their roofs for the summer season. We watched them for a moment. Then: "And Gorbachev?" I asked quietly.

He turned. "I first met him in 1982," he said. "He's a hard man to describe."

"He's been accused of being a ditherer, someone who didn't lead, but only responded to events."

"Oh, no—quite the opposite, I think. My impression is . . . well, I remember that when he asked me to stay on as foreign-policy advisor, he was rather perfunctory: he had none of the great warmth that Brezhnev had, for instance. He was not a good listener—which made it difficult for me later on, since I had to give him briefings. No, I think he was the opposite of what you say: he was in fact very decisive. He often made decisions in the face of Gromyko's advice, for example, which up to that time had been regarded as more or less sacrosanct."

"How do you rate him now as a politician?"

He laughed, then grimaced. He wouldn't be drawn.

"All right, then. Who's the most able politician you've known?"

"Brezhnev's successor, Yuri Andropov." We began to walk back through the village. "We were friends for thirty years. In fact he once worked under me, when Molotov came back to the Foreign Ministry in 1953, and there was talk of Andropov becoming ambas- sador in Denmark. I liked him very much; he was very intelligent and delicate, and probably the most interesting and able politician

of them all. His time as head of the KGB was perhaps unfortu-
nate—spending too much time with the security services can narrow
one's horizons. But ideologically he was on the same plane as I." He
paused as he opened the village gate to let me through. "Andropov
would never have allowed socialism to slide into capitalism. Never,"
he said.

Later, as we trudged out onto the road in Nikolina Gora by
Prokofiev's old house, he said: "Do you know what I saw last week,
Jo? In the *gastronom* near me in the city, kefir was on sale for a rouble
and eighty kopecks. People were buying it out of the back door for
three roubles, and selling it out front for ten. It's madness!" He
walked on for a moment in silence, then squinted up at the sun.
"You know, this is almost the first long walk I've taken since my
beloved [wife] Margarita died last year. And though there is not an
hour when I don't miss her terribly, I'm glad in a way that she died
when she did, so that she didn't have to see all the mess and chaos
that is happening today. I, too, have lived too long, I think. Perhaps
my whole generation. I'm ready to leave."

Andrei Alexandrov-Agentov is in his mid-seventies: a modest,
even ascetic man who survives today on a small pension. He lives
in Nikolina Gora in a two-storey dacha that used to belong to a man
named Gorbachev who was in charge of transport in occupied
Germany after World War II. (He is not a pushy man: he was kept
on a waiting list for seventeen years before he got it, during which
time two Central Committee members were turned down flat.)
Downstairs is a huge glassed-in terrace, and upstairs a fine, if rickety,
balcony, overlooking a rolling glade of tall, peaked conifers that
might be in Switzerland. At the other end of the overgrown garden,
by the gate into Kachalev Alley, is a low brick building where his
two daughters live during summer weekends. One is a special
internal-affairs correspondent for TASS; the other, after a time with
Coca-Cola, is the PR representative of a foreign oil company. Her

husband works for the Committee for Pan-European Cooperation on Energy and spends most of his time in Brussels. At a summer birthday party for the TASS correspondent daughter recently, one of the guests was the daughter of the onetime head of Goskomizdat, the state publishing organization. She was a doctor in a sanitarium and had a lot to say, amid much laughter, about Yeltsin's Monday rest cures after the excesses of his weekends.

These are the second-and-third-generation aristocracy of the Party: now either disillusioned and old, or else happily scattered, under the new dispensation, into the professions, state service abroad, joint ventures, and foreign companies. A lot of the houses in Nikolina Gora tell different versions of the same story—though undercut, often, by the sort of hair-raising ironies in which the history of this country seems to specialize. On one side of Alexandrov-Agentov's house, for example, is the dacha of Tupolev, the plane builder who designed aircraft for Stalin in a special prison camp like that described by Solzhenitsyn in *The First Circle,* and where his son, also a plane maker, now works for an industry almost totally dependent for its survival on foreign investment. On the other side is the house of the deputy chief of Stalin's bodyguard—a man much feared in his time in the village—which his granddaughter, married to a man said to be high in military intelligence, is anxious to rent to foreigners for $1,000 (or about five years' average salary) a month.

2

Things have changed in Nikolina Gora in the two and a half years that Yelena and I have been here. It has lost its innocence; the outside world has invaded it. When we first arrived in 1990, the dachas here had no particular value, except that they were in a nice, relatively remote place, with tennis and volleyball courts and a pleasant beach along the river. Painters and writers rented space in them when they could find it. Occasionally one would change hands when a family moved away or there was no one to inherit. But the council still had to approve any and all newcomers; and in any case there was little money (by Western standards) involved. So most of the houses remained what they had always been: a family place in the country; privileged, certainly, but rundown, endlessly patched-up, with outhouses rotting away for lack of materials to hold them together. Permission was given that year by the coopera-tive to put up new buildings on the dacha properties, but for most people it remained only an academic option. Wood was virtually impossible to get; nails hadn't been seen in large quantities for ages; and the waiting list for bricks in the central Moscow outlet was fifteen years long. Besides, though the *dachniki* owned a share in the cooperative, they didn't (technically speaking) own their dachas or the land they stood on, which had been rented from the beginning from the local soviet. There was still no such thing as private ownership; the whole business was extremely uncertain.

Only Guram, the Georgian brain surgeon, of all our friends, was prepared to buck odds as long as these. He'd somehow got hold of bits and pieces of land two villages away from us—not far from Gryaz (or Mud)—which he'd managed to parlay into a single holding. And he'd sold everything of value he had—an old Mer-cedes, some computer equipment—to buy gifts and construction materials and huge numbers of bottles of champagne and vodka ("liquid money") for the building of a dacha. He used to pass by, that first summer, with an almost continuous, hilarious nightclub act about his latest dodge or wrinkle: how he'd paid off the *militsia* to hire him a truck straight off the Garden Ring, for example; how he'd posed as a young Komsomol leader to find the secret entrance to the crucial brick factory; how he'd stood knee-deep in the snow, handing out tiny amounts of forbidden-fruit dollars to this or that plant manager; and how he'd been forced into demented, terrifying binges with electricians or builders to prove to them that he was a Georgian, not a Jew. It was all very funny. And it didn't occur to me till much later that to build something as overt as a private dacha in those days required equal amounts of *blat* and sheer nerve. To do it, Guram had to commit himself (on a large scale) to the twilight, half-criminal world where crooked officials, the Mafia, and foreign traders met.

In the summer of 1990, too, a dacha in Nikolina Gora changed hands for serious money for the first time. Yuri Bashmet, the viola player who looked like a Beatle or the young Ilie Nastase, bought a dacha compound near the road to the beach in Nikolina Gora for a reported $40,000. This was actually both illicit and meaningless, since (a) dealing in any currency except the rouble was against the law, and (b) the only thing that could be legally bought in any case was a cooperative share. But Bashmet was the sort of person the council approved of: he'd rented a house in Nikolina Gora before; he'd given concerts in the little hut on the village green. So it was all seen as something more or less normal, and not as a kind of writing on the wall.

It all seemed normal then, in fact. A number of years before, some of the more awful anomalies of the village's past had been corrected. The cooperative had done whatever it could to compen-sate the rehabilitated victims of the orgy of arrests and imprisonments that had spread through Nikolina Gora (as everywhere else) in the late twenties and the thirties. The son of a murdered doctor had been given land on which to build. The wife of an economist who died in the camps had been offered new housing. Sometimes dachas had had to be split in two to satisfy all parties. Not far away from Fyodor's house, for example, was a dacha which had been divided to accommodate the families of two physiologists, one of whom had been eaten up by the Gulag, the other of whom had been his legitimate successor when the house had been confiscated. Next door to us, too, the two daughters of a famous lawyer—both of whom had been arrested and imprisoned—had been given back half the house which an architect and his family had taken over. Now, though, the legacy of Stalin's assault on the village had been finally settled—with the return from the state and the disposition of what was still called the Vishinsky House.

The Vishinsky House lay directly opposite the tennis court; it lowered over the main road behind an elaborate gateway, and had originally belonged to a well-known historian named Gordon. He was arrested and disappeared in the first wave of purges, and it was then taken over by an old Bolshevik called Serebriakov (who may or may not have been responsible for Gordon's disappearance). Not far from him, though, in a wooden dacha, lived the odious state Prosecutor General Andrei Yanuaryevich Vishinsky, whom Alex-androv-Agentov later knew at the Foreign Ministry. Vishinsky was at the time Stalin's legal hatchet man: he orchestrated the most important of the purge trials (of Bukharin, Zinoviev, Kamenev, etc.) and decimated the leadership of the Red Army. In a 1937 report, he gave an account of his approach to his job. In interroga-tion and trial, he wrote, it was only ever possible to establish relative guilt, so it was useless to try to find absolute evidence. Proofs of guilt were approximate and could be found, he added, without the investigator having to leave his office, "basing his conclusions not only on his own intellect but also on his Party sensitivity, his moral forces, and his character." For these office musings of his and for the rabid accusations that followed, the defendants invariably thanked him, promptly admitted to conspiracy, praised Stalin, and begged for the most severe sentences—which is exactly what they got. When he died in 1954, in the vulgar Park Avenue mansion the Soviets bought from an American millionaire, United Nations Secretary General Dag Hammarskjöld and French Prime Minister Pierre

Mendès-France rushed to pay their respects. Singer Paul Robeson burst into tears at the sight of his black-rimmed portrait. Harold Laski described him sadly as "a man whose passion was law reform."

They remember him differently in Nikolina Gora. For this passionate jurisprudent, not content with his wooden dacha and envying Serebriakov's, simply had Serebriakov arrested and shot. He himself moved in, taking over much of the property next door, and occupied it until his death, when he left it to the state. The matter of its rightful ownership wasn't resolved until a couple of years before Yelena and I arrived there, when after a long battle it was finally returned to the cooperative. The council then sat in judgment and announced that it should be divided in half and given to the nearest surviving descendants of both Gordon and the old Bolshevik Serebriakov. They had recently moved in side by side: two elderly women, one who had spent her childhood in the camps, the other a translator, a member of the Writers' Union.

The cooperative council was proud of this Solomonic judgment. And though there were still some residents it regretted having given space to in the past—like the son of Brezhnev's disgraced minister of the interior, Igor Shchelokov, and the children of the corrupt minister for state planning, Nikolai Baibakov, who lived in an area at the end of the village known as "the kindergarten"—the mixture of inhabitants was much what it had always been from the beginning: instrumentalists, composers, painters, scientists, and workers in the Institutes. In 1990, Viktor Sukhadrev, Khrushchev's and Brezhnev's interpreter, came back with his wife, Inga, from his job at the UN to give his astonishing impression of a sauntering English clubman. Kolya Petrov and Sviatoslav Richter both gave concerts on the village green. The children practised for the volleyball competition. The tennis competition went off on time. Sacha Lipnitsky, it's true, rented his apartment in the city to a foreign correspondent for hard currency. But apart from him—and the musicians who worked abroad—no one seemed to have much money, or to be much bothered by its absence. People took offerings to each other's dachas—fruit or vodka or a bakery cake, whatever they could afford. Rock music was still listened to. People still went to the cinema and to the theatre. And, though a certain exhaustion was beginning to settle in, people were still reading the thick journals from cover to cover. Conversation, in the Russian way, was still never small.

3

By 1991, though, things had changed. The winter had been impos-sibly hard. In October, only sixty million tons of harvest had been delivered to the state; more than half of Moscow's meat stores had had nothing at all to sell. In November the country's credit rating had dropped to thirty-fourth place out of one hundred and twelve; the city, this time, had run out of milk; Gorbachev had announced direct presidential rule, and Shevardnadze had promptly resigned, warning of a right-wing coup. In December, meat had disappeared even from the farmers' markets when the city's Executive Committee had tried to impose price ceilings; and the first European Commu-nity aid had arrived, as if Moscow were the capital of some third-world country. In January, things had got even worse: the government had suddenly declared all fifty- and one-hundred-rouble notes simply null and void—a move, it said, that was aimed at the Mafias, but which in the end took money out of ordinary people's pockets. By the time Yelena, Katya, and I arrived back in Moscow for the big pro-Yeltsin demonstration (and Katya's first birthday) at the end of March, the mood in the city was grim and apocalyptic. It wasn't surprising that Gorbachev believed all the stories that were told him about gangs of toughs gathering together all over the city and about demonstrators being ready to invade the Kremlin. On the morning of the demonstration, we were fairly jittery ourselves. There were fifty thousand soldiers guarding the only country that Gorba-chev could be said to rule with confidence any longer: the area around the Kremlin girded by the city's Boulevard Ring. Every-where else there seemed to be nothing but bitterness and chaos.

The demonstration was huge. (It was a rehearsal, as somebody later put it, for the defence of the White House, just as the OMON killings in Lithuania two and a half months before had been a dry run for the putsch.) But it was entirely—and astonishingly—peace-ful. The weather was warm; foreign TV cameras were everywhere (on the ground, on the roofs above us); Ksiyusha and I met a lot of people we knew. But then, five days after it, came "the day of mourning," or "Paul's day," when Prime Minister Pavlov cynically raised consumer prices, as if to see whether Moscow and the Soviet Union could take any more. Children's shoes went up overnight by three hundred percent; school uniforms by five hundred; pens by two hundred and fifty. Flour, rice, meat, and some kinds of bread more than tripled in price. Tatiana Samoilovna cackled exasperatedly when she came home that evening. "Another brilliant day! Those people in the government, what do they imagine this is all for?"

"To stimulate investment?" I suggested, straight-faced.

"Ha! Then they're even stupider than they look. All that's happening is that money's being taken from those who don't have any and given to those who do! The bosses and the Mafia! They'll just take it and run."

It was hard to fault her. New businesses—kiosks and so-called "commercial" shops—were springing up all over the city. The city's hotels were swarming with smugglers and small-time entrepreneurs from Eastern Europe. Lorries were pouring in from the West—often rented by Russian emigrés—carrying secondhand goods, bin ends, and finished lines: anything at all that would sell. The fixed prices in the farmers' markets were rising, it seemed, almost daily. People were being separated from their money just in order to be able to survive. I remember sitting with Yelena in a hard-currency restaurant one day and listening all around us to business chatter: talk of cooperatives and market outlets and the problems of buying wholesale in the West. Yelena said: "I recognize half the people here, Jo. It's unbelievable. They're the old pimps and hookers from the National Hotel bar."

Fyodor came in from Nikolina Gora in the middle of April to get an advance on his rent for the summer. "It can't go on like this," he said. "It's crazy. Everybody knows it. It's like Chicago in the thirties. It's like Nero playing the violin while Rome's burning. There'll be a putsch—the army and the right wing will take over— and people will be glad." He told me the salaries he got from Moscow University and the Academy of Sciences and added on the sixty roubles that had been handed out as compensation for the price rises. It was what I spent in the market in four or five days. "I'm doing some private work," he said, "a geological survey for some people in the north. But if it wasn't for you, I don't think I would survive."

Most of our friends were just as depressed—and as desperate. Tolya, the film fixer, whom I'd recommended to a number of British producers, had been visiting lawyers, anxiously trying to find some legal means of doing what he was doing: i.e., working for hard currency. The lawyers had hemmed and hawed and charged him a fortune. Then they'd finally advised him to do it na lyevo. Nobody, they said, knew what the laws on hard currency were or whether they would be allowed to operate at Tolya's level. Besides, if he went through official channels, they told him, first he'd have to pay enormous bribes, and second, he'd never know if his name hadn't been sold off, as a potential profit earner, to a Mafia protection racket.

Tomas, too, was facing problems. The bribery necessary to get

his plant operating was mounting, he said; the city's central administration and its district executives were fighting for control and money
in different parts of the city, almost building by building. Meanwhile, he said, he just wasn't earning enough roubles to live. He
wanted me to help him with the idea of a series of films to be made
from the KGB archives—he'd just taken on an ex–KGB officer
who, Yelena said, had been her protector when she'd worked for
Goskino. But though we went to the Lubyanka building together
to see a KGB general and his staff, it soon became clear that, like
everybody else, they too were waiting for the highest hard-currency
bidder. Everyone who had anything to do with the film business
(like Tomas) was waiting: everyone had a perhaps deal with David
Puttnam or was just finishing a script for Meryl Streep. The native
film industry had more or less disappeared in a dream of the West.
As for the KGB, well, they too were doing what they could: later
in the year they offered sanitized tours of the Lubyanka at thirty
dollars a head. Tourists were told that sadly they could not take
photographs, since they would not then buy the postcards that "the
friends" had for sale.

Guram, when he came to the apartment, was as obsessed as the
KGB with the problem of earning hard currency. In his cups one
night, he confessed that he hadn't performed a brain operation since
the previous May. He'd taken a leave of absence from his institute
to start his dacha, and now he'd been put in charge of a neurological
conference that was due to be held during the summer in Moscow.
A large number of neurologists and brain surgeons were coming
from abroad—and a lot of hard currency was being generated. Joint
ventures and cooperatives were circling like sharks, and he had to
deal with them. He'd been threatened and offered bribes, he said; he
couldn't take it anymore. He simply had to get out and go into
business for himself. ("I can no longer afford to be a doctor," he said
sadly.) The problem was that, though he had immense energy, he

didn't really know how to be a businessman at all (any more than I did). Through some contact or other, he later found some aluminium that could be offered for sale to the West; but when he sent a fax to a London metal broker I knew, he overestimated its amount by a factor of a thousand and so wasn't taken seriously. And when I introduced him to an Englishman who owned a pub in Moscow to talk about the cost of importing Western beer, he immediately hatched a scheme to sell a proportion of it cheaply for roubles, a scheme that would have beggared him—eaten up his profits and more—before he'd even begun. The failure of these ideas, though, only seemed to make him more desperate. "There's so much money out there, Jo," he said one evening. "I went to see a friend of mine the other day, and there was a case in the hallway. 'What's that?' I said. And he said: 'Oh, a friend came up from the south. He wants me to buy something for him, anything.' It was thirty million roubles in *cash,* Jo!" I went with him one day to his institute, to make a telephone call—the most prestigious institute for neurosurgery in the Soviet Union. There was a nameless ooze of rubbish in the forecourt; the stairways smelled of cat piss. He showed me a ruinous building site at the back of his office. "What can I do, Jo?" he said. "That's our new building. They've been working on it now for eight years."

4

By the time we got to Nikolina Gora in June—just after Boris Yeltsin had been elected Russia's president—Fyodor had decided that his only option was to leave the country. "I can't go on doing nothing but patch up this dacha," he said. "I have to work. Grisha"—his son—"is going to San Diego with his mother. Yelena"—his second wife—"is Jewish. We can go to Israel."

"There's not much work for a geologist in Israel," I said.

"I know, Jo. But some people from the United Emirates are interested in my work. And then people came from Switzerland, looking for inventions, and my assay technique was one of the only two or three they thought good enough to take back." Fyodor had developed with a colleague a technique of assaying drill samples on-site, and assessing them quickly for the presence of oil, diamonds, and precious metals. It seemed to me, on the face of it—from his figures—much cheaper and better than Western methods. (I'd writ-ten some letters on his behalf to Australia.) "But here they'll never let me develop it or use it, Jo. The professors and people in the industry say: 'Yes, that's very interesting. But it's not the way we do it here.' They have their vested interests, you see. They try to steal the work, because of their contacts. But they'll never admit that they're wrong and we're right."

"What will you do about the dacha?"

"It's the only thing I possess. I'll have to sell it to give me a start in the West. People come all the time asking to buy it: maybe for fifty thousand dollars. There's a market here now."

There was indeed a market in Nikolina Gora. Below us, on the riverfront, a joint venture of some kind had fenced off a meadow and had put up picnic tables. Access to its (previously free) stretch of the river was now for credit cards only. Diplomats' Beach, too, was beginning to change; it was increasingly crowded at weekends with foreign cars with ordinary Moscow number plates, which could later be seen prowling the lanes, looking for property. At the "kindergarten" end of the village, new dachas were being built on tiny pieces of land, by the national skating coach Tatiana Tarasova and her classical-pianist husband; by a famous singer from the 1960s; and by the Baibakov children, one of whom was married to the general manager of the city's world trade complex. There was a scandal, moreover, in Nikolina Gora that year: Deputy Prime Minister Alexandra Biryukova had made a sweetheart deal on a state dacha not far from Prokofiev's house, buying it for a laughable seventeen thousand roubles. There were rumours all over the village that worse was to come: joint ventures, people said, were coming in to take over state houses and compounds, with Igor Shchelokov as their point man and local real-estate broker; the soviet which owned the land, they said, was on the point of putting up the cooperative's rents to something totally unmanageable. The only option the (mostly elderly) owners felt they had was to join forces with their children and put up second dachas on their plots of land. That way, it might be possible to sell off one to stem the coming tide.

The tide could already be seen rising in the villages on the far side of Nikolina Gora. Everywhere, even in open fields, foundations were being laid; piles of bricks and wood and scaffolding were rising. It was plain that the bosses of the local soviet and the farms were lining their pockets. (I was offered a small plot of land near one of the villages for fifteen thousand dollars.) I went out to see Guram at his unfinished dacha one day—he now had a dream of starting a medical insurance company. "Who are all these people who're building out here?" I asked. He shrugged his shoulders. "People with joint ventures," he said, "people who work with foreign companies." He introduced me to one of his future neighbours, one of the Russian managers for Mercedes-Benz. He looked, of course, like a middle-level Party apparatchik—which is exactly, presumably, what he had been until then.

5

"Soon it will just be a dormitory suburb for Moscow, I'm afraid," said Sacha Lipnitsky one day, as we were walking his dog, Uziya, through Nikolina Gora. "It will be subdivided and subdivided out of existence because of the problem of money."

Yelena and I spent a lot of time that summer—both before and after the coup—with Sacha Lipnitsky and his wife, Ina. Sacha's band, Zvuki Mu—after touring in Britain and America (and making a record with Brian Eno)—had fallen apart. Its lead singer, Peter Mamonov, once a legendary drunk, had dried out and become an actor instead. "He is now only interested in material things, I'm afraid." So Sacha still rented out his apartment in the city, and lived in Nikolina Gora year round with his wife, a country woman from near Arkhangelskoye, and their two young children. "I want to make sure they have a good start in life," he said.

Sacha was in his late thirties—bearded, full-lipped, with a taste for embroidered, slightly ecclesiastical-looking shirts and caps that gave him the look of a senior acolyte or a junior imam. He also had an absolutely natural, instinctive generosity, which meant that his house was always open to all comers. Artyom and Svetlana came out and stayed with him often; so did Boris Grebenshchikov whenever he came to Moscow. And so did an odd assortment of people, all roughly speaking his own age, who gathered together for occasional parties. Some were brokers at the new exchanges; some were returned emigrés now in business; one or two had been in the camps. There were filmmakers and philosophers; Party *apparatchiki* sozzled with drink; even a well-known Moscow hooker. One day I asked Sacha how he knew them all.

"They're my Big Chill, Jo," he said. "I know it's very hard for you to understand. But they're all that's left of my generation, the Brezhnev generation. How can I explain to you? Well, you see, look, the invasion of Czechoslovakia in 1968 was very important to us; it was our coming of age. But there was nothing we could do about it. We were completely impotent; we had no stake in the country or in the culture; we had nothing. So after that came what I call the long loss of the seventies. It was a time of total cynicism— and of alcohol. Stagnation equalled alcohol—and psychiatric hospitals. My brother lost his brain, his health, and his life, as did many others. Fyodor wasted time. I lost ten years of my life, the years between twenty and thirty. I spent seven years in journalism school, but it was a total waste of time. I was also in the icon business. Did you know?"

"Yes." I'd heard he'd been a dealer in icons, a restorer, a black marketeer, protected, it was said, by his stepfather, the interpreter Viktor Sukhadrev, who some people insisted was a full colonel in the KGB.

"Well, I did that," he said. "And others did other things, took different ways out. Some of them became currency dealers and were arrested. Some emigrated. Some became Party bureaucrats. Some of the women became prostitutes, trying to attract foreigners and escape. But many stayed here and were destroyed by alcohol—many. I can show you dachas round here where friends of mine died, dead drunk, in fires. There's another dacha that belonged to a friend of my parents, a composer. There was a drunken party there, and some friends of the son, Genya, took the father's car and a girl with them. They crashed the car and the girl died; they panicked and buried her and ran away. The composer had a stroke and died soon afterwards." He stared bleakly at the table. "It was a time," he said, echoing Boris Grebenshchikov three years before, "of great . . . sin. We were all part of the same sin. Otherwise we might have become fighters."

"What changed it?" I asked.

"Well, the dissident movement and samizdat helped. I remember when Artyom gave me a samizdat copy of Aksyonov's *Island in the Crimea* to read overnight, it changed my life. And then, well, in my case there was the band, Zvuki Mu. Do you know that my dacha was the scene of one of the most famous concerts in Russian rock history?"

"No."

He laughed. "Well, the first concert we ever gave was in 1984, when Chernenko was organizing the KGB against rock. It was for a school reunion at the school which Peter Mamonov and I had both been thrown out of. I somehow persuaded the director that we would provide the music, which he clearly thought would be waltzes and so on. Instead, we had Viktor Tsoy, and it was Bravo's second concert; and the word, of course, got around; and all the rock people were there. A friend of mine brought a video camera, one of the first we'd ever seen. He had no idea what he was doing and the result was very weak, but there are all these huge close-ups of people who became big heroes. The director of the school, I'm afraid, later had big trouble from the KGB, and I was arrested as I came out of my flat on some trumped-up passport charge. Chernenko was very stupid, I think, and I was very brave that year.

"Well, we had to go on having concerts, you know, but I couldn't think where—except, maybe, out here. So I asked the director of the little music festival in Nikolina Gora, where Bashmet and Richter had played, whether we could perform a concert. She agreed and even the police had no objection—they were completely ignorant; they gave us permission to play till eleven at night. We were going to have Aquarium, Viktor Tsoy, and Mike Naumenko of Zoopark.

"But then the KGB went into action. They went to Mike Naumenko's place of work and warned him off. They visited Artyom and threatened him. And then, after the bands from Leningrad had arrived in Nikolina Gora in a big bus, six or seven black Volgas appeared through the trees. It was very sinister. KGB men got out and started asking questions about what the council had organized in such a small, poor place. The colonel in charge said it was obviously a diversion and provocation from the West. The director, the widow of a famous composer, was very frightened. And so were the Moscow bands when they arrived—they'd been intercepted by the KGB along the way. Last Chance came, and

Bravo—though their lead singer, Zhanna Aguzarova, was in prison at the time—to join Kino and Aquarium and Zvuki Mu. The KGB told all of them to take their equipment and send their fans away—there was going to be no concert.

"Well, I was very strong. I said: 'Show me your instructions. Either arrest us or show us your instructions. Otherwise we're going to play.' There was a whole argument then about whether we had official stamps on our lyrics, and if we didn't, whether we could still perform without lyrics or not. And then they just got bored. They brought over the head of the local soviet, who said that he'd cancelled the concert series (which was a lie). And then the KGB colonel simply announced that he would arrest everybody if we tried to play anywhere else but at the dacha. So we brought about a hundred fans up here, followed by the KGB, who remained on duty at the gates until the evening of the following day. We set up the amplifiers on the steps, with me terrified of the Politburo house down the road behind us—though for some reason they were as quiet as a mouse that night. Kino gave their first electric concert. It was really serious, and probably dangerous, what with the rain falling on the cables. A hundred people slept in the house that night; a mere twenty has never fazed me since. My grandmother"—a famous actress who'd spent years in the camps after Stalin's purge of those with contacts with the West—"had a very good time."

"Were there any repercussions afterwards?" I asked.

"There's a legend that Gorbachev spoke at length about this concert to the Central Committee and said that plotters against the state had organized it. No one in Nikolina Gora said hello to me for months afterwards. When the Festival of Youth opened the following year, Gorbachev—who'd taken over by then—was very careful. The festival was strongly controlled by the KGB, and all rock concerts were banned."

6

When winter came, we moved three doors away from Sacha, into Andrei Alexandrov-Agentov's dacha, which had a heated kitchen. And from there we watched the slow disintegration of the Soviet Union; the renaming of St. Petersburg; the gathering paranoia of Gamsakhurdia in Georgia; the birth of Boris Yeltsin's Commonwealth of Independent States; and the resignation of Gorbachev. I went little into the city; Yelena took over the running of our lives. She bought potatoes and pickled cucumbers and mushrooms from a local carpenter. She found a distant cousin of hers, an old primary-school teacher, to come sometimes from Moscow to help with Katya. She found someone to clean at the nearby Council of Ministers' sanitarium, and—through Artyom's wife, Svetlana—a driver, a grizzled retired Red Army colonel, who would take her twice a week in his battered Volga to the shops in Moscow. "There's absolutely no point in going in there!" boomed Kolya Petrov one evening, when he came on a visit. "The old Moscow doesn't exist anymore. There's no theatre or cinema; no premières and poetry readings. There's not even any decent conversation anymore. All people can talk about is money!" Kolya was the last person I knew, I think, to read every journal that came into his house. In winter, he was like an animal in hibernation, with a larder full of newspapers and magazines.

We did go in from time to time, for celebrations and parties. But everything in the city that winter had either a slightly sinister edge or some undercutting tow of sadness. The big New Year's party at Dom Kino, one of the great highlights of the winter season, had the artificial, drunken overexuberance of a wake, as if people realized that, with prices due to rise at least three times in a few days, they wouldn't be able to afford it ever again. A concert by Boris's new band was a chaos of people fighting their way in; and though Boris's music was fine—the best he'd written for years, I thought—the audience laughed and smoked and lolled out of their seats, as if they'd really only come to see each other. Two faintly disturbing snapshots, too, remain in my mind from parties at which there were Georgians. At one, a superbly well-dressed man boasted of how he'd gone that day with his gunmen to protect Shevardnadze against assassination by Gamsakhurdia's emissaries. And at another—Guram's birthday party—he introduced us to a friend of his, who was now a bank president but had once been a government minister. I couldn't help noticing—in one of those persuasive little epiphanies that perhaps mean nothing—that he had a tattoo on his hand.

Only the Russian Christmas Eve party which Sacha and Ina invited us to sticks in my mind with the bright clarity of happiness. It was at Tsaritsyno, the palace that Catherine the Great had abandoned, half-finished. (She hated Moscow; she called it a place full of sloth. "The opportunities for corruption in Moscow," she wrote presciently, "are greater than anywhere else on earth.") One of the buildings, which was partly a museum, had been taken over by a joint venture, and for this evening by a group of film actors. They had organized mummers' plays, singers and dancers in peasant costumes, fireworks, a military band, even horse-drawn sleighs. We went to the church and lit candles among wreaths and bundles of fir branches. We drank vodka and champagne; Ksiyusha, Yelena, and I danced in the snow. It may have been kitschy, designed (perhaps) for the tourists. But in an anxious, fraught winter, it was suddenly like a love letter from the past.

Ksiyusha and Tatiana Samoilovna came out to Nikolina Gora at weekends through January. And from them I heard what was happening in the city. Tatiana Samoilovna said that prices had risen, not three times, as Yeltsin had forecast, but five times, some-times more; and salaries hadn't yet begun to match them. There was almost no work at her laboratory, she said, and she was afraid that she would lose her job. Ksiyusha said that students, too, were having an increasingly miserable time. Their scholarships were now only enough for about one meal in the canteen a day. So a lot of them, she said, were trying to give lessons, or were singing or playing instruments in underground passages. University lavatories and hostels had been turned into bazaars where goods were desperately traded, "like miniature versions of the markets or commodity exchanges."

Guram, too, came by, on his way through the snow to and from his dacha, which was virtually finished. He was by now deeply involved in the medical insurance business. His company had been registered; he'd secured a large bank loan to employ a lawyer and economists; and he was already doing deals, he said, with doctors, hospitals, and large factories. He bubbled over with plans for improving Russian medicine; for paying doctors properly; for getting equipment from abroad; even for putting up new clinics. He was now lobbying the government, he said, for tax concessions, since what he was proposing would take a considerable burden off the shoulders of the state. "And since some of the people I'm dealing with can't offer money but only goods and raw materials," he said cheerfully, "I'm having to be a little bit of a trader as well." I was sceptical about all this—not about Guram's intentions, but because buying medical insurance for a large plant's workers seemed to me, whatever its benefits, a perfect scam for turning still-cashless state resources into money. I hoped that Guram could handle the inevitable call—from ministry officials, hospital administrators, and industrial bosses—of "What exactly is in it for me?"

This was a problem that Tomas, who came most Sundays, was having to face increasingly. He'd left his wife, Galya, and their apartment by now, and was living with his Yelena—who'd blossomed out, become confident—in a home for old actors. And he was desperate to raise money for a place of his own. Given the situation on Moscow's housing market, though, this meant that he'd have to have hard currency. So he was trying to earn it by brokering a real-estate deal between a foreign company and the Moscow officials he'd got to know when setting up his factory. "Oh, but it's so difficult, Jo," he said one Sunday. "These people are so greedy. On one deal alone, they want more than a million dollars." Tomas—straight Tomas, who was Katya's godfather— like most Russian businessmen, carried a gun with him in his car for protection.

On January 26, 1992, a poll conducted for *Moscow News* showed that more than half the population had no idea what democracy was. Three days later, on January 29, Boris Yeltsin issued a decree making it legal for private citizens to sell goods on the streets. On March 25, the astronaut Sergei Krikalyov—dubbed "Major Tom" by the Western press—returned to earth after three hundred and thirteen days in space. (There hadn't been enough money available to bring him down before.) Krikalyov had left the planet shortly after Yeltsin had visited France, to be snubbed and met in a corridor for a few brief minutes by President Mitterrand; at around the time when Gamsakhurdia had been elected president in Georgia by an eighty-seven percent majority. He arrived back to find himself in a totally different country. Shevardnadze was the chairman of Georgia's State Council; Yeltsin had recently come back from a triumphal progress through the United States and France. Moscow had become Dodge City or Chicago. It was a different place.

We did what we could, that winter. Sacha tithed himself, spending a tenth of his income on icons for the churches that were beginning to be restored and reconsecrated in the villages around us. I gave money to, and tried to help, *Novy Mir,* the most famous of the thick journals, which, because of the rise in the cost of paper (and everything else), was now losing millions of roubles a month.

I drafted letters to the Western press, to friends at UNESCO and in New York. I wrote advertising copy and elaborate *cris de coeur* to supporters of the magazine, like Brodsky and Solzhenitsyn, saying that to lose *Novy Mir* would be to lose an indispensable part of the culture, like the Tretyakov Gallery. I suggested setting up the Friends of *Novy Mir;* I proposed benefit concerts and finding sponsorship among the businessmen who'd come from the universities and hospitals in the first wave of the cooperative movement. But it all came to nothing.

"The problem is that they despise us," said Vadim Borisov one evening in his apartment. Borisov, Solzhenitsyn's editor, was the smartest and most interesting man I knew. "They think we belong to the past."

"Who?"

"The businessmen. They're only interested in sponsoring things that will keep people asleep: pop concerts, terrible things on television." Then, after a pause: "Did you know that I didn't work for twelve years? We were constantly harassed by the KGB; they even tried to burn down the apartment." He laughed. "It must seem funny to you."

"No. What surprises me is that it seems funny to you."

"Why not?" He threw his hands wide. "We were young. We were in love. There was everything to believe in. Now, well, now all that's happening is that the worst of the West is flooding in, and the best of Russia is dying."

7

We moved back to Fyodor's in the early summer, and we've been here ever since. As I write, the fields beyond Nikolina Gora are filling up with dachas and markedout plots of land. The Volvos and Mercedeses of the new *dachniki* are travelling down Otto

Schmidt Prospekt at speed, dodging past the lorries filled with lumber and bricks and sand. In the next village, the children of Brezhnev's minister of culture have opened a restaurant. In Nikolina Gora, Igor Shchelokov is said to be trying to start a casino in the old Politburo house behind Sacha Lipnitsky. He already has a buried interest in the *shashlik* stand near Diplomats' Beach—which this year sells Western candy and biscuits, vodka, red wine, and champagne. There is an all-night disco there, too, where the local kids buy drink and fill the night with noise. There've been fights and fracases and a drunken car accident in which a young *dachnik* was decapitated. Our clothes have been stolen from off our washing line; and Sacha's icons have disappeared from the church being restored a mile or two up the road. Kolya and I have offered a reward to the police.

The dollar has arrived, too, in Nikolina Gora. A CNN correspondent has rented a dacha at one end of the village; and there are people from the Washington *Post* in a house at the other. An owner of a Moscow hard-currency supermarket has just moved into the Serebriakov half of the old Vishinsky House. Sacha Lipnitsky, too, has let his dacha for the year to a Western company—though he's moved, for weekends, into another house nearby. He says it's time for his children to get used to city life—"they were getting too wild in the country. Besides, too many of my friends have died in the past year, Jo, almost all of them from drink. It's like the Brezhnev years all over. Mike Naumenko is dead; a film director; other friends—I seem to have been going to memorials and funerals all summer. I've vegetated too long, I think. I must get on with my life." Today, he's in Finland, touring with an all-female band that he manages. His wife, Ina, wants to go to university.

Autumn is now on its way; the leaves are turning; and on almost every plot of land, it seems, new houses are going up. The wood that has been sitting on Fyodor's property all year (as a favour to a friend) is now being picked up by lorries. Fyodor is still here—all his plans for jobs abroad seem to have fallen through—and he's spent the summer completely restoring a wrecked car, helped by an endless succession of neighbours. But he's been accepted now as an immigrant by Germany, and he's filed for privatization of his dacha with the local district, paying a little something extra to jump the line. "I will sell it if I go," he says. "I may have to sell it even if I don't. They say that two different soviets are now claiming that they own the land here; and they're fighting with the council and between themselves about whether it should be classified as agricultural or urban land. Ha! When my grandfather came here, there was nothing but forest, with a little shrine to St. Nicholas down by the river. Now greed will make it cost a fortune to remain."

Andrei AlexandrovAgentov will remain, supported by the rent we mean to pay him this winter. And Kolya and Larisa Petrov will stay, whatever it costs. They've recently bought Andropov's huge apartment in the building on Kutuzovsky Prospekt in which Brezhnev once lived. But though Kolya is enthusiastic about the amount of cable they found under the floors—"The KGB must have been bugging him up his ass!"—he's not really interested. All he wants to do is stay in Nikolina Gora—almost without practising—and leave only to make music. Like anybody here with access to hard currency, he is now rich. When I first came to Moscow, a dollar was worth fiftysix kopecks; now the exchange rate is well over three hundred roubles and rising.

Guram, too, will remain. His dacha is finished: a handsome, gabled brick building, with a sauna, big timbered bedrooms, and a househigh atrium surrounded by balconies. He is now the president of the Association of Medical Insurers, and serves on government advisory panels. And though his wife, Yelena, seemed little interested while he was building the house, she is out in the country on most weekends, happily entertaining the aristocracy of the new rich: television-show hosts and members of Yeltsin's entourage. Guram has changed little in all of this: he is still charming and voluble, an actor capable of any part. But there is a tightness in him these days: the small brush, I sometimes think, of fear. The Mafia have been eyeing his house with envy, I know; and he has talked to me, slightly hollowly, about "the powerful people" he has to have behind him as protection. Once, in his cups, he told me of a potential client who tried to involve him in medical murder.

Tomas, too, will stay. The cassette business he started has run foul of the piracy and flouting of copyright that's fundamental to what is still a multibillion-dollar underground business. So he's withdrawn from it a little. He's still a consultant and he still has his company Mercedes. But he's also become an advisor to a British merchant bank. The bank has taken a lease on a number of dachas the other side of the river from Nikolina Gora, and Tomas will finally have a home there perhaps.

So, too, will Boris Yeltsin. Not long ago he took away Gorbachev's government Zil—the car he swore (as the people's Boris) he himself would never ride in again. Now he is building a large dacha for himself near the turn off the Royal Road to Nikolina Gora. Recently he sent his bodyguards to reclaim yet another dacha not far away, which Gorbachev had given to the local community. Yeltsin is now said to have at least seven dachas, two of which his wife and son are building. He and his colleagues in the Kremlin, too, are said to have restocked all the "special" shops, and to be indulging in an orgy of conspicuous consumption unknown under his predecessor. To the victors go the spoils—until the next victor comes along. "Hurry, hurry!" It is the Russian way.

8

We pack up our rooms at Fyodor's dacha for the winter and go into the city, buying apples and potatoes from the old women in the villages along the way. As we pass down Chekhov Street, the currency dealers outside the local bank are offering almost a hundred more roubles to the dollar than they were a week ago. Volodya, the dancer from upstairs, helps us take the bags out of the car in the courtyard at Vorotnikovsky Alley. His Toyota, he says, has recently been attacked three times in the streets—foreign-made cars have become a target for ordinary people's frustration. The special summer dance-and-opera season at the Stanislavsky Theatre—aimed at hard-currency tourists—has also been a disaster. Black marketeers somehow took it over; there was forging of tickets; and most of the money ended up in an unknown American bank account. Volodya doesn't yet know whether there'll be enough left over for the performers to be paid.

Tanya, Yelena's friend at the Aeroflot office, has another horrifying story to tell. During the summer, she says, she answered an advertisement offering an apartment for sale. She met a well-dressed man—a painter, he said—and saw the apartment, which was rundown but structurally in good shape. They came to terms: nine thousand dollars, provided that some renovation work was done before she moved in. He agreed; the contract was signed at a lawyer's office; and the money—which she'd somehow managed to gather together—was handed over. Then she later went to see how the work was getting on in her new apartment. She let herself in. "There were some drunks there," she says. "They demanded to know what on earth I was doing there; they said it was *their* apartment! I fled. I telephoned the man who'd sold it to me. He said he'd never heard of me before in his whole life. So I called the *militsia*. They went first to the lawyer and asked him why my contract had been signed without witnesses. (I didn't know it had to be.) He said: 'Because I handle all his legal business; I trust him.' Then they went to see the man. He broke down and promised to pay me the money back. But now he's disappeared. And when the *militsia* ask his mother where he is, she says she doesn't know—'and what mother would tell you, even if I did?' " In the evening, depressed, we go to the Taganka Theatre to see Lyubimov's production of *Electra,* which has just come back from its opening at the Athens Festival. The theatre is packed, for old times' sake. But Lyubimov has recently privatized the building, after a sweetheart deal with Mayor Popov, and has sacked large numbers of the fiercely loyal actors and techni-cians who founded the company with him and fought for his return from exile. The production is artificial and self-important—it is definitely Lyubimov's, not Sophocles' *Electra.* It leaves a bad taste in the mouth. When we go to dinner afterwards at Dom Kino, we run into Elem Klimov, the young Turk whose election as the head of the Union of Film Workers was seen as one of the first signs of *glasnost* in action. When Yelena greets him, he stares at her glassily. He is drunk.

The next day, there is more of the same. We go to the Sov-remennik Theatre for a rehearsal of Ariel Dorfman's *Death and the Maiden,* for which I helped the theatre get the Russian rights, and which Yelena translated with a friend during the summer. I talk to the cast about my memories of the London production, and then the director, Galina Volchak, draws me aside. She says that the produc-tion is already immersed in the jealousy and money hunger so typical of Moscow these days. A rival dramaturge has contacted Dorfman's New York agent to say that the translation is disastrous, even though he hasn't seen it and he doesn't speak English. I promise to do what I can to help.

At the Vorotnikovsky Alley apartment, meanwhile, the telephone never stops ringing. The official who deals with Yelena's passport calls to say that his wife has an ulcer, and can we help him find Western medicine? A doctor friend calls to say she desperately needs money for her sick child. A filmmaker friend says that children are now being given two hundred roubles a month for breakfast, so that they won't arrive at school hungry. Only those who earn dollars sound at all confident about surviving the winter. Tolya, the film fixer, is working with a Western crew and making a year's average salary a day. Artyom has a regular column with a new Moscow daily and is still much sought after as an interviewee by Western television. He has a new apartment, bought with hard currency, and he's also building a dacha. He, too, though, is touched by what's happening. He says: "Both Svetlana's parents have lost their jobs, and her father has started drinking. I do what I can, Jo, but I've told Svetlana that she has to come back from London soon to help." He is disillusioned and frustrated by his job in Russian television: he can do nothing to stem the tide of Western imports and garish pop extravaganzas. Instead, somewhat cynically, I think, he has ridden it. During the summer, to the derision of his friends, he was one of the judges at a television pop competition in the Baltics.

Boris Grebenshchikov also calls from St. Petersburg. A tour in Germany that was to have been organized by an emigré friend has just fallen through. He now has to come to Moscow to see if he can get money out of a frozen account at Vneshekonombank. "I have a fan there," he says, "so maybe it'll be all right. Otherwise I'm broke." He's forming a new band, he says, with one of the musicians from his old Aquarium—and he sounds hopeful, as ever. But I sense that he too is finding his own form of escape—into the druggy, dippy, mystical world he discovered in America. He will never be a spokesman for his generation again.

9

The night before I leave for London, we sit down for a family dinner. Ksiyusha has become very beautiful. But she is more and more confused by the times. "In some of the university schools," she says, "work has just stopped. The students have just become dealers. They rent their rooms in the hostels to people from outside the university. They buy and sell stuff to take to Poland and Hungary. You can get everything there: clothes, invitations from abroad, everything. Even the teachers are involved." She herself escapes from all this into poetry and philosophy, she says; she spends a lot of time in the library. But even in this embattled, private little world of hers, there is intense confusion. For the seventy-five percent of world culture that the Communist Party used to keep at bay has now flooded into Moscow and into students' lives in translations and foreign editions: novels and poetry, Sartre and Husserl, semiotics and structuralism and deconstructionism. It's extremely hard for serious students like Ksiyusha to get their intellectual bearings. She belongs to a little group that reads Heidegger obsessively; she's signed up for a course in ancient Greek; she's writing a paper on the poetry of Yeats. But all of these things seem to bleed together in her head, together with all the things she reads in the library, to form a morass of half-digested, overlapping ideas. Meanwhile, she thinks that, even though she loves her world of escape, real life is somehow passing her by. She is fond of a young student who is very smart, she says. "But he was once involved in the black market, and he now drinks too much, out of some strange disappointment with life. I don't know what to do about it."

Tatiana Samoilovna, too—I think, as we raise glasses of Rus-sian champagne to each other, smiling—has found her own means of escape. She says (again) that she's worried for her job at the

Documentary Film Studios. "There's a new chief," she says, "and he's intriguing against our boss in the laboratories. I'm afraid he wants to close our section down." But she's very cheerful; it's as if it's not quite real. Much more real to her these days are the new soap operas now on Russian television: "Santa Barbara," the two endless Mexican soaps ("The Rich Also Cry" and "No One But You"), and the new Brazilian one that's just starting up. Everyone in the country seems to be watching them: customers and counter workers at the airport, street fighters, even nationalist militias. There was a letter recently from an old man in one of the newspapers, saying that he would die soon and wished to offer his life savings to anyone who could tell him what happened at the end of "The Rich Also Cry." One of its Mexican stars recently arrived in Moscow to be fêted and mobbed as if she were a goddess, a myth made flesh. Tatiana Samoilovna gossips about all the daily doings on television with her workmates and on the telephone. And she also watches (like every‑ one else) the faith healer Alan Chumak whenever he is on. Chu‑ mak is the man who charged the evening newspaper with healing power and sells water infused with his healing energy (sent over to the brewery in the form of recorded silence). "He's just opened a gallery," I tell Tatiana Samoilovna, "where he sells paintings he's laid hands on, guaranteed to leak good vibrations into any room you hang them in."

"Yes," she says. "And not long ago he went to the Chaika swimming pool to bless the water. Ever since then, there've been queues of swimmers round the block!"

Katya rushes in and out of the room as we eat, chattering away in a mixture of Russian and the English I've talked with her for two hours every morning—after getting her up—throughout the sum‑ mer. She has learned the English alphabet on my word processor, and can sing a few recognizable English songs. But she now talks Russian faster and with more precision than I can; she can recite pages of Russian children's poetry by heart. Now she scrambles up onto Ksiyusha's lap, impressed by the fact that she's been allowed to stay up and eat with the adults. "When are you going to London, Katya?" asks Ksiyusha.

"When I've finished my book," she says in English trium-phantly.

When I've bathed Katya and put her to sleep, and as Ksiyusha and Tatiana Samoilovna wash up, Yelena and I sit at the table. I toast her with the remains of the champagne. "Here's to my beauti-ful, impossible Yelena," I say. "Thank you for being so patient with me, for helping me try to understand."

"You make it sound like an ending, Jo."

"No," I say. "Haven't you noticed? You've made me almost as Russian as you."

10

The next morning, we all sit down in the hallway, surrounded by my bags. We're silent for a long moment. Then Tatiana Samoi-lovna pushes Katya to her feet. We stand one by one. Yelena hangs on my neck. As always, when I leave alone for the West, she seems to think she'll never see me again, or that I'll call and put off her coming indefinitely, as if it were somewhere still very far away. She doesn't know that to me it's now the West that seems almost inexplicably foreign: noisy, theatrical, a place without secrets. I face it with the same buried anxiety I once brought here. Here, every-thing is impossible. But it's still alive with future possibility, the possibility of things that will astonish the world. I remember some-thing written by the German philosopher Walter Benjamin after a visit to Moscow nearly seventy years ago. Life in Moscow, he said, "is as insular and as eventful, as impoverished and yet in the same breath as full of possibilities as gold rush life in the Klondike." Or this, written by an Englishman at about the same time: "I can truthfully say that in no foreign country have I ever enjoyed myself so positively, been so sheltered from boredom, or felt such regret at departure."

Downstairs in the courtyard, we bundle my bags into the waiting Volga. We hug and embrace, and then I climb in. *"Khoro-sho,"* I say to Viacheslav Vasilyevich, the ex–Red Army colonel. *"Poyedem."* Let's go.

I I

On the plane I feel oddly apprehensive, as I used to feel when coming here—as if I'm now a Russian going to the West. London, I know from experience, will seem, after Moscow, garish and complicated, full of impossible confidence and speed: people on the run, having lunches and dates and appointments, ordering their days, living by the clock. It will also be hugely lonely. The apart-ment will echo with emptiness; it will take a week for me simply to learn how to be alone. Russians have no word for (or concept of) privacy; life is lived collectively; everything real happens indoors, away from the state. In the West, it is outside that constitutes the collective reality. Where you live is a retreat from all its sound and fury.

I look around. The Aeroflot plane is full. There are Pakistanis and Indians on their way from the subcontinent, and tall African women swirling down the aisles like butterflies in swathes of printed cotton. Behind me, three Russian businessmen are discussing what they are going to buy in the West, as they laugh and drink from a bottle of Georgian brandy. To my right, two more are talking about the special commission against corruption that Yeltsin has recently set up, to be headed by Vice-President Rutskoi. (They seem to find this particularly funny.) Around these two groups, jammed under their seats and into every available space, are cases and plastic bags tied up with string. The baggage handlers at Sheremetyevo Airport are now said to steal everything they can get their hands on. And besides, Aeroflot is charging astronomical amounts for every kilo of overweight that goes into the hold. My ten kilos have just cost me a hundred and fifty dollars—or eighteen months of Tatiana Samoilovna's salary. To emigrate with one's possessions is now beyond the means of virtually everyone—except those who are doing well under the new dispensation and no longer have the slightest need. They simply go to the West to visit their money. Though it's still illegal to have personal foreign bank accounts, even President Yeltsin has one, it's said, in a suburb of London.

I sit back in my seat, sipping the rusty-tasting mineral water that is about all the stewardess has to offer (except for sale, for hard currency), and listen to the chatter of a group of elderly British men and women, clustered together, hanging over the seats. They're talking about the wonderful time they've had in Russia, and are exchanging addresses, promising to keep in touch with each other, as if their package tour has been some extraordinary, bonding ordeal. I feel shut away from them, as I feel shut away from all the Westerners I meet these days who come to Moscow for the buzz of revelation and the infection of heroism against the odds. Recently, the Writer, with whom I first came to Moscow, returned on a visit; and her attention span seemed suddenly impossibly small. She was condescending, even rude to my Russian friends. And when she asked me at a large gathering in a restaurant to say something of what I'd learned about the city, she immediately turned her head away. She wasn't interested in anything that wasn't a story, that didn't fit the vision of the place she already had in mind.

What could I have told her, in any case, I think, that would have made sense as the sound bite she was looking for? What indeed have I learned in the past four and a half years, through my marriage to Yelena, through my disappearance into the (more or less) ordinary population? I've learned, I suppose, that Russia's long isolation has been, in the end, a tragedy—both for her and for us. For we in the West still know so little about the country that we continue to project onto its blank screen our own prejudices and histories, as I did when I saw in Boris Grebenshchikov and the politics of *glasnost* a rerunning of the sixties in the West. Russia is much older and odder than we imagine; and it's no use trying to foist off onto it ideas and solutions which have been forged—and look perfectly reason-able—elsewhere. What we fail to understand—as Lenin, in his way, did—is that imports from the West have a history in Russia of mutating rapidly into their opposites, or into something so im-moderate as to be virtually unrecognizable. Democracy, liberaliza-tion, the market economy, free trade, capitalism, and privatization—these things no doubt make total and delightful sense in the corridors of the International Monetary Fund. They ring like music in the ears of all those Western economists and politicians wanting to do their bit for poor old Mother Russia. But what do these things turn into on the ground when they become enshrined in public policy? Democracy in Russia has produced nothing but a ferment of traded insults and an endless, me-first clamour for public attention and position. (It is now, quite simply—and univer-sally—a dirty word.) Free trade has turned the streets of Moscow into a bazaar in which the same things—sometimes simply dreams—change hands again and again at higher and higher prices. Liberalization has stolen the money out of the pockets of ordinary people and pushed ninety percent of them below the poverty line. Capitalism has permitted whole ministries to turn themselves into "concerns" and "corporations" to the private profit of those who used to run them. And privatization . . . well, privatization, as I've said before, is an old Soviet institution. The only difference these days is that the opportunities presented by it for theft, bribery, and embezzlement have grown beyond the wildest of anyone's dreams.

What about us in the West? We failed from the beginning, I think, to see (and use) the good that lay alongside the bad in Gorbachev's Soviet Union: the God-haunted spirituality of Russians, their gift for friendship, their reverence for theatre, poetry, and art. It never occurred to us, in other words, that we might have something to learn from *them*. Instead, we simply pitied them because they hadn't had our advantages. We wanted them to be more like us. So we treated them as a huge new market of Western-style consumers in the making. And we failed to buttress those few institutions that were part of the consolation of Russian life: the thick journals, the theatres, the writers, television, even the church. And the result is that there is no single visible project in Moscow to advertise the goodwill and understanding of the West: no new St. Saviour's Cathedral, no monument to Stalin's victims, no libraries or parks or day-care centres or large-scale cultural foundations. We allowed our form of capitalism to dictate theirs. We did not insist on privatization before liberalization; it never occurred to us to suggest Draconian anticorruption legislation before Western aid and money began rolling in. Instead we sent to represent us in Russia freebooters and hustlers who were willing to join in the free-for-all in the old Soviet way, dealing with the Mafias and the new swashbuckling *nomenklatura,* greasing palms and stashing away money in bank accounts in Switzerland, Jersey, and anywhere else in the world the authorities didn't look too closely. Today, parents see their children wanting to go where the money is: to enrol in the Mafias or become hard-currency prostitutes. Not only "democracy" but also "Western" has become a dirty word.

The West, I think as the plane begins its long descent towards Heathrow Airport, has lost an extraordinary opportunity. With real aid, considered aid—not aid tied to commercial contracts, bank guarantees, and servicing of loan debts—it could have made an enormous difference to the future of Russia. Now, for all its good intentions, it has simply served to push Russia back towards the past, towards autocracy, chauvinism, corruption, and suspicion of the West. Whether the lasting autocrat of this new-old country will be Yeltsin remains to be seen, of course. But the effect will be the same. The Congress will be dismissed; the boss will rule by fiat; the princes of the command-administration will remain in place. Already there is talk in high places that the government has taken the wrong road; it should now follow the Chinese path to capitalism and the market.

And Yelena? I reach into my pocket and take out the photograph of her that I keep in my wallet: long, slanted eyes; a fall of black hair on either side of her face; staring into the camera. She's changed. Her terrible buying hunger has gone, her buried insecurity with people from the West. Soon she will go back to work, content to live wherever we finally choose. We two, I think as I put the photograph away, are the children of Gorbachev's *glasnost*. And now that it's over, we will still be able to keep one of the great gifts it brought with it. We will be able to come and go and live in Russia where we want. That, at least, whatever follows, now seems irreversible.

As we land, I look out at the neat fields and the drizzle. And then I pick up my bags and follow the crowd of passengers towards passport control. I am waved through: this is my home; this is where I belong. In the baggage hall, there are two of us at the mouth of the carousel as it begins to spit out luggage: I and a young man with spectacles and a backpack whom I'd seen joking in Russian to a KGB man at Sheremetyevo Airport. "What were you doing in Russia?" I ask.

"I'm a student. I'm studying Russian. I was staying with friends. It was my first time."

"And did you have a good time?"

"Oh, yes," he said. "It was astonishing. I hadn't expected it. I hadn't expected it to be so full of . . . love."

"So you're hooked."

"Oh, yes. Yes, I am, absolutely."

I held out my hand. "Welcome to the club," I said.

Permissions Acknowledgements

Grateful acknowledgement is made to the following for permission to reprint previously published material:

Basic Books: Excerpt from "Lament for Two Unborn Poems" from *Antiworlds and the Fifth Ace: Poetry* by Andrei Voznesensky, edited by Patricia Blake and Max Hayward, copyright © 1966, 1967 by Basic Books, Inc., copyright © 1963 by Encounter Ltd. Reprinted by permission of Basic Books, a division of HarperCollins Publishers, Inc.

Bloodaxe Books Ltd.: Excerpt from "The White-Hot Blizzard" from *No I'm Not Afraid* by Irina Ratushinskaya, translated by David McDuff (Bloodaxe Books Ltd., 1986). Reprinted by permission.

Farrar, Straus & Giroux, Inc.: Excerpt from "New Year's Greeting" by Marina Tsvetaeva, translated by Barry Rubin from "Footnote to a Poem" from *Less Than One* by Joseph Brodsky, copyright © 1986 by Joseph Brodsky. Reprinted by permission.

A Note About the Author

Jo Durden-Smith is the author of *Who Killed George Jackson?: Fantasies, Paranoia and the Revolution* (Knopf) and, with Diane DeSimone, of *Sex and the Brain* (Arbor House). He has written for *The Observer* and the *New York Times* as well as for virtually every major magazine in Canada and the United States. He has made films in Britain, Germany, Greece, Cyprus, the United States, and Russia.

A Note on the Type

The text of this book was set in Poliphilus, a facsimile of the typeface used by the Venetian printer Aldus Manutius in printing the famous *Hypnerotomachia Poliphili* in 1499. The modern cutting of this face was made by the Monotype Corporation, London, in 1923.

The italic used to accompany Poliphilus is called Blado, having been inspired by the chancery italic used by the printer Antonio Blado in Rome in the early fifteenth century.

Composed by ComCom, a division of Haddon Craftsmen,
Allentown, Pennsylvania

Printed and bound by R. R. Donnelley & Sons,
Harrisonburg, Virginia

Designed by Cassandra J. Pappas